INTERNATIONAL PERSPECTIVES ON

ADAPTED PHYSICAL ACTIVITY

INTERNATIONAL PERSPECTIVES ON

ADAPTED PHYSICAL ACTIVITY

Mavis E. Berridge, MS
University of Toronto

Graham R. Ward, PhD
University of Toronto

Editors

Human Kinetics Publishers, Inc.
Champaign, Illinois

Library of Congress Cataloging-in-Publication Data

International Symposium on Adapted Physical Activity
  (5th : 1985 : Toronto, Ont.)
  International perspectives on adapted physical activity.

  "Selected papers from the Fifth International Symposium on Adapted
Physical Activity held in Toronto, Canada, October 1-4, 1985"—T.p.
verso.
  1. Physical education for handicapped persons—Congresses. 2.
Handicapped—Recreation—Congresses. 3. Sports for the handicapped—
Congresses. I. Berridge, Mavis E., 1925–   . II. Ward, Graham R. III.
Title.
GV445.I57 1987   613.7'08808   86-18531
ISBN 0-87322-079-X

This volume contains selected papers from the Fifth International Symposium
on Adapted Physical Activity held in Toronto, Canada, October 1-4, 1985.

Developmental Editor: Laura E. Larson
Production Director: Ernest Noa
Assistant Production Director: Lezli Harris
Copy Editor: Barbara Cohen
Typesetter: Brad Colson
Proofreader: Jennifer Merrill
Text Layout: Mary Kay Dailey
Cover Design: Mary Kay Dailey
Printed By: Braun-Brumfield, Inc.

ISBN: 0-87322-079-X

Printed in the United States of America

10 9 8 7 6 5 4 3 2 1

Human Kinetics Publishers, Inc.
Box 5076, Champaign, IL 61820

Contents

Part I *Motor Development of Disabled Children*

Part II *Motor Skill Training*

Part III   *Physical Activity in Cardiac Conditions*

Part IV   *Programming for the Handicapped*

Part V   *Diagnosis and Physical Activity Prescription in Psychiatric Disorders*

Part VI   *Characteristics and Assessment of Disabled Athletes*

Part VII   *Sport and Recreation for the Disabled*

Part VIII   *Aging and Physical Activity Concerns of the Elderly*

Part IX *Programs for Seniors*

The Fifth International Symposium on Adapted Physical Activity

Cohosts

The School of Physical and Health Education, University of Toronto: The School of Physical and Health Education, University of Toronto is the first school in the British Commonwealth to grant a university degree. It has maintained a traditional link with the Health Science Faculties since its foundation in 1940 and now holds a leading position in the field of exercise science and physical education.

Variety Village: Variety Village is a sport training and fitness center catering to the disabled child and athlete in a modern, fully equipped activity facility that includes a 200-m Olympic-type track. The Electrolimb Production Centre at the Village makes some of the finest artificial limbs in the world.

Patron

The Honorable John Aird, Honorary Chair, Variety Village

Honorary President

Dr. Robert W. Jackson, past-president, International Stoke Mandeville Games Federation

Organizing Committee

Mavis E. Berridge, president, Fifth ISAPA; University of Toronto, Toronto, Canada

Dr. Graham R. Ward, chair, Program Committee, Fifth ISAPA; Variety Village, Scarborough, Canada, and University of Toronto, Canada

James R. Sinclair, chair, Hospitality Committee, Fifth ISAPA; Metro Toronto School Board, Toronto, Canada

Marilyn Soberman, secretary

Felicia Cukier, special assistant

Program Committee

Dr. Graham R. Ward (chair), Variety Village, Scarborough, Canada
Mavis E. Berridge, University of Toronto, Toronto, Canada
Dr. Jane Evans, Brock University, St. Catharines, Canada
Warren Campbell, Scarborough Board of Education, Scarborough, Canada
Dr. Glen Davis, Wright State University, Dayton, Ohio, U.S.A.
Jack Goodman, University of Toronto, Toronto, Canada
Mike Meadows, Ontario Association for the Mentally Retarded, Toronto, Canada
Dr. Morris Milner, Hugh MacMillan Medical Centre, Toronto, Canada

Hospital Committee

James R. Sinclair, Metro Toronto School Board, Toronto, Canada
Sheilah Rogers, Hospitality Toronto, Toronto, Canada

The International Federation of Adapted Physical Activity

The International Federation of Adapted Physical Activity (IFAPA/FIAPA) began in the Canadian province of Quebec in 1973. Since then it has rapidly expanded to become a worldwide organization with an international charter. It has sponsored five international symposia: Quebec, 1977; Brussels, Belgium, 1979; New Orleans, U.S.A., 1981; London, England, 1983; and Toronto, Canada, 1985. The Sixth International Symposium is scheduled for June 20–24, 1987, in Brisbane, Australia, and the seventh is planned for Berlin, West Germany in 1989.

The objective of IFAPA/FIAPA is to provide a global focus for professionals who use adapted physical activity for instruction, competition, recreation, remediation, and research. The biennial symposium serves as a forum to bring together people, programs, and research for the benefit of disabled people the world over.

Board of Directors, IFAPA/FIAPA

Dr. Jean Claude Pageot, president, IFAPA/FIAPA, University of Ottawa, Ottawa, Canada

David E. Jones, vice-president, IFAPA/FIAPA, Brisbane College of Advanced Education, Clayfield, Australia

Dr. Jean-Claude de Potter, secretary, IFAPA/FIAPA, Université Libre de Bruxelles, Bruxelles, Belgium

Dr. Gudrun M. Doll-Tepper, treasurer, IFAPA/FIAPA, Freie Universität Berlin, Berlin, West Germany

Dr. Dennis Drouin, Université Laval, Ste. Foy, Quebec, Canada

John A. Nesbitt, University of Iowa, Iowa City, Iowa, U.S.A.

Dr. Clermont Simard, Université Laval, Ste. Foy, Quebec, Canada

Dr. Julian U. Stein, George Mason University, Fairfax, Virginia, U.S.A.

Dr. Fernand Caron, University of Quebec at Trois Rivières, Trois Rivières, Quebec, Canada

Membership Information for IFAPA/FIAPA

Please contact: IFAPA Secretary/Secretariat de la FIAPA
Centre François-Charon
525, Boulevard Hamel
Quebec, Quebec
G1M 2S8 CANADA

Contributors

Adedoja, Dr. Taoheed A.
Dept. of Phys. & Health Ed.
University of Maiduguri
P.M.B. 1069
Maiduguri, NIGERIA

Bell, R. Gordon
Bellwood Health Services Inc.
1020 McNichol Avenue
Scarborough, Ontario
M1W 2J7 CANADA

Berridge, Mavis E.
School of Phys. & Health Ed.
University of Toronto
320 Huron Street
Toronto, Ontario
M5S 1A1 CANADA

Buell, Charles E.
33905 Calle Acordarse
San Juan Capistrano, California
92675 U.S.A.

Butterfield, Stephen A.
Dept. of Phys. Ed.
University of Maine at Orono
115 Lengyel Hall
Orono, Maine
04469 U.S.A.

Canabal, Maria Y.
PO Box 23661
Texas Woman's University
TWU Station
Denton, Texas
76204 U.S.A.

Chrétien, Romain
602, rue Chabanel
Chicoutimi, Quebec
G7H 3S7 CANADA

Cowin, Lloyd W.
Leisure Services Dept.
Royal Ottawa Rehab. Centre
505 Smyth Road
Ottawa, Ontario
K1H 8M2 CANADA

Croce, Ronald V.
Dept. of Phys. Ed.
University of New Hampshire
New Hampshire Hall
Durham, New Hampshire
03824 U.S.A.

Davis, Walter E.
162 Memorial Annex
School of Phys. Ed., Rec. & Dance
Kent State University
Kent, Ohio
44242 U.S.A.

de Potter, Jean-Claude
Institut Supérieur d'Education
   Physique et de Kinesithérapie
Laboratoire de l'Effort
Université Libre de Bruxelles
28, avenue Paul Heger (CP 168)
1050 Bruxelles
BELGIUM

Doll-Tepper, Gudrun M.
Institut für Sportwissenschaft
FU Berlin
Hittorfstr. 16
1000 Berlin 33
WEST GERMANY

Ferguson, Ronald J.
Dept. of Physical Education
University of Montreal
2100 Boulevard Edouard Montpetit
Montreal, Quebec
H3C 3J7 CANADA

Godin, Gaston
School of Nursing
Laval University
Ste. Foy, Quebec
G1K 7P4 CANADA

Gorman, Dean R.
Adapted Physical Education
HPER 308N
University of Arkansas

Fayetteville, Arkansas
72701 USA

Higgs, Colin
School of Phys. Ed. & Rec.
Memorial University
St. John's, Newfoundland
A1C 5S7 CANADA

Johannsen, Shirley
Box 27
Old Chelsea, Quebec
J0X 2N0 CANADA

Longmuir, Patricia E.
159 Broadlands Blvd.
Don Mills, Ontario
M3A 1K1 CANADA

Mälkiä, Esko Antero
Department of Health Sciences
University of Jyväskylä
Seminaarinkatu 15
SF-40740 Jyväskylä
FINLAND

McCubbin, Jeffrey A.
Dept. of Phys. Ed.
PO Box 32901
Texas Christian University
Fort Worth, Texas
76129 U.S.A.

Pageot, Jean Claude
Dept. of Recreology
Faculty of Social Sciences
University of Ottawa
550 Cumberland
Ottawa, Ontario
K1N 6N5 CANADA

Pasek, Tadeusz
Faculty of Medicine
University of Poznan
Poznan, POLAND

Rainbolt, Wanda Jean
PO Box 22293
Texas Woman's University
TWU Station
Denton, Texas
76204 U.S.A.

Roeren, Finn Richard
PO Box 1376 Vika
0114 Oslo 1
NORWAY

Rosenzweig, Marcee
Community Assoc. for Riding for
   the Disabled
4777 Dufferin Street
Downsview, Ontario
M3H 5T3 CANADA

Schulz, Linda
Director, Let's Play To Grow
1350 New York Avenue, NW
Suite 500
Washingon, DC
20005 U.S.A.

Shephard, Roy J.
School of Phys. & Health Ed.
University of Toronto
320 Huron Street
Toronto, Ontario
M5S 1A1 CANADA

Sherborne, Veronica
26 Hanbury Road
Bristol, ENGLAND
BS8 2EP

Simard, Clermont P.
Department of Phys. Ed.
Laval University
Ste. Foy, Quebec
G1K 7P4 CANADA

Sloman, Leon
Clarke Inst. of Psychiatry
250 College Street
Toronto, Ontario
M5T 1R8 CANADA

Tilley, Anne D.
School of Phys. Ed. & Rec.
University of British Columbia
6081 University Boulevard
Vancouver, British Columbia
V6T 1W5 CANADA

Vanlerberghe, J.O.C.
Kerkstraat 82

B-3200 Leuven
BELGIUM

Weingarden-Albert, Pamela
Dance Movement Therapist
The Wagman Centre
55 Ameer Avenue
Toronto, Ontario
M6A 2Z1 CANADA

Foreword

These proceedings of the Fifth International Symposium on Adapted Physical Activity are a stepping-stone in the history of the International Federation of Adapted Physical Activity (IFAPA/FIAPA). A decade ago, a group of researchers from Canada, the United States, Belgium, Germany, and Australia decided to join their efforts to promote physical activity among populations that were in a special situation and to build an international network to promote research and to exchange information.

The Fifth International Symposium was the biggest to date, with representation from 13 countries, in the form of 167 free communications and 7 minisymposia. It was also an occasion to observe new programs, to discuss new ideas, and to test research projects among colleagues.

In 1983 Human Kinetics Publishers, with the federation and the organizing committee of the third symposium, published the proceedings of that symposium. At the time the editors wrote a preface comparing the role of the federation to the agent described in the Parable of the Sower. It was then hoped that the works done by the federation and the papers presented at the third symposium would fall on good soil.

The choice of the theme of the fifth symposium is already an answer indicating that the soil was good. Function, fitness, and fun were chosen to serve as a common ground for discussions and presentation of papers. Two of these words can be used only when the basic idea and principle of an action are accepted. They are *function* and *fun*.

Function implies that something is already implemented and that efficiency is researched, whereas *fun* can be attained when people have some freedom to enjoy what they are doing. Thus, if the idea of using physical activities to improve the life-style of a special population had not begun to be accepted, it would have been impossible to rally on these two topics.

This does not mean that the role of the federation is over. On the contrary, there are still many countries that have to be contacted, the information network has to be improved, and there will always be new special populations to be served, such as the women at home, the unemployed, students, and many more. On the other hand, traditional special populations, such as the disabled, the aged, and the mentally handicapped, will always need new programs to keep up with what happens in the so-called normal population.

It is hoped that by indicating the state of the art these papers will encourage those who are already working to improve the life-style of special populations and will motivate others to become involved in an area where there is still so much to be done.

Finally, the role of Human Kinetics Publishers has to be commended. They were with us in 1983 to publish the proceedings at a time when the concept of adapted physical activity was almost unknown. Nevertheless, they showed the federation that they were good soil and had the pioneer spirit. Later on, they decided to publish a journal, *Adapted Physical Activity Quarterly,* and they are now collaborating with these proceedings. These are the kinds of collaboration that help researchers and other professionals in the field in their efforts to create better living conditions for those in special situations.

Jean Claude Pageot
President, IFAPA/FIAPA

Preface

This book represents a further step in the attempt to understand disabling conditions and to improve the quality of life for disabled people by documenting some of the research findings and new ideas in physical education and recreation programs that were presented at the Fifth International Symposium on Adapted Physical Activity.

The planning committee of the Fifth ISAPA was fortunate to secure, as its venue, the Metro Toronto Convention Centre and the adjoining L'Hotel, both in their first year of operation and each designed to accommodate disabled persons. Rising above the symposium site to a height of 1,815 ft (553 m) was the world's tallest free-standing structure—the CN Tower. Delegates, including the 10 members of the MacKay Centre Stage in their electric wheelchairs, attended the opening reception at the top of the tower and saw the sun set on Toronto and the lights come on in the great metropolis. The logo of the CN Tower was adopted for the Fifth ISAPA as a symbol of the heights to which human beings can aspire when given a chance.

The notion of adapted physical activity as a "freshly planted seed," put forward by the planning committee of the Third ISAPA held in 1981 in New Orleans, Louisiana, U.S.A., was an apt one. The past few years have seen a number of positive steps toward improved life-style for disabled people. Public awareness of their needs is increasing; legislation about their rights in education and community life is in effect in many countries, and the benefits of physical activity in terms of human resources instead of economic liabilities are beginning to be felt. Three hundred sixty-two delegates attended the Fifth ISAPA, representing among them 13 countries. The record number of 170 free communication papers submitted for presentation in 1985 is testimony to the fact that the "seed" has indeed fallen on good soil and has taken root.

Many presentations were practical demonstrations or film and video showings that did not lend themselves to written documentation. Some authors did not wish to publish or are seeking publication elsewhere. Nevertheless, the task of selecting the articles appearing in this volume was a difficult one. The referees were highly positive about the majority of papers, but the space for publication was limited. On the one hand, it was very hard to leave out some excellent papers from well-seasoned researchers and workers in the field; on the other, it was a delight to be able to include papers on the leading edge of new topics written by lesser known authors who show great promise for the future.

Selection was made on the basis of pertinence to the conference theme (Function-Fitness-Fun) and originality of topic. The resulting book represents the breadth of the field from the motor development of disabled children to programs for seniors, covering psychiatric disorders, post-cardiac rehabilitation, and concerns of disabled athletes along the way.

Thanks to our arrangement with Human Kinetics Publishers, the papers that do not appear here will be sent, with their authors' permission, to the *Adapted Physical Activity Quarterly* for publication. Thus none of the publishable papers from the Fifth ISAPA will be lost.

It is the editors' hope that this book will add to the growing body of knowledge in the area of adapted physical activity by highlighting several aspects of the field not widely documented.

Mavis E. Berridge
Graham R. Ward

Acknowledgments

A multifaceted conference depends greatly on funds and teamwork. Special thanks are due to WINTARIO for granting the funds to launch the Fifth ISAPA. Thanks also to the many donors who contributed financially to help keep down costs to individual delegates:

Adidas Canada Ltd.
Air Canada
Avon Sportswear
Campbell Soup Company Ltd.
Canadian Mental Health Association (Ontario Division)
Canadian Pacific Air
Canadian Reassurance Company
Canon Canada Inc.
Carling O'Keefe Breweries Ltd.
Fitness Canada
General Motors of Canada Ltd.
Gulf Canada Ltd.
Health and Welfare Canada
Hospital for Sick Children Foundation
Labatt's Ontario Breweries Ltd.
Manulife
Ministry of Community and Social Services, Prov. of Ontario
Ministry of Intergovernmental Affairs, Prov. of Ontario
Ministry of Tourism and Recreation, Prov. of Ontario
Participaction
Perfect Pen Company
Sanyo Canada Ltd.
Shoppers Drug Mart
The Eaton Foundation
The Toronto Dominion Bank
Union Carbide
University of Toronto, School of Physical and Health Education
University of Toronto, Office of the Vice-President, Institutional Relations
Wm. C. Brown Publishers

Appreciation is also expressed to the following institutions that opened their facilities to provide professional visits to the delegates: Variety Village, the Hugh MacMillan Medical Centre, Toronto Rehabilitation Centre, the Bob Rumball Centre for the Deaf, and Riverdale Hospital.

PART I

Motor Development of Disabled Children

Movement Observation and Practice

Veronica Sherborne

I have worked with children with a variety of handicaps and with student teachers and teachers in special education for the past 27 years. My training is in physical education, physiotherapy, and in the methods of Rudolf Laban.

After many years in normal education, I started to work with severely retarded children and found no one to turn to for help. I developed my ideas through trial and error, critical self-assessment, questionnaires, feedback from student teachers and teachers, and video and film. I have continued to experiment and to learn from experience and have slowly developed a program that works for children and teachers.

I realized that the severely retarded child has two basic requirements before he or she can learn and develop. These are self-awareness (or body concept) and awareness of others (the capacity to make relationships). Put simply, you cannot learn about the world unless you have a starting place—an identity—and you cannot learn from other people unless you can relate to them. Other people confirm that you exist and strengthen your sense of identity, and this helps you to relate better.

Self-Awareness

I will begin with self-awareness. The retarded child takes longer than a normal child to develop some degree of body awareness and needs constant reinforcement and encouragement. The severely retarded child needs to experience and to concentrate on messages coming from within his or her body. If the child has a good relationship with his or her body, the child can learn from experiences and has more confidence in tackling new skills. There must be a balance between providing subjective, internal learning experiences and objective, external learning experiences. Children find it easier to focus on external objects, thus avoiding relating to themselves. They need constant encouragement to concentrate on what is happening within their bodies and to listen to their bodies. On the whole, physical education programs stress the use of external stimuli and the acquiring of objective skills.

I work on two parts of the body, the trunk and the weight-bearing parts. It is not enough just to name sections of the body; they have to be experienced through sensory means and through developing physical control.

3

The trunk is often the least known part of the body, and many children move in an empty, disconnected way. It is essential to educate the trunk because it is the central link between the extremities, and children need to move as a coordinated whole. Activities that teach children that they have trunks are all kinds of rolling, all kinds of falling, and all the ways of transferring weight from shoulder to hips, from front to back. Children experience their bodies against the ground or other supporting surfaces. They learn to transfer weight comfortably and fluently in a variety of tumbling and somersaulting agilities. Children slowly gain confidence to try more challenging activities such as jumping and landing from a height. Children who can commit their weight to the ground or to the support of a partner indicate that they are self-confident. Anxious children will not let go of weight.

Children also need to develop flexible trunks. This can be done through lizardlike creeping and in successive movement in rolling, where part follows part of the body, producing a twist. Children with rigid, tense trunks are unlikely to be able to absorb new experiences, and the teacher needs to help such a child to mobilize what is so often a stiff, unknown area of the body. When the child's body is well supported on the ground, it can move in a more coordinated, fluent, and flexible way than when the child is standing.

Another need is to discover that the body has a center to which one can curl up. Normal children can do this between the ages of 4 and 5 and can maintain this against resistance. Retarded children need help with curling up but can develop a strong sense of a center. Without a lively center their movement is disconnected. Sequential movement, such as spinning on hips, falling, and rolling over, teaches free flow of weight experience and helps the child to adapt and respond quickly to changing situations. All these ground-based activities are presented as play, using gymnastic mats and crash mats, and are much enjoyed by children.

A teacher who is educating the trunk also has to develop awareness of the weight-bearing parts of the body. Severely retarded children often walk with a wide gait, find running difficult, and dare not risk jumping. The knee is the most important joint for maintaining balance, for acting as a shock absorber, and for all kinds of locomotion. Control of the knee joints and strength in the thigh muscles are essential for all sport, dance, and outdoor pursuits, as well as in daily life. Awareness of knees begins in sitting on the floor, where the knees are easily seen and can move freely without bearing weight. Children hold their knees while bending and extending them; knees are hammered with fists, smacked noisily, rubbed, patted, and connected to the elbows and chin. Sensory stimuli of all kinds are essential for the development of body awareness. Through kneeling, crawling, and squatting activities, awareness of knees continues into running, jumping, and landing. Awareness of knees is much enjoyed by children because knees have comic possibilities, and children's variations produce a great variety of different walks. The wide, empty gait becomes narrower as children learn to control the weight of the body in walking, running, and all forms of locomotion.

Awareness of Others

Awareness of others should be presented in a constructive and rewarding way, and children should be successful in all these activities because they are within their competence. Relationship play, or partner play, may involve a retarded child working with an adult, with a normal older child, with a retarded older child, with parents, or with partners in a class. Partner work is rewarding for all participants, feeds self-confidence and self-esteem, and provides a simple, practical way of helping retarded children to interact. Communication skills, such as making eye contact, increasing vocabulary, and developing the ability to play with another person, are developed, as well as the ability to initiate and invent.

There are three kinds of relationships. *With* relationships involve partners in caring, containing, and supporting activities. For example, different ways of rolling a partner, sliding, or supporting a partner strengthen the bond between people. When children allow their partners to take their weight and support them, they show confidence in themselves as well as trust in their partners. Partners must reverse roles so that retarded children can learn to look after and be responsible for other persons.

Relationships *against* a partner involve activities such as pushing back-to-back sitting on the floor, testing a curled up package or parcel, and testing a partner's ability to stick to the floor, or stability. When the older partner tests the retarded child's strength, the partner must understand the concept of testing as opposed to winning. The aim is to build up the retarded child's strength and not to destroy it. When retarded children work against their partners, they must be successful, but they must work for it. Older partners need to be sensitive to the degree of strength of which their partners are capable. Retarded children slowly gather their energy and learn to focus it. Severely retarded children can develop firmness and strength. They increase their concentration span and, paradoxically, become more capable of being gentle.

Shared relationships are demanding because they require simultaneous mutual dependence and mutual support. This is seen when partners sit facing each other and make a seesaw. Balancing a partner in standing is more advanced but can be achieved. Partners have to listen to their own bodies and to their partners' bodies at the same time. Working with one partner progresses to work in threes, fours, and larger groups. All these aspects of relationship play are illustrated in my recent film *Good Companions* (1985).

There are different stages in relationship play, beginning with the severely retarded child passively receiving movement experiences of being cradled, slid, or swung. This is seen when working with multiply handicapped children or with some long-term residents in a subnormality hospital. The next stage arises when retarded children respond to their partners, reciprocal play develops, and eventually the children begin to take the initiative. Finally, the retarded child is able to work with another retarded or disturbed child. The older partner is a facilitator who helps the younger child to develop skills in relating.

I am particularly interested in children who actively avoid making relationships. A postgraduate student teacher spent 1 day a week for 6 weeks trying to make a study of a boy who continually avoided all her efforts to make contact with him. By chance I was asked to supervise at the end of this time, and at my suggestion we went into the school hall. Children love free-flow movement, so I began by sliding the boy along the floor, and he looked up at me with some surprise. Eye contact is essential in making relationships and is best achieved when the child is higher than the adult or when the older partner is higher. The strangeness of seeing a person in an unfamiliar relationship seems to help; to gaze on the horizontal is sometimes threatening to children. I came down to floor level, and after some other activities I went on all fours and asked the student teacher to help the boy to sit on my back. I took him for a careful ride, and after about 10 minutes' play we finished with him sitting between my legs, leaning back and resting against me. This was an important statement from a nervous, tense child with autistic tendencies. I asked the student teacher to go through the sequence of movements I had just done, which she did. When she and the boy stood up to leave the hall, the boy lifted up his arms to her, silently asking her to pick him up. After weeks of frustration she had at last got through to him.

I worked in my college for 8 weeks with an extremely hyperactive and disturbed boy. He came once a week with a group of severely retarded children who were partnered by student teachers. We made no progress with this boy, partly because his partner, a mature man with children of his own, had difficulty himself with relationship play. The boy continually ran away, and when we had gymnastic apparatus he flitted from one piece to another and experienced nothing. However, his parents said the only nights he slept well were after the sessions in our gymnasium. On the last afternoon this boy worked by chance with a young woman student whom I describe as an earthy type, good at communicating through physical play. The boy played on a crash mat with her, somersaulting, rolling, and climbing under and over her. This was the longest time he spent with one person doing one kind of activity. At the end of the session his first partner made a "house" on all fours, and the boy spontaneously crept inside and stayed there. Unfortunately, it is sad when you get to the end of a series of sessions and cannot build on progress made, especially when that progress has taken so long to achieve. As he became older this boy became totally uncontrollable, and his parents had to put him in a subnormality hospital.

I have learned a lot from hyperactive children and have developed various strategies. I noticed years ago in Norway that an extremely hyperactive boy in a hospital became calmer and able to cooperate after his partner lay back on him and squashed him. I had discovered this myself earlier and have since recommended it to a special education adviser who was exhausted trying to work with a hyperactive boy. Children enjoy being squashed, and it calms them down. Children also enjoy being held in a "prison" made by the adult in a sitting position. The child is encouraged to escape, and the adult makes this difficult so that the child has to work hard. Eventually the child succeeds in getting out and promptly jumps in again for another go. Some normal 5-year-olds I taught from a socially deprived area found it so comforting to be held in the tight grip of the adult that they preferred to stay inside. On two occasions I have had to ask teachers not to let go of their hyperactive partners. In one case the boy had such an enjoyable play experience with one of the best teachers I have trained that he no longer wanted to run away, and there was no further need to physically contain him. The secret is to give children movement experiences that they crave so that they find it more rewarding to stay with the adult than run away. On the other occasion the boy was contained in sitting inside his partner's "house" with some difficulty. However, he watched the movement session of his classmates, and when it was over he performed the activities they had done all by himself. In the next session, with another partner, he joined in quite normally with his class.

Hyperactive children are hungry for free-flow experiences, and sometimes, in order to begin a relationship, one has to satisfy this need. I sometimes grasp the child around the waist and swing him or her around me. Invariably the child comes back for another swing. The child must accept the physical contact in order to get the swing. If a child demands to be swung by the hands and ankles by two people, the back can be swept along the floor so that the child gets the free-flow slide he or she wants but is "earthed" at the same time.

Working with educable retarded teenagers I was told that one girl would not let anyone touch her. I have been told this about other children, too, but in every case the child concerned has forgotten eventually to protect himself or herself. On this occasion three people knelt down on all fours, side by side, making a flat supporting surface with their backs that a child could lie on and be swayed gently from side to side. The girl who watched the session could not resist taking her turn, and she lay on the people's backs. This also illustrates that relationship through the back is often more acceptable and less threatening than working face to face with a partner.

Relationship play is similar to the rough-and-tumble play of parents with their children, but it has to be structured according to the needs of retarded and disturbed children. Tense children often develop quickly in weekly one-to-one movement sessions. Progress can be seen in increasing confidence, increasing movement vocabulary, increasing involvement and motivation, and an increase in the ability to concentrate and to repeat actions.

Directions in Space

We have considered what parts of the body are moving and with whom the child is moving. We must now look at where the child can move. Awareness of directions in space is a difficult concept for the severely retarded child, but it can develop to some degree as a result of increasing body awareness. For example, retarded children find it difficult to move backward and to extend a leg into space behind them because the action is out of sight. I saw one of my own children coming backward downstairs at the age of 8 months, extending a leg behind him to feel the next step. It is interesting to compare the age at which a normal child develops skills compared with a retarded child. Movement behind and movement low down are often neglected. Teachers have to encourage the child's experience of directions in space, and words such as *behind, in front, up, down, under,* and *over* are best learned as physical experiences.

Gravity

Gravity is the force that the child has to relate to, whether giving in to it or fighting against it. These opposite attitudes are experienced in jumping and in falling. Jumping has a stimulating effect, and rolling, which involves the smallest fall the body can do, has a harmonizing, calming effect. We are aware of the strong force of gravity when helping a multiply handicapped child to lift his or her head from prone lying and when helping the child to sit and stand with support. Gravity is the architect of the body, and all human movement is governed by it.

Movement Qualities

It is relatively easy to see what parts of the body are moving and where the body is moving. We must now consider *how* the body moves, and this is more difficult. Through a lifetime's work I have found the observation of how people move the most important skill I have. Just as gravity is always with us, so are the motion factors of energy, flow, space, and time. I put them in that order because it is the developmental sequence I have observed. There are opposite attitudes to these four motion factors, and people tend to prefer one way of moving and to neglect the opposite way. The aim is to work from people's strengths and to carefully introduce the undeveloped movement qualities. The goal is to balance the opposites while being aware that it will take a long time to achieve this.

Taking *energy* first, the child can move strongly and firmly or lightly and gently. Children need to learn how to use energy appropriately, knowing when to use strength and when to move sensitively. Strength usually develops first, whereas fine touch and sensitivity may demand greater maturity. Down's syndrome children sometimes show great delicacy in the way they use their hands. I have worked with four boys with abnormal strength and have seen one of them learn to control it through good movement teaching.

The opposite attitudes to the *flow* of movement are expressed in free-flow movement, which cannot be stopped easily once started, and controlled-flow (or bound-flow) movement, which is under the control of the will and can be arrested at once. Free-flow movement comes naturally to the majority of children and is much enjoyed. Swinging, sliding, and bouncing are provided by playground equipment. Controlled flow is seen when a child writes or draws carefully, and this type of flow requires concentration and certain maturity. Children need plenty of free-flow experiences, such as running, jumping, and tumbling, but a diet of too much free flow can increase hyperactivity. Too long an experience of controlled flow will cause children to explode wildly afterward. Down's syndrome children often move with natural freeflow.

Opposite attitudes to *space* produce movement that is three-dimensional, using flexible pathways in space, or movement that is confined to one direct pathway and is linear. Both aspects are needed. A flexible, mobile body that moves freely in space can be developed, and at the other end of the scale the retarded child can learn to focus and direct attention along a straight line. Direct attention is developed in pushing or pulling a partner, and the capacity to focus on a job slowly increases.

Opposite ways of using *time* are easily seen in quick, sudden movement and in slow, sustained movement. Children need encouragement to experience different tempos and to develop the ones they use least. On the whole young children move quickly, and slow movement is more difficult for them. It is useful to mix older retarded adolescents with younger retarded children because the younger ones, being more lively, stimulate the older children and because the adolescents calm the younger ones.

On the whole the movement qualities that come naturally to children are strong, free-flowing, flexible, and quick, and children need help with gentle, controlled, direct, and slow movement. Most severely retarded children operate in the middle ranges of energy, flow, space, and time, and they have to extend their repertoire. This is particularly important when helping severely retarded children discover some strength and some degree of sensitivity. Disturbed children show extremes of, for example, exaggerated strength, exaggerated free flow combined with great speed, and no sign of direct attention. Their range is lopsided, but in time and with good teaching they can achieve some degree of balance.

Good movement teaching depends on the teacher's skill in observing the children. The teacher chooses activities that are most acceptable to the children to start with, and slowly the teacher pushes the boundaries out so that the children's experience of movement is extended and their movement vocabulary is enriched. The teacher also has to be aware of his or her own preferences in ways of moving because these will influence what and how he or she teaches, which in turn will limit the movement vocabulary of the children.

We will now look at three activities and see what is involved in each of them. *Rolling* combines free flow of weight, giving in to gravity, and involvement of the whole body with the main emphasis on the trunk. *Back-to-back pushing* involves the trunk along with strength in the legs and arms and direct movement backward. *Two people helping a third to jump* shows strength, free flow, and the aim to go high. The coordination of three people's efforts is required.

I have covered briefly what parts of the child are moving, with whom the child is moving, where the child can move, and how the child moves. I have also covered briefly what to teach and why, but I have not attempted to describe how to teach. The teacher's aim is to give the child a sense of security—security in relation to the ground, the child's base, and security within the body, the child's center.

Everything I have learned about severely retarded children through observation and experience has illuminated my understanding of normal children, and my knowledge of normal children has helped me to understand the severely retarded. My aim is to develop in all children the inner resources that they have and that they will need to get the most out of their lives. Many people do not see that movement experiences are fundamental to the development of all children and are particularly important for the developmentally retarded child. Communication of aims, methods, and philosophy is almost impossible without personal experience of practice and theory. I have made four films of work with severely retarded children and adults, and they provide useful illustrations of theory and practice.

I have learned a great deal from student teachers, teachers, and countless children, and I hope I shall go on learning.

References

Sherborne, V. (Producer & Director). (1965). *In touch: Movement for mentally handicapped children* [Film]. Ipswich, England: Concord Films Council.

Sherborne, V. (Producer & Director). (1976). *A sense of movement: Movement for mentally handicapped children* [Film]. Ipswich, England: Concord Films Council.

Sherborne, V. (Producer & Director). (1982). *Building bridges: Movement for mentally handicapped adults* [Film]. Ipswich, England: Concord Films Council.

Sherborne, V. (Producer & Director). (1985). *Good companions: Movement for the mentally handicapped and normal children* [Film]. Ipswich, England: Concord Films Council.

Helping Special Families Grow Through Play

Linda L. Schulz

The United States National Center for Health Statistics estimates that there are 6 million American children under 18 with disabilities severe enough to prevent them from carrying out some major life activity. This number comprises about 10% of the total population of children from birth through age 18. It can be assumed that this number is fairly typical of most of the industrialized nations and is probably higher in poorer countries.

The impact of these statistics on the social and economic fabric of society has not been adequately assessed; however, it is clear that the costs are high. This is the case not only for society at large but also for those individuals and their families who must face the many personal challenges posed by disability. One of the most important factors affecting this situation arises from the fact that whereas in the past many parents would have been encouraged to place their handicapped child in institutional care, increasingly they are encouraged to care for their handicapped child at home. In fact, the U.S. Administration on Developmental Disabilities estimates that 80 to 90% of all developmentally disabled children are now being cared for at home. In theory, at least, this is good for the child. On the other hand, this results in extraordinary stresses on the family unit and on community-based services, which are often not adequate to provide for the needs of children with disabilities or their families.

Being successful parents of any child is difficult at best. Even the most loving, best intentioned mothers and fathers may not have all the skills they need to provide a healthy and positive environment in which to nurture the growth and development of their children.

Of course, the presence of a handicapped child in the family often compounds this problem. Parents of special children frequently find that the problems of day-to-day living that accompany a disability are all-consuming, devastating, and complex. They need even more help than the average parent in coping with the demands of parenthood.

Buscaglia (1975) noted, "Perhaps one of the greatest, and most painful problems parents who have disabled infants will have to be prepared for is that of the social deprivation which his [sic] impairment may create" (p. 34). He noted that parents are often not equipped to understand the special needs of their handicapped child and may find it very difficult to interact in a relaxed and playful manner or even to find playmates for the child. This social deprivation can severely inhibit the child's physical, intellectual, emotional, and social growth.

On the brighter side, as Buscaglia observed, when parents of handicapped children are provided with adequate support and training and are encouraged to assume an active role in the education and rehabilitation of their child, both the parents and the special child grow and find added strength, confidence, and achievement.

The Importance of Play

For children in the early developmental stages, almost every activity contains some element of play. What many parents may not understand is that "child's play" is not just a convenient but trivial way to keep children busy and content. Researchers such as Ainsworth, Bell, and Stayton (1974), Bowlby (1969), Brazelton, Koslowski, and Main (1974), and Piaget and Inhelder (1958) have demonstrated that play is the most important vehicle for the child's intellectual, social, emotional, and physical development and that parents and family play a crucial role in this process. While physical or mental impairments may limit the special child's ability to explore, the need to learn through play remains. Parents of a child with disabilities must learn to adapt the environment to ensure that the special child gets important early play experiences.

Unfortunately, relaxed family play is often a casualty of the many challenges families face when they have children with special needs. These challenges may include the special child's chronic medical condition, difficult behavior, or need for special educational therapies. They may also include adjustments to the fact that their disabled family member may not be like other children in looks, behavior, or ability, as well as society's prejudices regarding disability.

Independent recreation skills are also an important component of a healthy and productive life-style for teens and adults with disabilities. In fact, Wuerch and Voeltz (1982) report that research has shown that success in community placements of developmentally disabled persons appears to be related to constructive use of leisure time. Unfortunately, training in recreation skills is generally not a high priority of education and rehabilitation programs for severely handicapped individuals (Voeltz & Wuerch, 1981).

The Let's Play To Grow Program

Created and administered by the Joseph P. Kennedy, Jr. Foundation as a companion program to Special Olympics, Let's Play To Grow began in 1977 as a series of play guides for parents of handicapped children and relevant professionals. It was quickly discovered that parents found the printed materials useful for a limited time but then often left them to gather dust on the shelf. The concept of the Let's Play To Grow club was developed to provide a structured program that would bring families together to enjoy group recreational activities as a more effective vehicle for keeping families involved and motivated.

The purpose of Let's Play To Grow clubs is to help parents learn how to bring the benefits of play into the lives of their handicapped children, to build confidence in their abilities as parents, and to create an environment where special families can feel a part of a community. Let's Play To Grow provides a vehicle for special families to come together to enjoy the important physical and spiritual benefits of play.

Since 1980, in a network of 200 family clubs across the U.S.A. and internationally, mothers, fathers, sisters, brothers, handicapped children, professionals, and other volunteers have shared play and leisure time. Let's Play To Grow currently serves approximately 2,000 families in 31 states, the Virgin Islands, the United Kingdom, Canada, Mexico, Bermuda, and India.

The Let's Play To Grow Club Concept

The club concept is both simple and unique. There are four main ingredients of a Let's Play To Grow club:

- A group of families (5 to 10 is a good number to start with; Let's Play To Grow clubs currently have up to 60 members)
- A sponsoring agency (this can be any agency interested in serving the needs of families with a handicapped child; agencies sponsoring Let's Play To Grow clubs have included schools, recreation departments, nongovernmental charities, churches, institutions, hospitals, even businesses; sponsorship can involve providing a place to meet, financial assistance, and recruiting families and volunteers)
- A club leader (a parent, human service professional, or other volunteer)
- Activity leaders and other volunteers (people who have a special skill or interest they can share with club members or those who are interested in assisting with the club)

To the furthest extent possible, parents are encouraged to take responsibility for running their club. They choose the activities based on their children's needs and abilities, decide when, where, and how often the club will meet, and take on varying degrees of the leadership.

Clubs meet on an average of once a month for 2 to 4 hours, often on Sunday afternoons or weekday evenings when parents and siblings are free to participate. The activities are as diverse as the membership. Some emphasize a particular theme, such as camping, square dancing, roller skating, or community outings; most provide a wide variety of group recreational activities from art to zoo trips. Some are purely recreational; others provide a formal parent-training or educational component.

The national office of Let's Play To Grow offers ongoing assistance to those starting or running clubs. This assistance includes training workshops and materials, play guides for parents, general printed information, audiovisual materials, and individualized technical assistance. In addition, 20 volunteer coordinators in states and other countries provide localized assistance.

Unique Aspects of Let's Play To Grow

Let's Play To Grow is different from other parent-support or recreation programs for five reasons. First, because it is volunteer run, Let's Play To Grow does not cost a lot to organize or run. An average club costs under $200 per year. Second, Let's Play To Grow is fun. Unlike other support programs, Let's Play To Grow does not focus on problems or heavy subjects. Sharing problems and emotional support are a by-product of the friendships that develop in a relaxed, playful atmosphere. Third, unlike many other programs designed for the handicapped child, which often ignore the needs and potential contributions of the father, brothers, and sisters, Let's Play To Grow is not just a "babysitter" service for the child, nor is it a program for mother and child alone. It is a program for the entire family. Fourth, Let's Play To Grow is parent run. Parents come to see themselves as part of the solution rather than part of the problem. Finally, Let's Play To Grow is adaptable to different ages, disabilities, sponsoring agencies, and income groups.

Effective Aspects of Let's Play To Grow

Evaluations of Let's Play To Grow have found that the program addresses the needs of families with special children or young adults in four ways:

Let's Play To Grow gives parents specific techniques for teaching their handicapped child play and recreational activities.   Play can provide tremendous spiritual, emotional, and physical benefits to anyone. However, persons with disabilities are often left out of family recreational activities. As one Let's Play To Grow parent said, "Club activities have reemphasized the fact that my handicapped child is a child first who enjoys fun, laughter, recreation, and being with others. Through Let's Play To Grow we have been able to observe our child in as natural a play situation as possible. We have a better idea of his abilities, and we have learned ways to make the best of them."

Families are given tools to help themselves.   Often parents feel dependent on professionals, treated as clients or patients rather than as equal partners. Evaluation studies have shown that even low-income parents involved in Let's Play To Grow find they no longer feel uncomfortable working with teachers and other professionals in promoting their special children's development. Said one father, "The program is geared so you make it happen for yourself, so you decide what you want to do; and when you decide what you want to do and make it happen for yourself, you're going to have fun."

Let's Play To Grow provides structured time for families to learn or re-learn how to have fun together.   Dealing with the many problems of having a handicapped child may leave parents with few emotional resources for having fun and enjoying their handicapped child or family. Parents find, as one mother put it, that Let's Play To Grow is a "place where everyone is OK and you can come together and play."

During club meetings parents have the opportunity to meet and share experiences with other parents of handicapped children.   They can observe and become acquainted with the other handicapped children in the group, can learn what to expect of their own child at different age levels, and can get tips on ways to help siblings and other family members adapt to having a handicapped child in the family. Parents find, as one mother said, that "The Let's Play To Grow Club helped me to let go a little. There was that support from other families and the Let's Play To Grow staff. With this club has grown real friendship between families with similar problems."

Examples of Program Successes

One Family's Experience with Let's Play To Grow

Kerri and Jim Rymash of Noank, Connecticut, have been active Let's Play To Grow participants for almost 5 years. They began their involvement in Let's Play To Grow when their son Todd, now 7, was 3 years old. Todd has Down's syndrome and a severe heart defect. They and three other families of handicapped children founded their club with the help of professionals from the nearby Seaside Regional Center for the Developmentally Disabled. Let's Play To Grow staff from the national headquarters provided initial training for club leaders and continues to provide support and technical assistance.

Currently, Mrs. Rymash is coleader of the club along with the father of another handicapped child. Six families meet monthly to enjoy music, swimming, jumping on a trampoline, playing ball, or other recreational activities. The activities, meeting times, and other arrangements are organized by parents.

Mrs. Rymash, a former elementary schoolteacher, says that Let's Play To Grow has benefited every member of her family. She says that because Todd is very shy he has a hard time interacting with people outside the family, even at school. At Let's Play To Grow meetings Todd has so much fun that he does not even think about hanging back. "He's almost forced to interact," she says.

Todd's sister, Brooke, has also benefited. Mrs. Rymash reports that Brooke will never have the feeling, as so many siblings of handicapped children do, that she is the only one facing such a challenge. She will also never feel uncomfortable around other individuals with handicaps; even now she counts Todd's mentally retarded friends as her own, recently inviting them to her sixth birthday party.

A significant characteristic of the program is high father participation, averaging 75%. Jim Rymash says that club activities help him structure his schedule so that he spends more time enjoying family recreational activities. He is impressed with the large number of fathers in the program and says, "When I come to a meeting, I see other fathers there, and that's very important to me, to know that I'm not any less of a person or a man because my child is handicapped."

Omaha's Let's Play To Grow Club

Li'l Champs Club in Omaha, Nebraska, is an example of a Let's Play To Grow program that serves children from birth to age 5, during the crucial years when play is the main vehicle for the child's development. At a recent meeting of Li'l Champs, the 40 handicapped children, their parents, brothers, and sisters enjoyed an evening of music donated by a local pop band. Children, mothers, and fathers clapped, marched, and danced to the strains of children's tunes such as "She'll be Coming 'Round the Mountain When She Comes" and "Skip to My Lou" as well as country and western and rock and roll favorites. Even the nonhandicapped brothers and sisters actively participated.

Parents observed their own children and others, some expressing surprise that their child was capable of doing some of the activities. One mother said she did not know that her son could march to music and would try to play games that would encourage him to move to music at home. Before the meeting ended, the special education teacher who assists with the club provided guidance to the parents on simple music activities and games the families can do at home, such as some finger plays and use of homemade percussion instruments.

One mother summed up her Let's Play To Grow experience: "My child will have to live in a nonhandicapped world. At Let's Play To Grow he learns to interact with nonhandicapped adults and children who understand him, and he learns recreational and social skills he would never get with only other handicapped kids, like there are in his class at school. As a family we've found a place where we belong, where we're not isolated or separate or different just because we have a handicapped child. Just knowing that has given us a lot of support and hope."

References

Ainsworth, M. D. S., Bell, S. M., & Stayton, D. J. (1974). Infant-mother attachment and social development: "Socialization" as a product of reciprocal responsiveness to signals. In M. P. M. Richards (Ed.), *The integration of the child into a social world* (pp. 99-135). New York: Cambridge University Press.

Bowlby, J. (1969). *Attachment and loss: Attachment*. New York: Basic Books.

Brazelton, T. B., Koslowski, B., & Main, M. (1974). The origins of reciprocity: The early mother-infant interaction. In M. Lewis & L. Rosenbaum (Eds.), *The effect of the infant on its caregiver* (pp. 49-76). New York: Wiley and Sons.

Buscaglia, L. (1975). *The disabled and their parents: A counselling challenge.* Thorofare, NJ: Charles B. Slack.

Piaget, J., & Inhelder, B. (1958). *The growth of logical thinking from childhood to adolescence.* New York: Basic Books.

Voeltz, L. M., & Wuerch, B. B. (1981). A comprehensive approach to leisure education and leisure counseling for the severely handicapped person. *Therapeutic Recreational Journal,* **15**, 24-35.

Wuerch, B. B., & Voeltz, L. M. (1982). *Longitudinal leisure skills for severely handicapped learners: The ho'onanea curriculum component.* Baltimore: Paul H. Brookes.

Effects of Physical Education on Children With Learning Disabilities

Gudrun M. Doll-Tepper

Generally speaking, the Federal Republic of Germany's educational system provides special schooling for children and adolescents who are disabled. Exceptions to this rule are a number of projects aimed at the integration of handicapped children, chiefly at primary schools, in which disabled children (e.g., physically handicapped children or children with impaired vision) are taught alongside nonhandicapped children on an experimental basis.

Ten different types of special schools are distinguishable; in terms of pupil percentages, the largest share is taken up by schools for children with learning disabilities. In this type of school, pupils are taught who are distinctly of below-average intelligence or who have generalized learning disabilities (Kanter, 1980). Physical education at schools for children with learning disabilities is beset by a great number of problems that are largely connected with the heterogeneous composition of the pupils with regard to motor, cognitive, psychic-emotional, and social makeup.

Within the framework of the present field study, the questions examined were the extent to which motor skills of pupils at this special type of school deviated from those of other pupils of the same age and the effects of specially designed physical education aimed at furthering motor development as compared with conventional physical education lessons given at schools. For example, changes in the day-to-day routine of the school, increases in the number of lessons, the participation of additional physical education staff, or changes in the use of rooms and materials were excluded in order to simulate normal working conditions.

Methods

The pupils of two schools for children with learning disabilities were involved in the study. In all, 160 children between 6 and 16 years of age were tested according to the body coordination test for children, the Körperkoordinationstest für Kinder (KTK) (Kiphard & Schilling, 1974). This test procedure consists of four tasks that serve to evaluate the motor dimension "overall body control and coordination" and is well suited to assess the level of motor development in children between the ages of 5 and 14 years. It can also be implemented to measure the effectiveness of therapy and, according to Schilling (1974), can also be applied to older handicapped adolescents. The data from the motor-skill test were supplemented by a number of other variables thought to be closely linked to motor achievement.

Information about the existence of further disturbances or disabilities, such as impairments of vision, hearing, and speech, cerebral dysfunctions, and convulsive disorders, was based on medical and psychological examinations; inquiries were also made with regard to the pupils' participation in additional therapeutic measures (physiotherapy, occupational therapy). In the 20 weeks of the study, which represented one-half year of school, the pupils of both schools had three physical education lessons per week, in keeping with the time allotted for physical education in the timetable of this type of school.

For reasons of expediency, the division of the children into experimental and control groups was made according to the schools they attended. Physical education lessons in the experimental group were based on a special concept intended to further motor development. In this concept, which took account of the motopedagogic approach (Irmischer, 1984; Kiphard, 1979) and was aimed mainly at improving competence in motor acts, the following two aspects were of fundamental importance in the planning of the physical education lessons: Each single pupil should be given the opportunity to perform a wide variety of movements with a high degree of intensity; and account should be taken of each pupil's level of development and achievement in all kinds of exercise.

The lessons were characterized by alternation of phases guided by the teacher and phases in which the pupils were given the chance to develop their own ideas. Teaching in the experimental group was marked by a social-integrational style of teacher behavior. In all classes the lessons comprised the following components (although the weighting of each component differed from class to class): movement games, trampoline tumbling, swimming, exercises/games with apparatus, and circuit training. Lessons in the control group were given in accordance with the official curriculum; there was no special planning among the staff with regard to contents, methods, or teacher behavior.

At the end of the study the KTK (Kiphard & Schilling, 1974) was again used to assess changes in motor achievement in both groups.

Results

The score obtained in the KTK as a measure of motor coordination ability is expressed by the "motor quotient" (MQ), whereby a score of 100 ± 15 represents age-matched development. As a first result of the study, the scores achieved in the initial motor-skill test revealed—for the entire 160 children with learning disabilities taking part in the study—that the motor response of these children deviated considerably from that of normally developed children and adolescents. The average score of the group as a whole was MQ = 64, a figure that lies in the region of disturbed motor response. Overall, 56.9% of the children tested were found to have motor response deficiencies, 25% showed noticeable motor weaknesses, whereas 18.1% exhibited a response in keeping with their age. Because, when viewed separately, the scores of the initial test differed between the experimental and the control group, the dependence of motor skill on other variables was determined individually for both groups.

It must be stressed that no differences were found in motor skill between sexes, impairments of vision and hearing, and convulsive disorders. Significantly poor results, however, were obtained by pupils of the experimental group with speech impediments. In both groups motor response among pupils with symptoms of cerebral dysfunction was found to be considerably worse than that of their fellow pupils. It was also revealed, especially in the experimental group, that pupils who took advantage of sports activities outside the regular school physical education lessons achieved a higher score in the initial test. In the final test at the end of the study, higher scores were obtained in both the experimental and control groups.

Because the achievement of both groups differed at the beginning of the study, it was necessary—in the comparison of the two groups—to use the differences between the initial and final test scores to calculate the changes in motor skill. Comparison of the mean values of these differentials revealed a substantial difference between both groups with regard to the overall MQ score. Using covariance analysis, it was established that there was no significant influence of the initial score on improved achievement. Partialling out the initial MQ values leads to substantial differences between both groups.

The influence of the specially devised physical education lessons in connection with the various other variables was determined by means of two-factor variance analysis to gain information on each subgroup. In all cases the special lessons were allotted a high proportion of the affirmed variance. In the experimental group the factor "additional sport" was also of significance. In this subgroup—as mentioned above—not only the initial test score was higher than that of other pupils, but also the improvement in achievement was higher.

Discussion

The results of the initial motor-skill test clearly revealed that motor coordination among children with learning disabilities/subnormal learners is considerably weaker than that of normally developed children and adolescents (measured by the KTK). Over 75% of all the pupils tested exhibited more or less severe problems of coordination, and barely 25% possessed motor skills appropriate for their age. The results of these tests, when compared with other, although predominantly older studies of motor response among children with learning disabilities (Kiphard, 1973; Woschkind, 1967) with the exception of Schilling (1984), make clear that among this group of schoolchildren much greater difficulties of motor response must be expected than was hitherto supposed. Further, one must take note of not only the mean test score, which was distinctly below average, but also the great divergence of the test scores.

In the teaching process, increased attention must be paid to this divergence. The results of the longitudinal study demonstrate the positive effect of specially devised physical education lessons compared with conventional physical education in schools. A particularly positive result is verification of the fact that special lessons are equally effective among pupils who are affected to a greater or lesser extent by additional handicaps, such as cerebral symptoms and speech impediments. The effect of additional motor activity, neglected in studies on the effectiveness of sports programs up to now, is a question to which more attention must be paid in the future.

As already noted in a number of studies (Kluge, 1979; Wocken, 1982), only a very small percentage of children with learning disabilities take part in sports activities in formal groups, and this is plainly confirmed by the results of the present study. The significant differences of achievement in favor of the pupils who regularly took part in sports activities gave rise to the presumption that children with learning disabilities are assisted in their motor development by their membership in a group and that this has a positive influence on their level of achievement. At the same time, it must be supposed that only pupils with a higher level of achievement than their fellow pupils as far as motor skills are concerned develop an interest in regular sports activities. Apparently only those who feel accepted because of their motor ability have enough confidence to join a group, as Moegling (1982) noted in a pilot project. With regard to the integration of handicapped children, it can, therefore, be concluded that motor skills must be specially furthered if children with learning disabilities are to be given the chance to take part in games and sports along with other children, and not only during school hours.

Conclusions

Investigations undertaken to date on the motor responses of children with learning disabilities have revealed that among this group there is an increased incidence of noticeable weaknesses and disturbances in motor response, which corresponds to a restricted potential of the prerequisites for learning. Considering this, one can only speak of physical education lessons that offer an adequate amount of opportunity when qualitative improvements are introduced in schools in the field of physical education to further all-around development. The results of the longitudinal study can be interpreted as a possible step in this direction, and they support the thesis that it is possible to achieve these aims under normal school conditions. In other words, it is possible to intensify physical education teaching within the existing structure of school organization. Despite the positive effects of a special concept of lessons devised for this study, the fact cannot be ignored that the majority of children with learning disabilities achieved scores in the tests that were distinctly below average for their age. It would seem advisable, therefore, to give equal regard to both pedagogic and therapeutic objectives.

Seen in this light, physical education at schools for subnormal learners is not to be regarded only as compensation or rehabilitation; in addition, the preventive aspect must be taken into account. This means that through continuous efforts to further development starting as early as possible, the current difference in levels of achievement between large numbers of children with learning abilities and their contemporaries who are normally developed for their age must not be allowed to remain, let alone grow. Beyond this, the attempt must be made to improve individual ability through motor processes that offer enjoyment and adventure, thus providing the basis for better learning.

In general terms, furthering motor development can be regarded as helping individuals to help themselves. To achieve these goals, the following demands can be formulated as far as physical education in schools is concerned: more effective use of available physical education lessons to further motor development, as was tried in this study with a special concept of lessons; and more opportunity for physical exercise in the school curriculum (e.g., increase in extra lessons for weaker pupils).

References

Irmischer, T. (1984). *Didaktik des Sportunterrichts an der Schule für Lernbehinderte* [Didactics of physical education in schools for children with learning disabilities]. Dortmund: Modernes Lernen.

Kanter, G. (1980). Lernbehinderungen und die Personengruppe der Lernbehinderten [Learning disabilities and the category of persons with learning disabilities]. In G. Kanter & O. Speck (Eds.), *Pädagogik der Lernbehinderten* (2nd ed.) (pp. 34-64). Berlin: Marhold.

Kiphard, E. J. (1973). Zum Problem der Bewegungsstörungen in der Lernbehindertenschule [The problem of motor disturbances in schools for children with learning disabilities]. In H. Rieder (Ed.), *Bewegungslehre des Sports* (pp. 123-136). Schorndorf: Hofmann.

Kiphard, E. J. (1979). *Motopädagogik* [Motopedagogy]. Dortmund: Modernes Lernen.

Kiphard, E. J., & Schilling, F. (1974). *Körperkoordinationstest für Kinder KTK* [Body coordination test for children]. Weinheim: Beltz.

Kluge, G. (1979). Freizeitpädagogik für Behinderte [Leisure pedagogy for the handicapped]. In H. Stadler (Ed.), *Handbuch der Behindertenpädagogik* (pp. 70-82). München: Kösel.

Moegling, K. (1982). Sozialarbeit im Sportverein: Gymnasiasten und Sonderschüler gemeinsam in einer Sportspielmannschaft [Social work in a sport club: High school students and special-school students participating together in team sport activities]. *Sonderpädagogik, 12*, 117-123.

Schilling, F. (1974). *Körperkoordinationstest für Kinder KTK, Manual* [Body coordination test for children, manual]. Weinheim: Beltz.

Schilling, F. (1984). Die pädagogische Förderung Behinderter im Aufgabenfeld Bewegung am Beispiel Psychomotorischer Erziehung (Motopädagogik) [The education of the handicapped with regard to movement, particularly psychomotor education (motopedagogy)]. In G. Kanter, H. Langenohl, & M. Sommer (Eds.), *Sportunterricht an der Lernbehindertenschule* (pp. 1-19). Berlin: Marhold.

Wocken, H. (1982). Freizeitinteressen und Freizeitverhalten lernbehinderter Schüler [Leisure-time interests and behavior of pupils with learning disabilities]. In W. Kerkhoff (Ed.), *Freizeitchancen und Freizeitlernen für behinderte Kinder und Jugendliche* (pp. 197-248). Berlin: Marhold.

Woschkind, U. (1967). Untersuchungen zur Motorik bei Volks- und Hilfsschulkindern [Studies on motor abilities of elementary school pupils and special-school pupils]. *Zeitschrift für Heilpädagogik, 18*, 18–32.

Psychological and Social Problems of Physical Disability: State of the Art and Relevance to Physical Education

Taoheed A. Adedoja

Program development for the physically handicapped requires an understanding of the psychological and social problems experienced by physically handicapped persons. Siller (1960) pointed out that psychological insights can help in the construction, design, prescription, and training in the use of prostheses for amputees and can assist in programming strategies for other types of orthopedic disabilities.

Although literature reviews by McDaniel (1969), Schontz (1975), and Siller (1974) revealed that there are no sufficient data to support disability-specific personality types, several other studies (Bogdan, 1977; Brown, 1981; Bruininks, 1978; Bryan, 1976; Bucher, 1983; Cohen, 1977; Cratty, 1980; Harper & Richman, 1980; Richardson & Green, 1971) have indicated that the handicapped exhibit some psychological and social behaviors, such as extreme maladjustment, social alienation, self-pity, feeling of rejection, depression, and compensatory efforts. A format for considering the effects of physical limitations on adjustment in the somato-psychological relationship was proposed by Wright (1960).

Many other explanations have been put forward to describe the behaviors of the nonhandicapped. Cratty (1980) stated that normal individuals react in various ways to handicapped persons. However, when confronted with the orthopedically handicapped, the primary social-psychological error committed by normals is to show pity rather than to offer help and useful support. Cratty further stated that the orthopedically handicapped are often reluctant to enter and compete in new social situations and that they may suffer from other problems, such as social overcompensation, speech and language difficulties, and other perceptual and conceptual problems that inhibit their total adaptation to society.

In research undertaken among children in Great Britain, Richardson and Green (1971) indicated that the major factor influencing children adversely against their fellows is neither color nor intelligence but visible deformity. Citing an example of a typical attitude toward the handicapped in many parts of the world, Mills (1960) offered this description, ''There they sit, fed and housed by more or perhaps less sympathetic relations, but regarded by all as useless and unproductive'' (p. 3). Such unfavorable attitudes toward the handicapped are seen throughout developing countries, of which Nigeria is an example (Nwaogu, 1979). Also, the stigma attached to being handicapped may take many forms: rejection as a person with whom to be associated; belief in God's punishment upon him or her; sins of parents; and strong disbelief in ability to be capable of approaching normality as a fellow citizen (Commonwealth Secretariat, 1972).

Barker, Wright, and Gonick (1983) stated that studies indicate rather consistently that physically disabled persons are more frequently maladjusted than physically normal persons. They also pointed out that the resulting maladjustment can take the following forms: withdrawal, retiring behavior; shyness; timidity, self-consciousness, and fearful behavior; serious, thoughtful behavior; refusal to recognize real conditions, concealment, and delusions. Others include feelings of inferiority; emotional and psychosexual immaturity; isolated asocial behavior; paranoid reactions, sensitivity, and suspicion; craving for attention, love of praise; extreme aggressiveness, competitive behavior; and anxiety, tension, nervousness, and temper tantrums. Furthermore, Dewey and Dewey (1974) stated that children with handicaps such as amputations, deformed hands, or "frozen" joints face a great psychological challenge. They know that their handicaps are visible and often must tolerate tactless reactions from others.

Matthew (1967) administered the Handicap Problems Inventory to a group of nonblind physically disabled people. Factor analysis of the responses to the inventory yielded six dimensions of psychological impact of physical disability: a feeling of personal rejection; a need to be normal; denial of disability; guilt; despair; and nonacceptance of self. In a study cited by Love (1978), it was reported that the effects of crippling conditions on intelligence, school achievement, and emotional adjustment of 270 physically handicapped children aged 5 through 16 was not significantly different from other nonhandicapped persons. An earlier study by Kanner (1972) postulated that emotional disturbance is not necessarily a characteristic of physical handicap. But the investigation by Harper and Richman (1980) showed that the orthopedically impaired group exhibits an isolative and passive orientation to interpersonal interactions as well as more generalized feelings of alienation.

Furthermore, the psychological impact of disability on body image has received considerable attention by researchers. The concept of body image or body schema has been referred to by Little (1974) as the mental idea and basic attitude a person has toward his or her own body and an idea of how the person perceives himself or herself physically, aesthetically, and socially. Body image also provides a clue as to how the person sees himself or herself in relation to the world, and this reflects the person's style of life. Joy, Reynolds, and Tishaw (1983) agreed that the language used to describe people and their abilities influences how people perceive themselves, how they believe others perceive them, and the way other people learn to describe the same people and abilities. Therefore, the term *person with a handicapping condition* has been suggested by Joy et al. rather than *handicapped person*, because, according to them, one may only experience a handicapping condition in certain situations and not in all situations. Meninger (1963), Szasz (1963, 1970), and Blatt (1970) also agreed that the terms used in describing the handicapped have both descriptive value and deleterious effect.

Brown (1981) stated that many factors influence the development of impaired persons, but it is their attitude about themselves that seems most significant. The amputee cannot find a place in his or her body image for the deformity. The amputee may even deny the deformity and resist efforts to use braces and crutches. Acceptance of the disability could be facilitated not only by various forms of physical therapy but also by various psychological means aimed at satisfying emotional and attitudinal needs and pressures and at social integration.

In a study of the body image of amputee children, Siller and Peizer (1957) found feelings of inferiority and shame to be important components in the psychological functioning of more than one third of the children studied, particularly among amputees of traumatic origin. Also, Garret and Levine (1962) stated that the word *cripple* comes to the amputee's mind along with its various connotations of inadequacy, charity, shame, punishment, and guilt. Garret and Levine further indicated that when individuals view themselves and feel that they are being viewed by others in these forms, they consider themselves objects of lessened respect and react to this changed status accordingly. Because these attitudes are not likely to enhance self-concept but rather devalue it, the handicapped may be expected to undertake defense against the effect of these attitudes on their integrity.

Extensive research studies have been done on the attitudes of peers, parents, students, the public, teachers, and administrators toward the handicapped. Almsgiving seems predominant in the charitable attitude of many Nigerian people toward the handicapped. Lenhart (1976) explained that the charitable act of almsgiving is done in many cases not because of a concern for the handicapped but because of the givers' selfish interest in seeking rewards and blessings from God. Mba (1978) also indicated that among factors contributing to the general apathy toward the handicapped in emerging countries of Africa are "superstitious beliefs that reward disability as a curse invoked by the gods who must be appeased in order to work off the evil Karma" (p. 30).

Goffman (1963) indicated that when an individual is identified as having a physical abnormality, people also assume that the person has some form of mental retardation. Such misunderstandings and attitudes about physically disabled students affect the development of educational programs as well as the methods used to implement these programs (Patton, 1979).

Peer reactions to handicapping conditions have also received attention in the literature. Brown (1981) commented that peers of orthopedically handicapped students are often moved by pity, which might cause them to overreact with concern or to be helpful beyond what is needed or wanted.

In a recent article on attitudes toward people with disabilities, Siller (1982) found seven stable factors describing attitudes of nondisabled people toward amputation and other physical disabilities. Six factors were clearly negative, and one that appears to be positive was interpreted as actually reflecting negativity. In another data-based study by Kennedy and Thurman (1982), they concluded that at a very early age children perceive incompetence in others without having seen it demonstrated. In addition, relatively young children, as determined by their investigation, ascribe negative status to handicapped children by referring to them as babies, young, and small. Kennedy and Thurman's data further suggested that attitudes toward handicapped children begin to develop even before the child enters school or comes into contact with handicapped children. They suggested that parent training in the preschool years might be the strongest influence in developing a child's concern for the welfare of others and tolerance and acceptance for those viewed as different. Brant (1979) agrees that parental attitude is very important in influencing a child's social and personal development.

Some parents have unrealistic ideas about their handicapped child, while others are able to accept their child's handicapping condition and try to utilize the best possible education opportunities (Kindred, 1976).

Furthermore, attitudes of teachers and administrators toward the handicapped have been studied and have been found woefully inadequate to meet the educational needs of the handicapped (Gickling & Theobold, 1975; Patton, 1979). Such negative attitudes by educators have been labeled the "two box" theory; that is, children are considered either exceptional or normal.

A summary of the psychological impact of being handicapped has been well presented by Cruickshank (1966). He suggested that the handicapped child might be involved with a success-prohibitory situation. Cruickshank defined the situation as follows:

> The handicap—sets into operation a circular situation: The handicap—is the barrier to success; frustration results; attempts are made to substitute satisfactions for the original activity; the handicap is again a barrier; greater frustration results; more activity, and more blocking ad infinitum. (p. 18)

Specific efforts designed to aid the disabled in developing competency in social and psychological situations and understanding of the roots of stigma should be considered as an integral part of programming for the handicapped (Rosenthal, 1973).

Relevant information on the psychological and social problems of the disabled gives a clear picture of some of the problems and challenges for physical education. The psychosocial profiles of the disabled relate to inadequate physical movement, poor or negative body image, and deteriorating effect on the self-esteem, physical development, socialization, and healthful experiences of the disabled.

Personality development and the achievement of desirable social adjustment have long been important objectives of physical education. It is considered important, therefore, that the physically disabled, no matter what type of rehabilitation program is provided, be taught or assisted to resist the tendency to adopt a completely sedentary life. Learning certain physical skills and activities within the limitation of the disability provides an acceptable outlet for the disabled.

Within the framework of organized physical education and sports, adapted physical education is expected to perform two major functions. First, it should provide the disabled with an opportunity to learn and to participate actively in a number of physical education activities and appropriate recreational and leisure time sports. Second, it should help disabled students develop a feeling of self-worth and value through success-oriented activities. Specifically, a program of physical education for the disabled should provide activities adapted to the needs, interests, and capabilities of the disabled and promote greater physical and emotional relaxation. It should create a variety of activities in order to discover the special interests of the disabled and to aid the disabled in resocialization into the mainstream of society. As researchers, we hope that it will also develop their feelings of self-worth and value and that they can compensate for their specific disability by mastering it and finding personal achievement and success in other areas of life.

Early intervention through programs of physical education, recreation, and sensory stimulation can help the disabled in making developmental gains characteristic of their age level as well as help impede further deterioration in social, psychological, and physical development. Because of the social and psychological deviations of the disabled as reviewed in this article, a multidisciplinary approach consisting of interactions among many fields is most desirable. For physical educators to be very successful in their mission of providing purposeful movement activities and counseling for the disabled, other professionals in social work, physical and occupational therapy, medicine, communication disorder, psychology, and special education must cooperate. The role of members of the public in serving as volunteers and peers in physical education and recreation activities will gradually and significantly influence the attitude of others toward the disabled.

References

Barker, R. G., Wright, B. A., & Gonick, H. R. (1983). Adjustment to physical handicap and illness: A survey of the social psychology of physique and disability. *Social Science Research Council Bulletin,* **55**(5), 5.

Blatt, B. (1970). *Exodus from pandemonium.* Boston: Allyn & Bacon.

Bogdan, R. (1977, March-April). Handicapism. *Social Policy,* **18**, 8-9.

Brant, L. (1979). *I like you when I know you.* Columbus, OH: Ohio State University.

Brown, F. M. (1981). *The attitudes of mainstreamed toward physical education.* Unpublished master's thesis, University of Wisconsin, La Crosse.

Bruininks, V. L. (1978). Peer status and personality characteristics of learning disabled and non-disabled students. *Journal of Learning Disabilities,* **11**(18), 484-489.

Bryan, E. (1976). Come on dummy: An observational study of children's communications. *Journal of Learning Disabilities, 9*(10), 66-69.

Bucher, C. A. (1983). *Administration of physical education and athletic programs.* St. Louis: C. V. Mosby.

Cohen, S. (1977). *Special people.* Englewood Cliffs, NJ: Prentice-Hall.

Commonwealth Secretariat (1972). *Special education in the developing countries of the Commonwealth.* London: Author.

Cratty, B. J. (1980). *Adapted physical education for the handicapped and youth.* Denver: Love Publishing.

Cruickshank, W. M. (1966). *Cerebral palsy—Its individual and community problems.* Syracuse, NY: Syracuse University Press.

Dewey, M. A., & Dewey, R. A. (1974). *Teaching physical education to special students.* Portland, ME: J. Weston Welch.

Garret, J. F., & Levine, E. (1962). *Psychological practices with the physically disabled.* New York: Columbia University Press.

Gickling, E. E., & Theobold, J. T. (1975). Mainstreaming effect or affect. *Journal of Special Education, 9,* 317-328.

Goffman, E. (1963). *Stigma: Notes on the management of spoiled identity.* Englewood Cliffs, NJ: Prentice-Hall.

Harper, D. C., & Richman, L. C. (1980). Personality profiles of physically impaired young adults. *Journal of Clinical Psychology, 36,* 668-671.

Joy, C., Reynolds, N., & Tishaw, K. (1983). *Leisure knows no handicap.* Stillwater, OK: Oklahoma Quality Printing.

Kanner, L. (1972). *Child psychiatry.* Springfield, IL: Charles C. Thomas.

Kennedy, A. B., & Thurman, S. K. (1982). Inclinations of nonhandicapped children to help their handicapped peers. *Journal of Special Education, 16*(3), 319-327.

Kindred, E. M. (1976). Integration at the secondary school level. *Volal Review, 78,* 35-43.

Lenhart, L. W. (1976). *The stigma of disability.* Unpublished doctoral dissertation, University of Oklahama, Norman.

Little, E. A. (1974). *Rehabilitation of the spinal cord injured* (Publication No. 806). Little Rock: University of Arkansas, Arkansas Rehabilitation Research and Training Center.

Love, H. D. (1978). *Teaching physically handicapped children.* Springfield, IL: Charles C. Thomas.

Matthew, J. P. (1967). Psychological impact of physical disability upon vocationally handicapped individuals. *Dissertation Abstracts International, 28,* 1204.

Mba, P. O. (1978). Priority needs of special education in developing countries: Nigeria. In F. H. Pink (Ed.), *International perspectives on future special education* (pp. 30-33). Reston, VA: Council for Exceptional Children.

McDaniel, J. W. (1969). *Physical disability and human behavior.* New York: Pergamon Press.

Meninger, K. (1963). *The vital balance.* New York: Viking Press.

Mills, R. (1960). *Nigeria's blind farmer.* London: Royal Commonwealth Society for the Blind.

Nwaogu, O. P. (1979). *A program for the education of the mentally retarded in a developing country: Nigeria.* Unpublished doctoral dissertation, Southern Illinois University, Carbondale.

Patton, J. M. (1979). *Teachers attitudes toward the special needs students: From research to practice* (ERIC Document Reproduction Service Number Ed. 181380). Petersburg, VA: Conference for Vocational Educators.

Richardson, S. A., & Green, A. (1971). When is black beautiful: Colored and white children's reaction to skin color. *British Journal of Educational Psychology, 41*(1), 62-69.

Rosenthal, R. (1973, September). The pygmalion effect lives. *Psychology Today,* 57-63.

Shontz, F. C. (1975). The psychological aspects of physical fitness and disability. New York: Macmillan.

Siller, J. S. (1960). Psychological concomitants of amputation in children. *Child Development, 31,* 109-120.

Siller, J. S. (1974). Psychological situation of the disabled with spinal cord injuries. In *Rehabilitation of the Spinal Cord Injured* (Publication No. 806). Little Rock: University of Arkansas, Arkansas Rehabilitation Research and Training Center.

Siller, J. S. (1982). Continuing research findings: Attitudes toward people with disabilities. *Rehabilitation Brief, 10,* 1-4.

Siller, J., & Peizer, E. (1957). Some problems of the amputee child in school. *Education, 78*(3), 141.

Szasz, T. (1963). *Law, liberty and psychiatry.* New York: Macmillan.

Szasz, T. (1970). *The manufacturer of madness.* New York: Macmillan.

Wright, B. A. (1960). *Physical disability—A psychological approach.* New York: Harper & Row.

PART II

Motor Skill Training

Motor Skill Training: A Neurobehavioral Approach

Ronald V. Croce

The acquisition of motor skills is important in all facets of human endeavor. Although many skills are learned through play experiences, the more complex skills that make up the majority of our movement repertoire require goal-directed instruction. As a general rule, the learning of a new motor skill occurs in three phases (Fitts & Posner, 1967). During the first phase, the performer consciously executes skills step by step and is extremely dependent on cognitive processes for adequate levels of performance. During the second phase, the primary concern is practice, error detection, and manipulation of the motor act. The third and final phase involves the automatic execution of the skill with minimal conscious involvement. Accordingly, the learner progresses from conscious involvement, where there are numerous responses of extraneous muscle tissue during skill execution and where the skill is crude and poorly coordinated, to an automatic posture, where skill execution occurs with minimal conscious involvement and proceeds in a highly efficient and coordinated manner.

The development of sound motor training programs for neurologically problematic youngsters (i.e., those children having neurological dysfunction) presents unique methodological problems for motor training and rehabilitation specialists. It is the purpose of this chapter to outline basic neurological and behavioral processes involved in motor control and to present an intervention program for the amelioration of motor dysfunction based on theories of motor control and learning.

Neuropsychological Aspects of Motor Control

Two preeminent operational modes exist in the control of human motor behavior. The first is the *central programming-output* mode, which includes the motivation, intention, and preparation of movement, the planning of movement, and the designing of an appropriate motor program. These functions are carried out by many different, yet constantly interacting, parts of the brain, such as the association cortices, basal ganglia, cerebellum, and motor cortex. The second is the *peripheral-input* mode, which involves the integration of sensory information into feedback systems, spinal and cortical reflexes, and servo-control mechanisms of movement.

In general, all voluntary muscular control originates in supraspinal motor centers, the most important being the cerebral cortex, which can be divided into three areas: the sensory area, where activity patterns of muscular contraction are modified; the association area, where intellectual processes occur and where motor acts are conceived; and the motor areas (primary and secondary), where bodily movements are initiated. Assisting the cerebral cortex in motor control are the basal ganglia, which are involved in the programming and initiation of motor behaviors, and the cerebellum, which provides movement-related feedback to the cerebral cortex as well as being involved in the preplanning and programming of motor cortex output (Brooks, 1983; Evarts, 1979; Marsden, 1980; Requin, 1980; Wise & Evarts, 1981).

Historically, two major theoretical models evolved to explain the locus of control of skilled motor behaviors. On the one hand, there were the peripheralists, who contended that movement is controlled by way of feedback either from the responding limbs (proprioception) or from the visual, auditory, or vestibular systems. This position has taken the form of a closed-loop hypothesis as espoused by Adams (1971). On the other hand, the centralists (Lashley, 1917) argued that movement is controlled by way of centrally stored motor progams and that these programs are organized in advance and then executed without the involvement of peripherally generated feedback.

Glencross (1977) stated that the evidence did not strongly favor one position of motor control over the other. He suggested a more integrated control model incorporating the use of both systems. In this two-stage model, Glencross suggested that during the early stages of motor learning the performer is feedback dependent (closed-loop control). Only with increased skill acquisition does the performer move into a more central, preprogrammed mode (open-loop control).

In order to resolve some of the processing limitations of open-loop and closed-loop theories, Schmidt (1975) proposed a schema theory of motor control and learning. Central to Schmidt's theory is the position of the *motor schema*. According to Schmidt, motor schemata are sets of rules that establish generalized motor programs for a given type of movement. Stronger motor schemata produce fewer errors in the initial trials of a novel skill governed by those schemata and lead to an increased rate of learning of new skills governed by those schemata.

The acquisition of new motor skills is predicated on the continuous repetition of a motor pattern (practice). This forms new motor engrams, which essentially produce automatization of the newly learned skill. Concurrently, conditioned reactions that support the movement pattern will be established. It is through previous motor experiences and practice of individual skills that most skills become so well learned that they become automatic and not under conscious thought. The more automatic a movement becomes, the less conscious involvement the performer needs. Less conscious control leads to faster processing of incoming information, at the same time freeing the performer to better interact with the environment.

Many individuals with brain damage lack some of the basic components of complex motor behaviors and, consequently, must be taught less complex patterns before more complex skills can be trained. Kottke (1980) asserted that motor engrams develop progressively by slow, precise practice of simple patterns, combined as they develop into more complex patterns and, ultimately, combined into the final skill. At that stage, the performer becomes less conscious of the details of the movement and can allocate more attention to environmental changes that may influence the response. In addition, the learning of new motor skills occurs only with active participation. Conscious muscular contraction is fundamental to the learning of muscular control.

Similarly, Brooks (1983) and Tatton and Bruce (1981) envisioned complex motor behaviors as containing more basic, fundamental movements. During the execution of simple motor patterns, one ordinarily uses sensory feedback to make adjustments, but one can, when the need arises, manage the motor response without it. This is not true for those motor responses that are not well learned and, consequently, not preprogrammed. The better a skill has been learned, the fewer the number of corrections that are needed. As a consequence, the movement becomes continuous, faster, and smoother. The learning of a new skill involves constant communication between sensory and motor systems and a continued use of adjusted programs.

Implications for Motor Rehabilitation

Although may therapeutic intervention programs have been pursued extensively for some time, their real value and effectiveness in motor reeducation have not been subject to sufficient controlled experimentation (Turnbull, 1982). In support of this position other authors have also questioned the efficacy of these intervention techniques (Brocklehurst, Andrews, Richards, & Laycock, 1978; Degangi, Hurley, & Linsheid, 1983; Ferry, 1981; Jones, 1974; Piper & Pless, 1980; Stern, McDowell, & Miller, 1970). In the January 1981 issue of *Pediatrics*, Ferry stated that therapists have unknowingly oversold developmental therapy, in effect promising that such programs will result in the growth of "new brain cells," though no direct evidence exists demonstrating such an effect. Ferry further stated that the literature does not yet provide any support for the claimed results of developmental therapy on the motor functioning of neurologically impaired children. She stated, "There is no valid scientific evidence that these programs do alter neurological development in high-risk or neurologically handicapped children" (p. 40).

Jones (1974) argued that many of the methods employed by therapists to improve motor control may be ineffective because they are based predominantly on the proprioceptive feedback theory of motor performance. (The current belief holds that movement is centrally initiated.) Jones strongly suggested that therapists need to develop new methods of motor reeducation that concentrate on teaching individuals to monitor their own voluntary motor responses.

This is not to say that no authors have found positive results with these motor therapy programs. Denhoff (1981) provided an extensive review on the subject and concluded that infant enrichment programs do provide benefits to handicapped children; however, Ferry (1981) strongly disagreed with Denhoff's conclusion. Ferry emphasized that there is inadequate documentation of program effects. Major problems encountered in the research include: (a) inappropriate and subjective evaluation instruments; (b) poorly designed experiments; (c) small numbers of subjects; (d) insufficient longitudinal follow-up; (e) the existence of confounding variables, the most notable being maturation of the subjects between pre- and posttests; and (f) the absence of matched control groups.

In response to the shortcomings of many of these intervention techniques, many authors have espoused a therapeutic approach based on theories of motor control and learning (Herman, 1982; Kottke, 1980; Marteniuk, 1979; McClenaghan, 1983; Turnbull, 1982). Turnbull stated, "This emphasis on learning is strongly implied in terms such as reeducation and rehabilitation. Learning theory, particularly motor learning, should then be fundamental to the body of knowledge associated with neurological physiotherapy" (p. 38).

Jones (1974) and Kottke (1980) stressed that the establishment of efference copies—or motor engrams—is essential for developing voluntary muscular control and should be the goal of therapeutic intervention programs. Kottke emphasized that automatic neuromuscular activity is the highest level of motor control. A perfected engram, which is only established by practice and repetition of the desired act, is voluntarily regulated only to the extent that the individual can initiate the movement, maintain it as long as desired, and terminate it at the end of the performance. Practice of the skill should be performed at a speed and with a force of muscular contraction at which each repetition can be performed precisely and successfully. The speed, force, and intensity of each practice session can be increased as performance levels improve. Correct motor engrams will be established only by repetition of precise movements at the actual speed and force that the movements will be performed; therefore, at the heart of any motor training or motor rehabilitation program is practice and repetition of specific, discrete skills (Kottke, 1980).

Marteniuk (1979) has provided a framework for educators and therapists to better understand how motor skill breakdown occurs and how they can best facilitate motor skill reacquisition. Though Marteniuk's article is beyond the scope of this chapter, the basic tenant of his approach, and consequently that of motor learning theory, is that of information processing.

The major theme of information processing theory is that all movement is the end product of a complex series of central nervous system events that includes such processes as perception, cognition, and motor planning. Marteniuk (1979) stressed that by understanding how motor skill acquisition is a function of information processing, as well as a function of several phases of learning (Fitts & Posner, 1967), the therapist or educator can utilize the basic principles of motor learning theory to analyze an individual's present level of motor functioning and better facilitate the acquisition of motor skills.

An individual's level of motor functioning is the product of genetic endowment, the degree of neurological or muscular dysfunction (both of

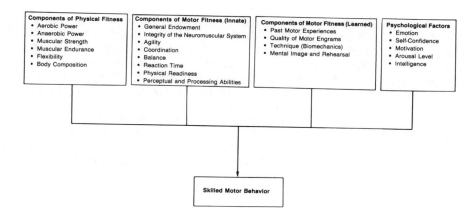

Components of Physical Fitness	Components of Motor Fitness (Innate)	Components of Motor Fitness (Learned)	Psychological Factors
• Aerobic Power • Anaerobic Power • Muscular Strength • Muscular Endurance • Flexibility • Body Composition	• General Endowment • Integrity of the Neuromuscular System • Agility • Coordination • Balance • Reaction Time • Physical Readiness • Perceptual and Processing Abilities	• Past Motor Experiences • Quality of Motor Engrams • Technique (Biomechanics) • Mental Image and Rehearsal	• Emotion • Self-Confidence • Motivation • Arousal Level • Intelligence

Skilled Motor Behavior

Figure 1   Factors affecting the acquisition of complex motor behaviors.

which cannot be changed significantly), and learning processes brought about by external and internal stimuli. The degree to which motor functioning can be optimized is predicated on the quality and quantity of the numerous stimuli imposed on the individual during the course of motor training and by individual capacity.

In order for motor training and rehabilitation specialists to construct the most appropriate training programs the following guidelines are suggested.

First and foremost, those factors that influence learning must be evaluated; that is; the learner's perceptual-motor and physical functioning must be evaluated. These factors include: the integrity of the neuromuscular system, balance, coordination, body build, strength, cardiovascular endurance, muscular endurance, and flexibility. It is important to note that the capacity to perform a particular motor skill is limited by the quality of the motor engram, which in turn is directly dependent on the interplay of strength, power, speed, flexibility, and somatotype; therefore, fundamental to motor skill acquisition is physical conditioning. It is, to borrow a metaphor, the foundation upon which all else is built.

Second, the learner's preparatory state must be analyzed. Attention level, motivational level, and physical and cognitive maturational and readiness levels must all be ascertained prior to the initiation of any motor training program.

Third, the motor training specialist must prepare an overall instructional strategy. Some pertinent questions include (a) what types of directions are best for the learner (i.e., are manual, visual, or verbal directions mandated); (b) what types of practice sessions are best for the learner, massed or distributed; (c) should the early stages of learning be geared for speed or accuracy; and (d) should whole, part, or whole-part instructional methodology be employed?

Finally, the motor training specialist must formulate, during practice and after practice, instructional strategies. These strategies include the type of reinforcement to use, the schedule of reinforcement to use, the quantity of feedback to use, the level of overlearning to use for maximizing retention of the skill, and ways of maximizing the potential for transfer of learning to other skills. Figure 1 is a diagram of factors that affect the acquisition of complex motor behaviors. Note that some factors are, to a large extent, genetically based and not trainable to any appreciable degree; however, many factors (learned components of motor fitness, physical fitness, and psychological factors) are trainable and can be manipulated by motor training and rehabilitation specialists to optimize motor skill acquisition and performance.

References

Adams, J. A. (1971). A closed-loop theory of motor behavior. *Journal of Motor Behavior*, **3**, 111-149.

Brocklehurst, J. L., Andrews, K., Richards, B., & Laycock, P. J. (1978). How much physiotherapy for patients with stroke? *British Medical Journal*, **1**, 1307-1310.

Brooks, V. B. (1983). Motor control: How posture and movement are governed. *Physical Therapy*, **63**, 664-673.

DeGangi, G. A., Hurley, L., & Linsheid, T.R. (1983). Toward a methodology of the short-term effects of neurodevelopmental treatment. *American Journal of Occupational Therapy*, **37**, 479-484.

Denhoff, E. (1981). Current status of infant stimulation or enrichment programs for children with developmental disabilities. *Pediatrics*, **67**, 32-37.

Evarts, E. V. (1979). Brain mechanisms of movement. *Scientific American*, **241**, 164-179.

Ferry, P. C. (1981). On growing new neurons: Are early intervention programs effective? *Pediatrics*, **67**, 38-41.

Fitts, P. M., & Posner, M. (1967). *Human performance*. Belmont, CA: Brooks/Cole.

Glencross, D. J. (1977). Control of skilled movements. *Psychological Bulletin*, **84**(1), 14-29.

Herman, R. (1982). A therapeutic approach based on theories of motor control. *International Rehabilitation Medicine*, **4**, 185-189.

Jones, B. (1974). The importance of memory traces of motor efferent discharges for learning skilled movements. *Developmental Medicine and Child Neurology*, **16**, 620-628.

Kottke, F. J. (1980). From reflex to skill: The training of coordination. *Archives of Physical Medicine and Rehabilitation*, **61**, 551-561.

Lashley, K. S. (1917). The accuracy of movement in the absence of excitation from the moving organ. *American Journal of Physiology,* **43,** 169-194.

Marsden, C. D. (1980). The enigma of the basal ganglia and movement. *Trends in Neuroscience,* **3,** 284-287.

Marteniuk, R. G. (1979). Motor skill performance and learning: Considerations for rehabilitation. *Physiotherapy* (Canada), **31**(4), 187-202.

McClenaghan, B. A. (1983). Motor rehabilitation: Application of instructional theory. *The Physical Educator,* **40,** 2-7.

Piper, M. C., & Pless, I. B. (1980). Early intervention for infants with Down's Syndrome: A controlled trail. *Pediatrics,* **65,** 463-468.

Requin, J. (1980). Toward a psychobiology of preparation for action. In G. E. Stelmach & J. Requin (Eds.), *Tutorials in motor behavior* (pp. 373-399). Amsterdam: North Holland.

Schmidt, R. A. (1975). A schema theory of discrete motor skill learning. *Psychological Review,* **82**(4), 225-260.

Stern, P. H., McDowell, F., & Miller, J. M. (1970). Effects of facilitation exercise techniques in stroke rehabilitation. *Archives of Physical Medicine and Rehabilitation,* **51,** 526-531.

Tatton, W. G., & Bruce, I. C. (1981). Comment: A schema for the interactions between motor programs and sensory input. *Canadian Journal of Physiology and Pharmacology,* **59,** 691-699.

Turnbull, G. I. (1982). Some learning theory implications in neurological physiotherapy. *Physiotherapy,* **68**(2), 38-41.

Wise, S. P., & Evarts, E. W. (1981). The role of the cerebral cortex in movement. *Trends in Neuroscience,* **4,** 297-300.

The Influence of Age, Sex, Hearing Loss, Etiology, and Balance Ability on the Fundamental Motor Skills of Deaf Children

Stephen A. Butterfield

Literature relative to the motor ability of deaf persons is sparse. This is especially apparent in the area of motor development. Although information relative to the motor development of deaf children would be useful to teachers, few such investigations have been reported in the professional literature. Generally, the available studies have focused on balance and selected motor fitness and physical fitness variables. For example, most studies agree that as a population the deaf are inferior to the normal population in performing tasks of static and dynamic balance (Boyd, 1967; Grimsley, 1972; Lindsey & O'Neal, 1976; Long, 1932; Vance, 1968). Investigators have also attempted to identify specific aspects of the physiology of deaf children thought to contribute to their inferior balance performances. The influence of etiology of deafness on balance ability was investigated by Myklebust (1964) and Padden (1959), who observed that impaired balance was more likely to occur if the child had had meningitis, a known cause of deafness and labyrinthal injury. This finding, however, was not confirmed by Boyd (1967), who found similar balance deficiencies across etiological categories. Other researchers have examined the roles of vision and amount of hearing loss with respect to balance-related tasks. Grimsley (1972) and Lindsey and O'Neal (1976) observed that the balance performances of deaf children were more adversely affected than those of hearing children when visual cues were removed, whereas Carlson (1972) found degree of hearing loss to be an insignificant factor in the performance of balance tasks. Other evidence suggests that the deaf may lag behind the normal in motor fitness (Vance, 1968) but may be superior in certain items of visual-motor control (Brunt and Broadhead, 1982).

The primary purpose of this study was to describe the fundamental motor and static and dynamic balance characteristics of hearing-impaired children aged 3 through 14. This was accomplished by means of a criterion-referenced assessment tool, The Ohio State University Scale of Intra Gross Motor Assessment (Loovis & Ersing, 1979), and selected balance items from the Bruininks-Oseretsky Test of Motor Proficiency (Bruininks, 1978). More precisely, this investigation attempted to ascertain the qualitative differences of this population in the performance of the skills of skipping, walking, climbing, running, hopping, jumping, throwing, catching, kicking, and striking. In addition, the study attempted to resolve the following related problems:

1. Do the basic fundamental motor skill performance and balance skills of hearing-impaired children differ with chronological age?
2. Do comparable levels of fundamental motor skill performance and balance skills exist for males and females?
3. Is there a relationship between balance performance and the performance of certain fundamental motor skills among hearing-impaired children?
4. To what extent are fundamental motor skills and balance performances influenced by etiology of hearing loss?
5. To what extent are fundamental motor skills and balance performances influenced by degree of hearing loss?

Method

Subjects

The subjects were 132 hearing-impaired children between the ages of 3 and 14 who met their state's criteria for placement in programs for deaf children. The children were enrolled in day or residential schools for the deaf in New York, Vermont, Rhode Island, and Ohio. Ninety-five percent of this sample had a hearing loss greater than 60 dB in the better ear. Mean hearing loss for the remaining subjects was 46 dB. Etiologies included 16 meningitis, 8 rubella, 23 genetic, 69 idiopathic, and 16 other causes. The subjects in the "other" category included children whose deafness was due to low-incidence etiologies, such as Treacher-Collins syndrome, cytomegalovirus, premature birth, or birth injury. All data relative to hearing loss and etiology were obtained from each subject's audiological and medical records. No subject was physically or mentally impaired.

Procedures

The Ohio State University Scale of Intra Gross Motor Assessment (OSU SIGMA) (Loovis & Ersing, 1979) was utilized to collect data on the subjects' basic gross motor skill performances. OSU SIGMA is a criterion-reference assessment tool and as such examines the quality of an individual's performance on basic gross motor skills from a developmental point of view rather than on performance results.

Through use of SIGMA, 11 basic motor skills can be evaluated qualitatively, including walking, running, jumping, hopping, skipping, catching, throwing, striking, kicking, ladder climbing, and stair climbing. Each skill is divided into four performance levels ranging from Level 1 (least mature) to Level 4 (the most mature functional level). Each level is defined by performance criteria stated in behavioral form. In each skill, the four re-spective levels reflect the sequential motor development of each skill and a score of 1, 2, 3, or 4 is awarded for the predominant behavior. Before initiating data collection procedures, a pilot study was conducted to estab-lish examiner reliability. Mean intrarater reliability for the principal investi-gator was .948 for the 11 SIGMA skills.

Data for the static and dynamic balance skills of the subjects were obtained through use of Subtest 2, Items 2 and 7 of the short form of the Bruininks-Oseretsky Test of Motor Proficiency (Bruininks, 1978). Static balance was assessed by the number of seconds, up to 10, the child was able to stand on his or her preferred leg while on a balance beam. Dynamic balance was measured by the number of heel-to-toe steps, up to six, the child was able to take while walking forward on a balance beam. Test-retest reliability coefficients for the balance items reported by Bruininks (1978) were .49 for Grade 6 and .64 for Grade 2.

In administering both tests, explicit directions were given in the child's preferred mode of communication, whether it be the oral (speech and lip-reading) or the total communication (speech, lipreading, signing, and finger-spelling) approach. In either case, communication with the subjects was based on the philosophy of the individual school. For some children, particularly those in the 3 to 5 year range, it was necessary to supplement verbal instructions and demonstrations with some physical prompting.

Design and Statistics

The basic design for this study was a cross-sectional correlational design. This may also be referred to as a prediction study whereby a set of predic-tor variables (age, sex, degree of hearing loss, etiology of hearing loss, static balance, and dynamic balance) was correlated with a set of criterion variables (Levels 1, 2, 3, 4 of OSU SIGMA) to determine the relative in-fluence of each on the subjects' fundamental motor skill development.

Because combinations of variables may result in a more accurate predic-tion than any single variable, a multiple regression analysis was performed to test these relationships. More specifically, the class of multiple regres-sion used in this study was linear discriminant analysis (Klecka, 1980) where the four OSU SIGMA levels of fundamental motor skill develop-ment formed the criterion variables, and subjects' age, sex, hearing loss, static balance, and dynamic balance served as the predictor variables. From these analyses, the standardized discriminant coefficients and struc-ture coefficients were interpreted for the significant discriminant func-tions. Due to the fact that, as nominal data, the numerical scores assigned to levels of etiology (genetic, other, rubella, meningitis, and idiopathic) would not be appropriate for discriminant analysis, chi-square analysis was selected as the most appropriate statistical technique to test this variable.

The subjects' raw scores for static and dynamic balance were also ana-lyzed to determine the possible influence of age, sex, and etiology on the

Table 1   Summary of Function 1 Linear Discriminant Analysis for Level of Fundamental Motor Skill Development and Five Predictor Variables

Skill	Wilks' lambda	Chi-square	df	Alpha	Canonical correlation
Stair climbing	.6809	48.4100	10	.0000**	.5480
Running	.6790	48.5680	5	.0000**	.5664
Throwing	.7403	37.8830	10	.0000**	.4757
Catching	.3724	123.9600	15	.0000**	.7708
Kicking	.6144	61.3720	10	.0000**	.6148
Jumping	.5831	67.1370	5	.0000**	.6456
Hopping	.4020	114.3500	15	.0000**	.7682
Skipping	.7247	40.5680	10	.0000**	.5202
Striking	.8512	20.2920	10	.0266*	.3398
Ladder climbing	.5759	69.5220	10	.0000**	.6475

$*p < .05.$ $**p < .001.$

performance of these tasks. For purposes of analysis, the subjects were assigned to six chronological age groups: 3 to 4, 5 to 6, 7 to 8, 9 to 10, 11 to 12, 13 to 14. A two-way analysis of variance was used to examine the main and interaction effects of age and sex. To determine if any significant performance differences existed among the etiological categories, a one-way analysis of variance was conducted with age as a covariate. Post hoc tests were run, for both age groups and etiological categories, using the Scheffe procedure for all possible pairwise comparisons. Pearson correlation coefficients were calculated to determine if a relationship existed between the subjects' degree of hearing loss and their performance on tasks of static and dynamic balance.

Results

Fundamental Motor Skills

The results of the discriminant analysis for stair climbing, running, throwing, catching, kicking, jumping, hopping, skipping, striking, and ladder climbing were significant for the first function (see Table 1).[1] The other skill, walking, was not included in the analysis because each subject performed at the mature level. To interpret and name the function, structure coefficients were calculated for each of the predictor variables for each skill.[2] A structure coefficient is a measure of the degree of relationship between a variable and a function. Consequently, as the magnitude of the co-

Table 2   Means and Standard Deviations for Static and Dynamic Balance by Age Group

Age group		Static balance		Dynamic balance	
	n	M	SD	M	SD
3- 4	16	1.81	2.46	.75	1.06
5- 6	18	3.22	3.02	1.05	1.63
7- 8	19	4.10	3.29	1.15	1.60
9-10	24	5.16	3.85	2.38	2.49
11-12	32	6.75	3.47	3.38	2.47
13-14	23	6.09	3.65	3.87	2.36

Note. Total *n* = 132.

Table 3   Means and Standard Deviations for Static and Dynamic Balance by Etiological Category

Etiology		Static balance		Dynamic balance	
	n	M	SD	M	SD
Genetic	23	7.04	3.29	3.52	2.10
Other	16	6.06	3.59	2.31	2.21
Rubella	8	5.25	3.88	3.12	2.16
Meningitis	16	4.18	3.78	1.93	2.40
Idiopathic	69	4.01	3.57	1.95	2.44

Note. Total *n* = 132.

efficient approaches +1.00, the function is carrying nearly the same information as the variable. Only structure coefficients having a greater value than .30 were used in the interpretation. For each of the skills analyzed, age, static balance, and dynamic balance gave meaning to the function. For the skill of kicking, hearing loss also gave meaning to the function. For all 10 skills, the higher the SIGMA level, the older the child was likely to be and the greater his or her performance scores in static and dynamic balance.

Static and Dynamic Balance

Mean performances for both static and dynamic balance increased with age (see Table 2). As expected, significant main effects for age were observed for both static balance ($F(5, 120) = 6.21$, $p < .01$) and dynamic balance ($F(5, 120) = 7.92, p < .01$). The post hoc analysis revealed significantly better performances ($p < .05$) for the two oldest groups (ages 11 to 12 and 13 to 14) over the three youngest groups (ages 3 to 4, 5 to 6, and 7 to 8) in dynamic balance and for the two oldest groups over the two youngest groups in static balance. There were no significant performance differences between males and females at any age.

With regard to etiology, the mean scores of the genetic group were superior in both static and dynamic balance (see Table 3). However, only one significant difference (genetic group exceeded the idiopathic group in static balance, $F(4, 126) = 3.79, p < .05$) emerged among the etiological categories. In addition, Pearson correlation coefficients revealed positive but low relationships between hearing loss and static ($r = .094$) and dynamic ($r = .134$) balance ability.

Discussion

In 10 of the fundamental motor skills examined in this study, age was a highly significant factor in the development of mature form. The other skill, walking, did not appear to depend on age within the age ranges evaluated in this study. This finding comes as no surprise and is in line with previous work in the area of motor development with nonhandicapped children. For example, Bayley (1935) observed large gains in jumping performance between ages of 28 and 54 months. Bruce (1966) found steady improvement with age in the skill of throwing; and Olson (1949) found age to be a significant factor in the development of the alternating foot pattern used for ascending and descending a flight of stairs.

In terms of balance performance, the significant difference among age levels within this population favored the older groups (ages 11 to 14). These findings are consistent with the work of Carlson (1972), Boyd (1967), and Brunt and Broadhead (1982), who also investigated the balance skills of deaf children.

Interestingly, the investigation failed to identify any significant differences between males and females for any of the fundamental motor skills or balance tasks. With regard to static and dynamic balance, these findings support the findings of Carlson (1972) and Lindsey and O'Neal (1976). More surprising, however, was the failure to find any significant sex differences in motor skill performance. Previous investigations have found significant differences favoring the females in skipping and hopping (Gutteridge, 1939) and males in throwing (Wickstrom, 1977) and kicking (Deach, 1950). This relative equality between the sexes in fundamental motor skill development may be due, in part, to the nature of physical education programming in schools for the deaf. Deaf children are often placed in special schools at as early as age 3. Physical education is usually considered an important part of the total curriculum in these schools. Consequently, children of both sexes participate together in physical education beginning at an early age and continue this throughout their schooling. This extensive programming, combined with the fact that deaf children living in institutions may be somewhat removed from cultural expectations that favor either males or females in certain skills, could be sufficient to account for the relative equality of performances of males and females in this study.

It is common knowledge that the ability to maintain equilibrium plays an important role in locomotor as well as other fundamental motor skills. The results of this study, which found a direct relationship between static and dynamic balance and motor skill development, merely confirm this fact within the deaf population. The implications, however, may be more far-reaching.

Additional programming designed to improve static and dynamic balance is likely to have a positive impact on a wide range of fundamental motor skills. Likewise, improved motor skill performance or at least increased opportunities to practice these skills might enhance balance performance—traditionally a weak area for many deaf children.

One of the principal objectives of this study was to determine if gross motor skill or balance performances were influenced by etiology of hearing loss. No relationship was found to exist between etiology of hearing loss and the attainment of mature functional performances in any of the 10 fundamental motor skills. However, with respect to balance, the genetic group was significantly superior ($p < .05$) to the idiopathic group in static balance. It should also be noted that mean performance scores for both static and dynamic balance favored the genetic group over all other etiological categories. These findings agree, to some extent, with the conclusions of Boyd (1967). Although Boyd did not observe any significant differences among etiological categories, he did observe that children with hereditary deafness functioned more closely to the subjects in a nonhandicapped control group than did subjects from other etiologies. Of further interest was the performance of the meningitis group, which did not differ significantly from the other etiologies. Again, this finding supports the findings of Boyd (1967), although it contradicts Padden (1959) and Myklebust (1964), who observed that inferior balance performances occurred significantly more often in individuals who had had meningitis.

Another important area of concern was the possible influence of hearing loss in decibels on motor skill performance. The effect of this variable on gross motor skills and balance appears to be negligible except for the skill of kicking, where significant results were obtained. The results showed that subjects who performed at the mature level tended to have the greatest hearing loss in decibels. Unfortunately, there is no explanation to account for this finding at the present time.

Due to the inconsistent and limited amount of evidence with respect to etiology, further studies should continue to control for this variable, taking into account new causes such as herpes and cytomegalovirus. Although it appears that gender and level of hearing loss do not influence motor performance, it may be necessary to investigate possible differences in child-rearing practices between deaf and nonhandicapped populations that could impact on motor performance.

50 Butterfield

Notes

1. The percent of cases correctly classified for each skill is available upon request from the author.

2. Standardized coefficients and structure coefficients are available upon request from the author.

References

Bayley, N. (1935). The development of motor behaviors during the first three years. *Monographs of the Society for Research in Child Development*, **1**, 1.

Boyd, J. (1967). Comparison of motor behavior in deaf and hearing boys. *American Annals of the Deaf*, **112**, 598-605.

Bruce, R. (1966). *The effects of variation in ball trajectory upon the catching performance of elementary school children*. Unpublished doctoral dissertation, University of Wisconsin, Madison.

Bruininks, R. H. (1978). *Bruininks-Oseretsky Test of Motor Proficiency examiners manual*. Circle Pines, MN: American Guidance Service.

Brunt, D., & Broadhead, G. D. (1982). Motor proficiency traits of deaf children. *Research Quarterly for Exercise and Sport*, **53**, 236-238.

Carlson, R. B. (1972). Assessment of motor ability of selected deaf children in Kansas. *Perceptual and Motor Skills*, **34**, 303-305.

Deach, D. (1950). *Genetic development of motor skills of children two through six years of age*. Unpublished doctoral dissertation, University of Michigan, Ann Arbor.

Grimsley, J. R. (1972). The effects of visual cueness and visual deprivation upon the acquisition and rate of learning of a balance skill among deaf individuals. *Dissertation Abstracts International*, **33**, 3354A.

Gutteridge, M. (1939). A study of motor achievements of young children. *Archives of Psychology*, **244**, 1-178.

Klecka, W. R. (1980). *Discriminant analysis*. London: Sage University Publications.

Lindsey, D., & O'Neal, J. (1976). Static and dynamic balance skills of eight-year-old deaf and hard of hearing children. *American Annals of the Deaf*, **121**, 49-55.

Long, T. (1932). *Motor abilities of deaf children*. Contributions to Education No. 914. New York: Columbia University Teachers' College.

Loovis, E., & Ersing, W. (1979). *Assessing and programming gross motor development for children*. Cleveland Heights, OH: Ohio Motor Assessment Associates.

Myklebust, H.R. (1964). *The psychology of deafness.* New York: Grune & Stratton.

Olson, W. (1949). *Child development.* Boston: D. C. Heath.

Padden, D. A. (1959). Ability of deaf swimmers to orient themselves when submerged in water. *Research Quarterly for Exercise and Sport, 30,* 214-226.

Vance, P. C. (1968). Motor characteristics of deaf children. *Dissertation Abstracts International, 29,* 1145-1146A.

Wickstrom, R. (1977). *Fundamental motor patterns.* Philadelphia: Lea & Febiger.

Evidence for Muscle Activation Deficiency in Mentally Handicapping Conditions

Walter E. Davis

Nearly all studies comparing nonhandicapped subjects to those labeled as mentally handicapped have shown a definite and often marked difference on a variety of motor performance measures. There are, of course, wide variations within the mentally handicapped population, and this is a very important note. The focus of many of these studies, however, has been on rather global measures that have provided few insights into understanding exactly why such motor deficiencies exist in mentally handicapping conditions. Thus it remains for us to pursue the task of identifying and more precisely describing the exact nature of this deficiency.

In a recent examination of existing data of motor control with this population (Davis, 1986a), I offered a tentative postulate regarding motor deficiency in mentally handicapped subjects. This postulate was made on the basis of the theoretical distinction between motor coordination and motor control (Kugler, Kelso, & Turvey, 1980) and was put forth as a departure point for further research. In the present chapter I examine these and some additional data from a more descriptive rather than theoretical perspective.

Precisely, from a physiological descriptive level, data seem to suggest that mentally handicapped subjects can be characterized as having a deficiency in muscle activation. That is, mentally handicapped subjects are unable to generate high levels of muscle activity (compared to their nonhandicapped peers) as measured by the electromyogram (EMG); EMG activity is more variable within the same task and between trials of the same task with this population—they appear not to be capable of maintaining constant levels of activity; and there is a marked delay in the onset of muscle activation. Moreover, this muscle activation deficiency appears to be even greater in Down's syndrome subjects than nondistinguished mentally handicapped subjects. We may further speculate that extreme slowness of movement, which so typically characterizes this population, may be an important manifestation of this muscle activation deficiency.

There have been few studies of EMG measures with mentally handicapped subjects, so these suggestions are tentative at best. And, to be clear, this hypothesized muscle activation deficiency is only another description of mentally handicapping conditions. It is a complement to, but at a different level than, previous behavioral descriptions. Therefore, it is not to be construed as an explanation of or as having causal linkage to motor performance decrements.

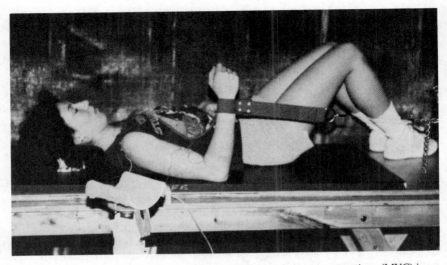

Figure 1 Experimental setup for obtaining maximum voluntary contractions (MVC) in an isometric condition. EMG recordings from the biceps brachii muscle were obtained using surface electrodes. Torque was measured with a strain gauge. These measures were fed into a physiograph. This same setup was utilized in the step-loading procedure.

Magnitude of EMG Activity

The first set of data relates to the magnitude of EMG activity generated that is thought to be related to maximum voluntary contractions (MVC), that is, muscular force production. The data come from a recent study by Davis and Sinning (in press) in which both Down's syndrome and non-distinguished mentally handicapped subjects as well as nonhandicapped subjects were asked to produce an MVC in the elbow flexor muscles in an isometric condition. The experimental setup is shown in Figure 1. EMG measures were taken from the bicep brachii muscle using surface electrodes, and the torque was measured with the use of a strain gauge. A minimum of two trials was conducted with a 2-min rest period between trials. Following the MVC measures, step-loading proceducres were conducted under these same isometric conditions. Subjects were asked to maintain a constant elbow joint angle (90°) against a series of loads that were applied for 2 s with a 1-min rest period between loads. These loads ranged from 5 pounds to 90% of the measured maximum.

Torque measures were calculated and plotted against the measures of the magnitude of Integrated EMG (IEMG). Samples of these plots of individual subjects from each group are shown in Figure 2. Statistical analysis of the group mean with respect to the slope of these plots revealed that significant differences do not exist between the three subject groups (Down's syndrome, mentally handicapped, and nonhandicapped subjects). This suggests that the relationship between force generation and

IEMG BY TORQUE FUNCTIONS

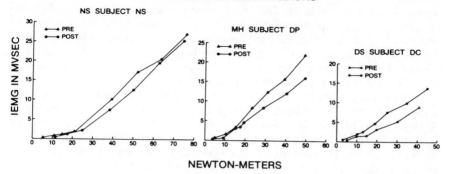

NEWTON-METERS

Figure 2 Individual IEMG by torque functions taken from the elbow flexor muscles contracted isometrically during a step-loading procedure. From "Muscle Stiffness in Down's Syndrome and Other Mentally Handicapped Subjects" by W. E. Davis and W. E. Sinning, in press. Reprinted by permission.

GROUP DIFFERENCES IN MEAN MAXIMUM VOLUNTARY CONTRACTIONS

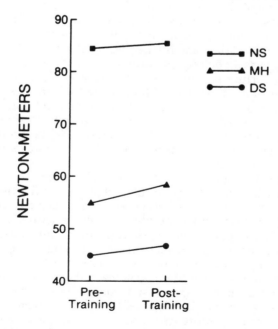

Figure 3 Group differences in mean maximum voluntary contractions of the elbow flexor muscles. From "Muscle Stiffness in Down's Syndrome and Other Mentally Handicapped Subjects" by W. E. Davis and W. E. Sinning, in press. Reprinted by permission.

EMG activity is the same for all subjects. The only difference among the subjects was in the magnitude of EMG activity generated. Statistical analysis showed that nonhandicapped subjects produced greater magnitude of EMG (as measured in millivolt seconds) than the mentally handicapped subjects, who in turn were superior to the Down's syndrome subjects. These findings were consistent with the results of the torque measures (MVC). The latter results are shown in Figure 3.

These results corroborate findings from other studies of strength measures in mentally handicapped subjects (e.g., Brown, 1977; Francis & Rarick, 1959; Molnar & Alexander, 1983). Exactly how strength relates to motor performance is a question yet unanswered (see Atwater, 1979). However, in tasks that require force production, mentally handicapped subjects are clearly deficient when compared to their nonhandicapped peers. For example, in a study of speed/accuracy of the overhand throw (Davis, 1986b), Down's syndrome and other mentally handicapped subjects were not only less accurate than the nonhandicapped subjects, but they also threw with significantly less velocity.

Maintenance of a Constant EMG Activity Level

The evidence for greater variability of EMG activity in mentally handicapped subjects comes from studies by Shumway-Cook and Woollacott (in press). These researchers measured the EMG activity of the gastrocnemius-tibialis anterior and quadriceps-hamstring agonist-antagonist muscle groups in Down's syndrome children and nonhandicapped subjects during a static balance task. Subjects stood on a platform that could be rotated or translated in order to perturb postural control of subjects. It was found that during these postural adjustments EMG activity of Down's syndrome subjects did follow the same proximal to distal muscle timing found in the nonhandicapped children. This was consistent with Nashner's (1977) results with nonhandicapped adults. However, the EMG responses in the Down's syndrome subjects were also more variable than responses in the nonhandicapped children.

Variability in EMG responses seems to be consonant with some of our movement data with Down's syndrome subjects. We (Davis & Kelso, 1982) found evidence that these subjects cannot maintain a constant level of muscle activity, at least under conditions of resistance (external force). This characteristic is implied from an examination of the movement tracings taken when subjects were asked to move their index finger to a specified target angle against a resistance. We compared the tracings from Down's syndrome and nonhandicapped subjects (Figure 4). They showed that in moving to the target, Down's syndrome subjects move in a step-like fashion, whereas the nonhandicapped subjects' movements may be characterized as smooth. Moreover, once the target was reached, the Down's syndrome subjects were less able to maintain that joint angle (see Figure 4b, tracing b). We did not record EMG activity during these movements.

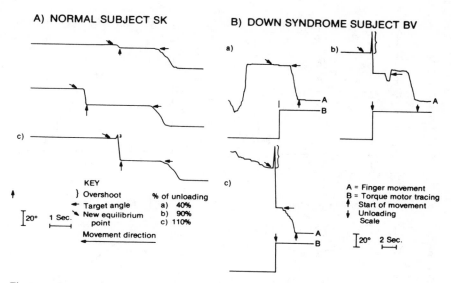

Figure 4 Tracings of finger movements of individual subjects. Tracings for nonhandicapped subjects were taken directly from the computer, and tracing from Down's syndrome subjects were taken from the visicorder. From "Analysis of 'Invariant Characteristics' in Motor Control of Down's Syndrome and Normal Subjects" by W. E. Davis and J. A. S. Kelso, 1982, *Journal of Motor Behavior*, **14**, p. 200. Copyright 1982 by Heldref. Reprinted by permission.

Delay in Muscle Activation

The slow reaction times of mentally handicapped subjects is a well-known and robust finding. A systematic and detailed analysis of this characteristic from a physiological level has been provided in a series of studies by Karrer and his colleagues (Karrer, 1985). Reaction time may be fractionated into components on the basis of the electrical activity in the brain and muscle (Weiss, 1965). Traditionally, these components are defined as premotor time (PMT), the onset of a stimulus to the initial appearance of EMG activity in the muscle, and motor time (MT), the onset of EMG activity to the onset of actual limb displacement.

We have obtained data on these measures but, unlike previous researchers, we made the distinction between Down's syndrome and other mentally handicapped subjects (Davis, Ward, & Sparrow, in press). Our study revealed some important differences between these two groups and thus we argued, as have others (e.g., Henderson, 1986; Johnson & Olley, 1971), that such subject distinctions ought to be made.

In our study (Davis et al., in press), subjects were asked to respond as quickly as possible to a light, sound, or light/sound combination signal by extending their arm at the elbow joint. They were to move their arm as rapidly as possible until it contacted a sponge-padded board. The electrical activity of the tricep muscle group was taken with surface electrodes and

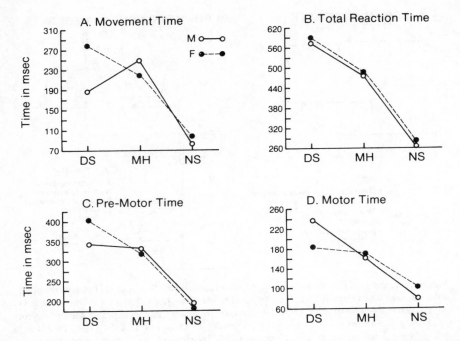

Figure 5 Group differences in movements time, total reaction time, premotor time, and motor time. Subjects reacted and moved as quickly as possible to sound, light, and light/ sound combination signals. Movement was elbow extension into a foam pad. The time was measured from starting point to the first 30° of movement. From "Fractionated Reaction Time in Down's Syndrome and Other Mentally Handicapped Adults" by W. E. Davis, T. Ward, and W. A. Sparrow, in press. Reprinted by permission.

used to start and stop a series of digital clocks. These clocks provided the premotor, motor, and movement times. Total reaction time was calculated by summing the premotor and motor times. Results indicate that the non-handicapped subjects were much faster on all measures than either group of mentally handicapped subjects (Figure 5). The mentally handicapped subjects were significantly faster than the Down's syndrome group on all measures except movement time.

To further determine the source of this delay, we calculated the means for the 10 fastest and 10 slowest trials for each of the three groups. This analysis suggests that the source of the delay, for all groups, lies in the premotor times rather than motor times (Figure 6). These findings support the results of Karrer (1985) and Lanphear (1972).

This delay in reaction time may be very important to the overall response time. However, as I previously argued in a paper presented at the American Alliance for Health, Physical Education, Recreation, and Dance (AAHPERD) (Davis, 1984), perhaps the speed of movement is more important to the actual task performance. This aspect of performance has been given little

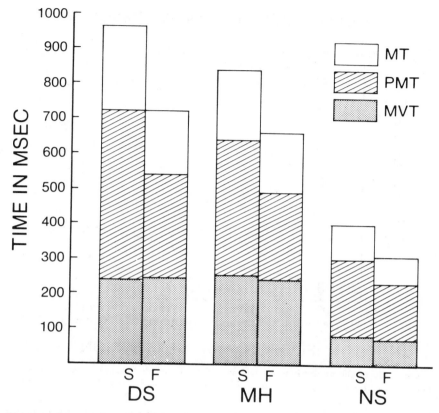

Figure 6 Group means for the 10 fastest (F) and 10 slowest (S) trails for each component (PMT and MT) and for movement time (MVT). From "Fractionated Reaction Time in Down's Syndrome and Other Mentally Handicapped Adults" by W. E. Davis, T. Ward, and W. A. Sparrow, in press. Reprinted by permission.

attention with mentally handicapped subjects. Although reaction time studies with mentally handicapped subjects abound, movement speed studies with this population are conspicuous by their absence. This absence is accentuated by the fact that movement speed in nonhandicapped subjects has received a great deal of attention in the motor control literature (e.g., Meyer, Smith, & Wright, 1982; Woodworth, 1899).

As previously noted, we (Davis et al., in press) found mentally handicapped subjects move their limbs much slower than their nonhandicapped peers (see Figures 5 and 6). Movement may be viewed as consisting of two phases, an acceleration and a deceleration phase (Meyer et al., 1982; Soechting & Lacquanti, 1981), which are symmetrical in rapid movements. From neurophysiological studies (e.g., Angel, 1975; Hallett, Shahani, & Young, 1975), it is shown that these phases are produced by an initial burst of force (an impulse) brought about by a cocontraction of the agonist and antagonist muscle groups. Two bursts of electrical activity occur in the

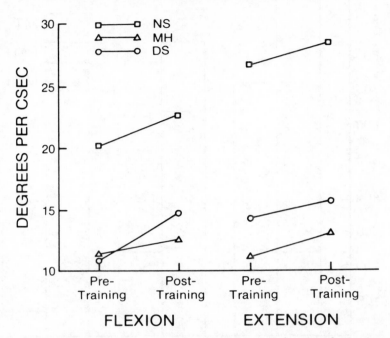

Figure 7   Group differences in mean average velocity for elbow flexion and extension movements. Measures were taken prior to and following an 8-week strength training program.

agonist muscle at the start of the movement and are associated with the acceleration phase. A single burst of the antagonist muscle, which occurs between the agonist bursts, decelerates the movement, aided by the visco-elastic properties of the muscle-joint system. It is important to recognize that both central (cortical) and peripheral (reflex) sources contribute to the summation of electrical activity at any given time (see Feldman & Latash, 1982).

Movement speed, then, is a result of the net positive force (an impulse) produced by the agonist versus antagonist contractions and influenced by changing external forces of inertia and gravity. Thus movement speed may be increased by increasing the speed and magnitude of muscle activation, but it is also influenced by the movement distance and load.

More recently we (Davis & Sinning, 1984) collected EMG data during a task in which subjects were asked to move as rapidly as possible to a visual target and to come to a stop as suddenly as possible. Both elbow flexion and extension movements were carried out. Again, the Down's syndrome and other mentally handicapped subjects moved significantly slower than the nonhandicapped subjects (Figure 7). Also, they were not able to stop as suddenly as the nonhandicapped subjects, as can be observed in Figure 7. The EMG data confirm the velocity measures (Figure 8). Nonhandi-

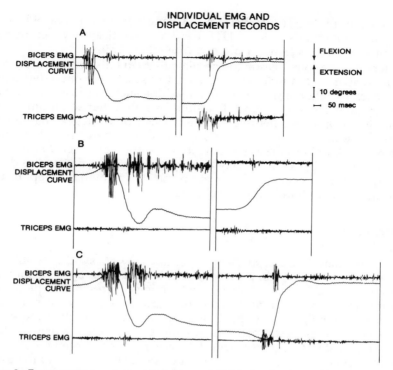

INDIVIDUAL EMG AND DISPLACEMENT RECORDS

Figure 8 Representative movement tracings and EMG records of individual subjects from each of the three groups (nonhandicapped, mentally handicapped, and Down's syndrome). EMG recordings are from the elbow flexor and extensor muscle groups taken with surface electrodes.

capped subjects consistently demonstrated the triphasic EMG bursts, whereas the mentally handicapped subjects did not. More typical of the responses of the mentally handicapped and Down's syndrome subjects were single EMG bursts from the agonist with a diminutive or an absence of antagonist burst.

If mentally handicapped and especially Down's syndrome subjects have a decreased efficiency in muscle activation, as the data here imply, the reason for this deficiency is not clear. There are studies suggesting that Down's syndrome subjects may have a biochemical deficiency in neural transmission and muscle contraction. Down's syndrome infants have been found to have low blood levels of the protein enzyme serotonin (Coleman, 1973; Pueschel, 1984), which is known to cross the blood-brain barrier (Viala & Buser, 1969). Animal research suggests that serotonin plays an important role in neural transmission and muscle contraction (Ahlman, Grillner, & Udo, 1971; Viala & Buser, 1969). Earlier studies had reported (Airaksinen, 1974) that the muscle tone of Down's syndrome infants increased when given 5-hydroxytryptophan (5-HTP), precursor of serotonin. However, a more recent and more extensive study did not concur with the previous findings (Pueschel, 1984). Changes in muscle tone of Down's syndrome infants receiving 5-HTP were not significantly different from a control group receiving a placebo (Pueschel, 1984).

There may be some reason to speculate that Down's syndrome subjects are less capable of muscle activation due to some biochemical deficiency, but extreme caution must be taken in reaching such conclusion until more substantial evidence is found. It should be noted that serotonin is only found in the brain as a neurotransmitter. This would suggest that the lack of muscle tone is a central nervous system rather than a peripheral phenomenon. Another possible explanation for the decreased MVC in the handicapped subjects, especially those with Down's syndrome, is differences in muscle fiber type. There are no studies known that report fiber type in mentally handicapped subjects.

Summary

Mentally handicapped subjects, especially Down's syndrome subjects, appear to experience comparative difficulty in activating their muscles. Empirical evidence supporting this contention was presented. Specifically, my research shows that mentally handicapped subjects are less capable of generating high levels of EMG activity, and such activity is more variable than in nonhandicapped subjects. Moreover, there is a marked delay in the onset of EMG activity. This delay is largely accounted for by an increase in premotor time (time of onset of signal to move until the initial appearance of EMG activity in the muscle). The reasons for this activation deficiency are not clear. It is suggested that slow movement speed may be an important manifestation of this hypothesized deficiency.

Acknowledgments

The author gratefully acknowledges the help of Alice Hyer and Janet Kotyk in the preparation of this manuscript. Work on this manuscript was supported, in part, by a grant awarded to the author by the U.S. Department of Education, Office of Special Education, No. G008301260-02.

References

Ahlman, H., Grillner, S., & Udo, M. (1971). The effect of 5-HTP on the static fusimotor activity and the tonic stretch reflex of an extensor motor. *Brain, 27*, 393-396.

Airaksinen, E. M. (1974). Tryptophan treatment of infants with Down's syndrome. *Annals of Clinical Research, 6*, 33-39.

Angel, R. W. (1975). Myoelectric patterns associated with ballistic movement: Effect of unexpected changes in load. *Journal of Human Movement Studies, 1*, 96-103.

Atwater, A. E. (1979). Biomechanics of overarm throwing movements and of throwing injuries. In R. S. Hutton & D. I. Miller (Eds.), *Exercise and sports sciences reviews* (Vol 7, pp. 43-85). Philadelphia, PA: Franklin Institute Press.

Brown, B. J. (1977). The effect of an isometric strength program on the intellectual and social development of trainable retarded males. *American Corrective Therapy Journal, 31*, 44-48.

Coleman, M. (1973). *Serotonin in Down's syndrome.* New York: American Elsevier.

Davis, W. E. (1984). *Movement speed of the mentally handicapped.* Paper presented at the Research Consortium, AAHPERD, Anaheim, CA.

Davis, W. E. (1986a). Development of coordination and control in the mentally handicapped. In M. G. Wade & H. T. A. Whiting (Eds.), *Issues in motor development.* Amsterdam: North Holland.

Davis, W. E. (1986b). Precise visual information and throwing accuracy of mentally handicapped subjects. In M. G. Wade (Ed.), *Motor skill acquisition of the mentally handicapped.* Amsterdam: North Holland.

Davis, W. E., & Kelso, J. A. S. (1982). Analysis of "invariant characteristics" in motor control of Down's syndrome and normal subjects. *Journal of Motor Behavior, 14*, 194-212.

Davis, W. E., & Sinning, W. E. (1984). Unpublished data.

Davis, W.E., & Sinning, W. E. (in press). *Muscle stiffness in Down's syndrome and other mentally handicapped subjects.* Manuscript submitted for publication.

Davis, W. E., Ward, T., & Sparrow, W. A. (in press). *Fractionated reaction time in Down's syndrome and other mentally handicapped adults.* Manuscript submitted for publication.

Feldman, A. G., & Latash, M. L. (1982). Interaction of afferent and efferent signals underlying joint position sense: Empirical and theoretical approaches. *Journal of Motor Behavior, 14*, 174-193.

Francis, R. J., & Rarick, G. L. (1959). Motor characteristics of the mentally retarded. *American Journal of Mental Deficiency, 63*, 792-811.

Hallett, M., Shahani, B. T., & Young, R. R. (1975). EMG analysis of stereotyped voluntary movements in man. *Journal of Neurology, Neurosurgery & Psychiatry, 38*, 1154-1162.

Henderson, S. E. (1986). Motor skills development in Down's syndrome. In D. Lane & B. Stratford (Eds.), *Current approaches to Down's syndrome.* London: Holt, Rinehart & Winston.

Johnson, J. T., Jr., & Olley, J. G. (1971). Behavioral comparisons of mongoloid and non-mongoloid retarded persons: A review. *American Journal of Mental Deficiency,* **75**, 546-559.

Karrer, R. (1985). Input, central and motor segments of response time in mentally retarded and normal children. In M. G. Wade (Ed.), *Motor skill acquisition of the mentally handicapped.* Amsterdam: North Holland.

Kugler, P. N., Kelso, J. A. S., & Turvey, M. T. (1980). On the concept of co-ordinative structures as dissipative structures: I. Theoretical lines of convergence. In G. E. Stelmach & J. Requin (Eds.), *Tutorials in motor behavior* (pp. 3-47). New York: North Holland.

Lanphear, J. L. (1972). *Fractionated reaction times and reflex times on 9 to 12 year old mentally retarded boys.* Unpublished master's thesis, University of Massachusetts.

Meyer, D. E., Smith, J. E. K., & Wright, C. E. (1982). Models for the speed and accuracy of aimed movements. *Psychological Review,* **89**, 449-482.

Molnar, G. E., & Alexander, J. (1983). Strength development in retarded children: A comparative study on the effect of intervention. In J. Hogg & P. J. Mittler (Eds.), *Advances in mental handicap research* (Vol. 2) (pp. 285-307). London: John Wiley and Sons.

Nashner, L. M. (1977). Fixed patterns of rapid postural responses among leg muscles during stance. *Experimental Brain Research,* **30**, 13-24.

Pueschel, S. M. (1984). *The young child with Down's syndrome.* New York: Human Sciences Press.

Shumway-Cook, A., & Woollacott, M. (in press). Dynamics of postural control in the child with Down's syndrome. *Physical Therapy.*

Soechting, J. F., & Lacquanti, F. (1981). Invariant characteristics of a pointing movement in man. *The Journal of Neuroscience,* **1**, 710-720.

Viala, D., & Buser, P. (1969). The effects of DOPA and 5-HTP on rhythmic efferent discharges in hind limb nerves in the rabbit. *Brain Research,* **12**, 437-443.

Weiss, A. D. (1965). Locus of reaction time with set, motivation and age. *Journal of Gerontology,* **20**, 60-64.

Woodworth, R. S. (1899). The accuracy of voluntary movement. *Psychological Monographs,* **3**(2, part 13), 1-113.

Effects of Relaxation on the Peripheral Chronaxie of Persons Having Multiple Sclerosis

Romain Chrétien
Clermont P. Simard
André Dorion

Multiple sclerosis (MS) is a degenerative neurological disorder characterized by extensive demyelination of the central nervous system (Wright, 1973). A majority of researchers agree with this definition. Most articles published on the subject seem to ignore the effects on the peripheral nervous system as well as the fact that the lesions barely affect the transition zone where the Schwann cells originate (Adams & Kubik, 1952; Lumsden, 1970, 1972). Nevertheless, several postmortem studies mention anomalies of the peripheral system of multiple sclerosis patients (Dawson, 1916; Hassin, 1921; Hasson, Terry, & Simmerman, 1958), whereas more recent studies have noted a drop in the peripheral nervous conduction velocity (Chrétien, Simard, & Dorion, 1984).

Research in this field primarily concerns the etiology and treatment of this disorder rather than an improved physical condition for the beneficiaries. To date, with the cause unknown, treatment of the symptoms is centered on physiotherapy and chemotherapy for treating complications such as muscular fatigue, weakness, spasms, and spasticity (Cook & Weistein, 1973; Illis, Oygar, & Sedgwick, 1967).

Some authors favor a program of specific and appropriate physical exercises to improve certain physical defects (Gordon & Carlson, 1951). They stress, among other things, active and passive movements, coordination, and neuromuscular-promoting exercises. These induce the mental effort of the desired movement while inhibiting the one to avoid. Thus the aim is to decrease or modify neuromuscular complications such as contractures, atrophy, or ataxia (Caillet, 1980).

Other authors tend to favor use of dynamic exercises (e.g., gymnastics, ergocycle, swimming) with the goal of maintaining an acceptable level of physical fitness and preventing complications due to inactivity. Russell (1976) correctly noted that an appropriate program of activities and rest counteracts the pathogenic evolution of the illness by eliminating the development of certain aspects of the multiple sclerosis.

This has led us to consider the efficiency of a relaxation program and its effects on the nervous conduction velocity of its beneficiaries. To be more precise, the aim of our study is to quantify the effects of relaxation on the peripheral chronaxie. The chronaxie provides a useful investigation tool that is likely to lead us to a better understanding of our patients and thus to orient better our actions and measures in establishing a program of physical activities that will maximize an improvement in these persons' condition. Therefore, our study intends to quantify the effect of a relaxation program adapted to the time required for an electric current to release a given muscle contraction.

Methodology

Subjects

Eighteen volunteer multiple sclerosis patients between the ages of 22 and 59 ($M = 40.5$, $\pm 10, 9$) were selected for this study. Eleven members of this group received treatment, whereas the other 7 comprised the control group.

Apparatus

The neurological problems of the type studied—multiple sclerosis—may lead to an increased cutaneous sensitivity and cause a certain muscular irritation (Hyman, 1968). In a previous test involving several patients, we noted that some have difficulty tolerating electrodes used in the monopolar (stylo) technique as opposed to the use of electrode stimulation of a larger surface. We have, therefore, chosen the latter technique, which is better tolerated by all.

To conduct this experiment, we used Siemens's "Neuroton Universal 626." The object of our study was the anterior ulnar nerve, which innervates, among others, the short adductor of the fifth finger. The motor point corresponding to the motor plaque of the muscle in question (i.e., the neuromuscular junction) is found at the hypothenar eminence of the hand. The investigating electrode at the motor point had a surface area of 4 cm², whereas the other had an area of 12 cm². The two electrodes were made of tin plates.

A galvanized impulsion current corresponding to a duration of 1,000 ms and a rest period of 2,000 ms was used to determine the rheobasis. By doubling the intensity of the latter and by using a rest period of an equal duration, at 2,000 ms, we determined the chronaxie (i.e., the time required under these conditions to release the contraction).

Procedure

The treatment consisted of a program of relaxation counseling lasting 1-1/2 hr at a time repeated twice a week. Sixty minutes were devoted to relaxation exercise and 30 min to counseling. Much importance was given

Table 1   Influence of Relaxation on Right and Left Chronaxie in the Experimental Group

Variables	Pretest		Posttest		t	df
	M	SD	M	SD		
Left chronaxie	0.032 ms	0.713	0.429 ms	1.136	2.673*	10
Right chronaxie	1.000 ms	0.475	0.464 ms	0.252	3.725**	10

*$p < .05$. **$p < .01$.

Table 2   Evolution of the Right and Left Chronaxie in the Control Group

Variables	Pretest		Posttest		t	df
	M	SD	M	SD		
Left chronaxie	0.900 ms	0.678	0.473 ms	0.185	1.705[ns]	6
Right chronaxie	1.207 ms	0.794	0.681 ms	0.422	1.543[ns]	6

Note.   [ns] = not significant.

to the position of the patients, to the relaxation techniques, to the relaxing exercises, and to counseling. The experiment took place in a favorable environment with appropriate background music.

Results

Table 1 shows the comparison between the left chronaxie and the right chronaxie in the pre- and posttest. We noted a significant difference in both the right and the left chronaxies between the pre- and posttest ($p < .05$) in the experimental group (Table 1). However, in the control group, no significant difference appeared between the two tests in relation to the dependent variables ($p < .05$) studied (Table 2).

Discussion

In this study, which concerned 18 patients suffering from multiple sclerosis, there was a significant difference between the pre- and posttests of those who followed the treatment, and this significant difference concerned both the right and left sides. This study tends, therefore, to confirm the conclusions of Dawson (1916/1977), Hassin (1921), and Hasson et al. (1958) that, in addition to the central nervous system, multiple sclerosis affects the peripheral nervous system.

Conclusion

It seems to us that persons suffering from multiple sclerosis react favorably to an adapted relaxation treatment, and, inversely, anxiety and muscular tension may constitute negative factors in their improved physical condition and in their functional evolution. Therefore, it would be desirable to incorporate into the usual treatment a parallel program of relaxation exercise for the functionally improved physical condition of these beneficiaries. On the other hand, it would be of interest to verify the influence of other forms of treatment on the chronaxie of these beneficiaries (i.e., other types of relaxation exercise programs).

References

Adams, R. D., & Kubik, C. S. (1952). The morbid anatomy of the demyelinative diseases. *American Journal of Medicine, 12,* 510-546.

Caillet, R. (1980). Exercise in multiple sclerosis. In J. V. Basmajian (Ed.), *Therapeutic exercise* (3rd ed.) (pp. 375–388). Baltimore, MD: Williams & Wilkins.

Chrétien, R., Simard, C., & Dorion, A. (1984). Sclérose en plaques et chronaxie périphérique. Communication à l'ACFAS [Multiple sclerosis and peripheral chronaxie. Paper presented to the Association Canadienne pour l'Avancement des Sciences (ACFAS)].

Cook, A. W., & Weistein, S. P. (1973). Chronic dorsal column stimulation in multiple sclerosis: Preliminary report N. Y. State. *Journal of Medicine, 73,* 2868-2872.

Dawson, J. W. (1977). The histoloy of disseminated sclerosis. *Annals of Neurology, 2,* 41-48. (Original work published 1916)

Gordon, E. E., & Carlson, E. E. (1951). Changing attitude toward multiple sclerosis. *Journal of the American Medical Association, 147,* 720-723.

Hassin, G. B. (1921). Pathology of multiple sclerosis. *Research Publications Association, 2,* 144-156.

Hasson, J., Terry, R. D., & Simmerman, H. M. (1958). Peripheral neuropathy in multiple sclerosis. *Neurology* (Minneapolis), *8,* 503-510.

Hyman, L. C. (1968). *A manual of electro-neuromyography.* Philadelphia: W. B. Saunders.

Illis, L. S., Oygar, A. W., & Sedgwick, E. M. (1967). Dorsal column stimulation in rehabilitation of patients with multiple sclerosis. *Hospital Practice*, **2**, 51-58.

Lumsden, C. E. (1970). The neuropathology of multiple sclerosis. In P.J. Vinken & G. W. Bruyn (Eds.), *Handbook of clinical neurology: Multiple sclerosis and other demyelinating diseases*. Amsterdam: North Holland.

Lumsden, C. E. (1972). An outline of the pathology of multiple sclerosis. In D. McAlpine, C. E. Lumsden, & E. D. Acheson (Eds.), *Multiple sclerosis: A reappraisal*. London: Churchill/Livingstone.

Russell, R. W. (1976). Disseminated sclerosis: Rest-exercise therapy. In R. W. Russell (Ed.), *Multiple sclerosis: Control of the disease* (pp. 67-76). New York: Pergamon Press.

Wright, S. (1973). *Physiologie appliquée à la médecine* [Physiology applied to medicine]. Paris: Flammarion, Médecine-sciences.

PART III

Physical Activity in Cardiac Conditions

Limitations to Exercise in Coronary Artery Disease Patients

Ronald J. Ferguson

Exercise has become an important tool in cardiology and particularly in the study of coronary artery disease (CAD). Exercise testing can aid in determining a diagnosis, establishing the severity of the patient's physical incapacity, and evaluating the effect of medical or surgical treatment. Exercise testing is also employed in establishing the efficacy of new antianginal drug therapy, and physical conditioning is now an accepted part of cardiac rehabilitation. Several factors can explain the limited exercise capacity in patients with CAD, and considerable research interest has been given to explaining the increase in "maximal" exercise capacity of CAD patients following a physical reconditioning program.

Total Body Oxygen Consumption Versus Myocardial Oxygen Consumption

In the following discussion a distinction is made between total body oxygen consumption (VO_2) and myocardial oxygen consumption (MVO_2), since a physiological difference exists between traditional tests of $\dot{V}O_2$max and "maximal" tests conducted in CAD patients with a limited MVO_2 reserve.

Total Body Oxygen Consumption (VO_2)

In dynamic exercise, total body oxygen consumption (VO_2) increases proportional to the intensity. The maximal oxygen consumption is a measure of the capacity of the cardiovascular system:

$$\dot{V}O_2max = \text{cardiac output} \times \text{arteriovenous } O_2 \text{ difference}$$

Maximal dynamic exercise is characterized by considerable skeletal muscle vasodilatation, lowered total peripheral resistance, and increased sympathetic drive, cardiac output, heart rate, stroke volume, and systolic blood pressure. The augmented arteriovenous oxygen difference in maximal exercise reflects the greater skeletal muscle oxygen extraction (from 20% at rest to over 70% in exercise) and the redistribution of cardiac output from the viscera and nonworking muscle to active muscle. In normal subjects the attainment of $\dot{V}O_2$max and the ensuing fatigue are accompanied by increased skeletal muscle and blood lactate concentrations (> 9 mM/1) reflecting the anaerobic reserve of skeletal muscle. Skeletal muscle contains a mixture of oxidative and glycolytic fibers, which facilitates this combination of aerobic and anaerobic metabolism.

Myocardial Oxygen Consumption (MVO_2)

Myocardial oxygen consumption is also directly related to the intensity of skeletal muscle dynamic exercise. Major determinants of MVO_2 include heart rate and ventricular pressure, volume, contractile state, and wall thickness. Sympathetic drive is augmented in exercise and results in increased MVO_2 secondary to the higher heart rate, ventricular pressure, and contractile state. Changes in MVO_2 with exercise can be estimated by determining the product of heart rate and systolic blood pressure (RPP). As with total body oxygen consumption, MVO_2 can be expressed in terms of oxygen transport and extraction as follows:

$$MVO_2 = \text{coronary blood flow} \times \text{arteriocoronary venous } O_2 \text{ difference}$$

The myocardial oxygen demands are met primarily by a locally mediated decrease in coronary vascular resistance causing an increase in coronary blood flow. The arteriocoronary venous O_2 difference changes little from rest to exercise because myocardial oxygen extraction, unlike that of skeletal muscle, is relatively high even at rest (70%). In addition, the MVO_2 represents the total energy demand of the heart even in intense exercise, because myocardial muscle fibers are oxidative and, therefore, adapted to the aerobic rather than anaerobic generation of ATP. Myocardial lactate production generally indicates hypoxia and a pathological condition.

Factors Limiting Exercise Capacity of CAD Patients

The presence of obstructions in the coronary arteries can cause regional imbalances between myocardial oxygen supply and demand. Exercise tests performed in coronary artery disease patients are usually terminated for reasons related to a limit in MVO_2 rather than in VO_2. From a physiological viewpoint they cannot be considered tests of $\dot{V}O_2$max, since the end point is determined by signs or symptoms of coronary insufficiency, such as chest pain, dyspnea, and electrocardiographic abnormalities (ST segment depression or significant dysrhythmia). The following factors are associated with a reduced exercise capacity in CAD patients: severity and extent of coronary artery lesions; patient category (symptomatic, postinfarction, postsurgery); ventricular dysfunction secondary to exercise-induced coronary insufficiency or to previous myocardial infarction; and deconditioned skeletal muscles. The heterogeneous nature of CAD can result in a combination of these factors limiting performance. The exercise position (erect or supine) and the type of exercise (static or dynamic) may also influence performance by altering the VO_2/MVO_2 relationship.

Severity and Extent of Coronary Artery Lesions

The severity of coronary artery narrowing and the extent of coronary disease both affect regional blood supply and limit myocardial oxygen delivery. There is an inverse relationship between exercise tolerance and the number of major vessels obstructed. We studied 100 male patients with normal resting electrocardiograms and no clinical evidence of myocardial infarction (Chaitman, Bourassa, Wagniart, Corbara, & Ferguson, 1978; Chaitman & Ferguson, 1980). Patients with obstructions greater than or equal to 70% of the luminal diameter in two or more vessels had lower exercise times on a Bruce treadmill test than did patients with single vessel disease or normal subjects. Whereas 97% of those with no obstructions entered Stage 3 of the Bruce test (540 s), only 21% and 9% of those with two and three vessel disease could attain this work level, respectively. Similarly, patients with a positive electrocardiogram (ECG) on a treadmill exercise (i.e., ST segment depression of 1.0 mv for 0.08 s) and multivessel disease cannot perform the same work load as patients with single vessel disease or normal coronary arteries.

An indication that exercise in these patients is influenced by limits on MVO_2 is the fact that the RPP at which the exercise ECG becomes positive is also inversely related to the number of vessels obstructed. In our study (Chaitman et al., 1978), the mean values for RPP $\times 10^{-3}$ were 24.5, 22.6, and 18.8 for patients with single, double, and triple vessel disease, respectively. In another study, Paine et al. (1978) reported similar results in patients with previous myocardial infarction. Mean duration of treadmill exercise (421 ± 24, 345 ± 21, 286 ± 25 s), peak heart rate (152 ± 4, 138 ± 4, 133 ± 4 beats/min), and rate-pressure product (23.8 ± 1.0, 20.4 ± 0.9, $20.2 \pm 1.0 \times 10^{-3}$) were found for patients with single, double, and triple vessel disease, respectively. There appears to be no significant difference in the above mentioned variables between normal individuals and patients with single vessel disease on the one hand or between those with double and triple vessel disease on the other.

Patient Category

Detry, Mengeot, and Brasseur (1978) obtained measures of cardiac output (direct Fick) during symptom-limited maximal exercise that demonstrate the influence of patient group on treadmill exercise capacity (Table 1). Exercise capacity (VO_2) was highest in patients without exertional angina pectoris and having no previous myocardial infarction ($M = 2.13$ l/min). Lowest values were obtained in patients with both angina pectoris and previous infarction (1.31 l/min). The cardiac output of patients with angina was limited primarily by a low maximal heart rate ($M = 138$ beats/min).

Table 1 Maximal Exercise and Hemodynamic Data in Different Patient Groups (Detry et al., 1978)

Patient group	n	Oxygen consumption (l/min)	Cardiac output (l/min)	Heart rate (beats/min)	Stroke volume (ml)	Arteriovenous oxygen difference (ml/l)
No angina in exercise						
No previous MI	9	2.13	14.8	163	91	144
Previous MI	17	1.96	13.2	171	77	148
Angina pectoris in exercise						
No previous MI	30	1.41	11.5	137	84	123
Previous MI	18	1.31	9.4	137	69	140

Note. MI = myocardial infarction.

Table 2   Comparison of Coronary Hemodynamic Data for Normal Young Subjects (Bertrand et al., 1977) and Patients With Angina Pectoris (Ferguson et al., 1978)

Testing variables	Normal individuals (n = 13)		Patients (n = 9)	
	Rest	Maximal exercise	Rest	Maximal exercise
	3.11 3.11	3.1 3.1	3.1 2.1	3.1 2.1
Coronary sinus blood flow (ml/min)	111 ± 119	433 ± 102	95 ± 25	200 ± 56
Left ventricular oxygen consumption (ml/min)	13.0 ± 2.1	55.0 ± 14.5	10.7 ± 4.3	25.2 ± 5.3
Arteriocoronary venous oxygen difference (ml/l)	11.62 ± 1.14	126 ± 11	110 ± 18	130 ± 18
Heart rate (beats/min)	84 ± 12	180 ± 14	78 ± 9	132 ± 18
RPP[a] × 10^{-3}	10.0 ± 2.1	29.5 ± 5.1	11.6 ± 1.8	24.2 ± 3.6
Work load (kgm/min)		950 ± 245		493 ± 100

Note. Normal individuals exercised in the supine position and patients in the upright position.

[a]RPP = heart rate × systolic blood pressure.

The cardiac output of patients with previous myocardial infarction was also limited by reduced maximal stroke volume (15% less). The greatest impairment in cardiac output was in angina patients with previous myocardial infarction.

Measures of coronary sinus blood flow during dynamic exercise by the thermodilution technique have been made in normal individuals (Bertrand et al., 1977) and in patients with CAD (Ferguson, Côté, Gauthier, & Bourassa, 1978) (Table 2). Normal subjects can increase coronary sinus blood flow and myocardial oxygen consumption from rest to exercise by about four times. In comparison, patients with exertional angina pectoris are only able to double the oxygen delivery to the myocardium. As mentioned previously, the arteriocoronary sinus oxygen difference does not increase significantly with exercise in normal subjects. However, the patients with angina pectoris in our study had a small but significant increase (18%) in arteriocoronary sinus oxygen difference from rest to exercise.

Type of Exercise

This review is concerned primarily with dynamic exercise. However, CAD patients often perform isometric work or dynamic exercise with a static component. These exercises are not generally recommended to the patient because of an alleged excess energy demand on the myocardium created by an elevated blood pressure. However, laboratory data have not confirmed this hypothesis, and handgrip tests fail to produce angina or ST segment depression in the majority of patients with known CAD (DeBusk, Pitts, Haskell, & Houston, 1979). Although isometric exercise produces a greater cardiovascular effect than dynamic exercise does for the same total body VO_2, the occurrence of myocardial ischemic responses is more closely related to the MVO_2. Sustained isometric exercise with a handgrip to fatigue at 30, 50, and 70% of maximal voluntary contraction failed to increase coronary sinus blood flow to those values obtained in the same patients in peak dynamic leg exercise at the onset of angina (Ferguson, Côté, Bourassa, & Corbara, 1981) (Table 3). Myocardial energy demands are lower in sustained isometric contraction because heart rate increases only slightly in this form of exercise. The increase in diastolic pressure in isometric exercise may improve coronary perfusion to pressure-dependent stenotic regions of the myocardium, and ventricular volumes may be lower than in dynamic work (Ludbrook, Koziol, & O'Rourke, 1974).

The coronary sinus flow values in Table 3 reflect global blood flow and oxygen consumption for the left ventricle, whereas it is well recognized that coronary insufficiency is a regional disorder. This can readily be seen from scintigraphy studies using Thallium-201 at rest and during exercise. The Thallium scan can show qualitatively equal perfusion throughout the left ventricular mass at rest and regions that were underperfused during exercise. The efficacy of combining exercise electrocardiography and Thallium-201 exercise scintigraphy in patient subgroups is under investigation.

Table 3   Comparison of Isometric and Maximal Dynamic Exercise in Patients With Exertional Angina Pectoris (Ferguson et al., 1981)

Exercise parameters	Coronary sinus blood flow (ml/min) 3/2	Heart rate (beats/min) 3/2	Systolic blood pressure (mmHg) 3/2	Diastolic blood pressure (mmHg) 3/2	RPP[a] $\times 10^{-3}$ 2.1/1.1
Rest	106 ± 22	76 ± 8	134 ± 13	81 ± 9	10.2 ± 1.5
Isometric 30%	144 ± 40	95 ± 19	179 ± 28	106 ± 17	17.3 ± 5.6
Isometric 50%	161 ± 43	97 ± 17	183 ± 26	109 ± 19	18.0 ± 5.0
Isometric 70%	180 ± 31	100 ± 15	183 ± 24	112 ± 18	18.4 ± 4.3
Dynamic	228 ± 77	134 ± 21	185 ± 19	92 ± 14	24.7 ± 4.3

Note. $n = 10$. Patients exercised in the upright position.
[a]RPP = heart rate × systolic blood pressure.

Ventricular Dysfunction Secondary to Exercise

Left ventricular dysfunction can be induced by exercise in patients with coronary insufficiency. Increases in left ventricular end-diastolic pressure, pulmonary wedge pressure, left ventricular volumes, decrease left ventricular ejection fraction,* and stroke volume as well as the presence of wall motion abnormalities are employed to evaluate left ventricular dysfunction. Recently, radionuclide cine-angiography has permitted the noninvasive evaluation of ventricular function during exercise. In subjects with normal coronary arteries, the left ventricular ejection fraction increases from rest to exercise, and left ventricular wall motion is normal (Borer et al., 1978). The increased ejection fraction with exercise is the result of greater systolic emptying (decreased end-systolic volume) with a constant or slightly increased end-diastolic volume (Rerych, Scholz, Newman, Sabiston, & Jones, 1978; Slutsky et al., 1979). However, in patients with CAD, ejection fraction fails to increase or decrease in exercise, and wall motion abnormalities may be seen (Borer et al., 1978). The decreased contractility secondary to the exercise induced regional ischemia may result in increases in end-diastolic or end-systolic volume. Several studies (Ferguson, Dupras, et al., 1981; Slutsky et al., 1979) of exercise performed in the supine position indicate that left ventricular end-diastolic volume does not change from rest to exercise in various patient groups. The fall in ejection fraction at angina in these patients was mainly due to an increased end-systolic volume. In a study (Rerych et al., 1978) of upright exercise, end-diastolic volume rose significantly over resting values in normal individuals (12 ml), patients with single vessel disease (39 ml), and patients with multivessel disease (78 ml). Whereas in exercise end-systolic volume decreased in the normal subjects, it increased significantly in the two patient groups (13 ml and 15 ml, respectively). Therefore, the stroke volume was maintained by the Frank-Starling mechanism in these patients exercising in the upright position.

Exercise Position

The importance of the exercise position is demonstrated from data (Table 4) obtained in CAD patients 8 to 12 weeks after aortocoronary bypass surgery (Ferguson, Dupras, et al., 1981). The supine position creates a larger oxygen demand on the myocardium even though there are no significant differences in RPP between position at rest and during exercise at 200 kgm/min. This is due to the significantly higher diastolic volume in the supine position (26 ml and 24 ml, respectively).

Exercise-induced ventricular dysfunction occurs at a lower work load in the supine position. In this position ejection fraction falls from 62% at 200 kgm/min to 49% at 400 kgm/min, and there is a significant fall in stroke volume, 94 ml to 79 ml, a plateau in cardiac output, and a significantly higher RPP. Even at 600 kgm/min performed in the upright position, stroke volume is maintained despite an increase in end-systolic volume

*Ejection fraction $= \dfrac{\text{Diastolic volume} - \text{systolic volume}}{\text{Diastolic volume}} = \dfrac{\text{Stroke volume}}{\text{Diastolic volume}}$

Table 4 Changes in Ventricular Function From Rest to Exercise by Patients 8-12 Weeks Postaortocoronary Bypass Surgery (Ferguson et al., 1981)

Testing variables	Rest				Exercise									
	Supine		Upright		200 kgm/min				400 kgm/min				600 kgm/min	
					Supine		Upright		Supine		Upright		Upright	
	3.1	2.1	3.1	2.1*	3.1	2.1	3.1	2.1*	3.1	2.1	3.1	2.1**	3.1	2.1
Ejection fraction[a] %	58 ± 10		48 ± 10*		62 ± 9		61 ± 9		49 ± 14		59 ± 7.2		54 ± 14	
Diastolic volume (ml)	151 ± 61		125 ± 43*		153 ± 58		129 ± 60**		155 ± 58		139 ± 68		157 ± 82	
Systolic volume (ml)	61 ± 21		63 ± 17		58 ± 24		50 ± 23		76 ± 31		57 ± 30		74 ± 52	
RPP[b] × 10^{-3}	11.9 ± 2.4		13.0 ± 2.9		20.6 ± 3.4		18.4 ± 1.9		28.2 ± 4.3		24.5 ± 3.4**		31.9 ± 3.5	
Heart rate (beats/min)	86 ± 12		94 ± 15*		124 ± 14		122 ± 14		146 ± 14		137 ± 13		158 ± 13	
Stroke volume (ml)	90 ± 46		62 ± 30*		94 ± 38		79 ± 41*		79 ± 42		82 ± 42		83 ± 40	
Cardiac output (ml)	7.5 ± 3.7		5.6 ± 2.3*		11.6 ± 4.4		9.6 ± 4.7*		11.3 ± 5.1		11.4 ± 6.4		12.9 ± 6	

Note. $n = 8$.
[a]Ejection fraction = (diastolic volume − systolic volume) / diastolic volume. [b]RPP = Heart rate × systolic blood pressure.
*$p < .05$. **$p < .01$.

Table 5 Skeletal Muscle Oxidative Capacity and Fiber Size in Normal Individuals and Patients With Coronary Artery Disease (Ferguson et al., 1982; Taylor et al., 1978)

Subjects	SDH (I.U.)	Fiber Area (μm^2)	
		Type I	Type II
Adolescent males	7.1	—	—
Young adult females	5.3	7252	7290
Young adult males	5.1	6224	5362
Middle-age patients	1.7	4364	4360

(50 ml to 74 ml). Cardiac output continued to increase (11.3 l/min to 12.9 l/min). The increased end-diastolic volume, which at this higher work load is now equal to the supine value (155 ml vs. 157 ml), contributed to the fall in ejection fraction (59% to 54%).

Deconditioned Skeletal Muscles

The deconditioned state of the skeletal muscles of inactive coronary artery disease patients can limit exercise capacity if local fatigue sets in before cardiac limitations. There is also evidence that a large part of the posttraining exercise bradycardia is related to changes in the trained skeletal muscles. Conversely, the relatively high heart rates observed in untrained coronary patients are partly due to the deconditioned state of skeletal muscles. The higher heart rate contributes to a higher MVO_2 for a given absolute work load VO_2. The mechanisms relating the state of training to exercise heart rate are not well described. Clausen (1976) implicates changes in skeletal muscle. An analysis of biopsies taken from the vastus lateralis of sedentary patients with exertional angina pectoris shows extremely low values for oxidative capacity and for both slow (Type I) and fast (Type II) twitch fiber areas (Table 5) (Ferguson et al., 1982). Glycogen levels have also been shown to be low and easily depleted in these patients (Taylor, Ferguson, Côté, Gauthier, & Bourassa, 1976).

To maximize the returns from clinical exercise testing, it is necessary to have clearly defined objectives, to understand the physiologic basis for terminating the test, and to distinguish between tests on healthy individuals versus patients with coronary artery disease. Exercise capacity will be affected by the severity of coronary artery lesions, the patient's functional capacity, the type of exercise, the degree of left ventricular dysfunction, and the exercise position.

References

Bertrand, M. E., Carre, A. G., Genistet, A. P., Lefebvre, J. M., Desplanque, L. A., & Lefieffre, J. P. (1977). Maximal exercise in normal subjects. Changes in coronary sinus blood flow, contractility and myocardial extraction of FFA and lactate. *European Journal of Cardiology*, **5**, 481-491.

Borer, J. S., Bacharach, S. L., Green, M. V., Kenneth, M. S., Kent, M., Johnston, G. S., & Epstein, S. E. (1978). Effect of nitroglycerin on exercise-induced abnormalities of left ventricular regional function and ejection fraction in coronary artery disease. *Circulation*, **57**, 314-320.

Chaitman, B. R., Bourassa, M. G., Wagniart, P., Corbara, F., Ferguson, R. J. (1978). Improved efficiency of treadmill exercise testing using a multiple lead ECG system and basic hemodynamic exercise response. *Circulation*, **57**, 71-79.

Chaitman, B. R., & Ferguson, R. J. (1980). Stress testing exercise physiology and cardiac rehabilitation. In K. M. Rosen (Ed.), *Current cardiology* (Vol. 2) (pp. 71-109). Boston: Houghton Mifflin.

Clausen, J. P. (1976). Circulatory adjustments to dynamic exercise and effect of physical training in normal subjects and patients with coronary artery disease. *Progress in Cardiovascular Disease*, **18**, 459-495.

DeBusk, R. F., Pitts, W., Haskell, W. L., & Houston, N. (1979). Comparison of cardiovascular responses to static-dynamic effort and dynamic effort alone in patients with chronic ischemic heart disease. *Circulation*, **59**, 977-984.

Detry, J. M. R., Mengeot, P., & Brasseur, L. A. (1978). Ventricular function in coronary disease. *Advances in Cardiology*, **24**, 37-46.

Ferguson, R. J., Côté, P., Bourassa, M. G., & Corbara, F. (1981). Coronary blood flow during isometric and dynamic exercise in angina pectoris patients. *Journal of Cardiovascular Rehabilitation*, **1**, 21-27.

Ferguson, R. J., Côté, P., Gauthier, P., & Bourassa, M. G. (1978). Changes in exercise coronary sinus blood flow with training in patients with angina pectoris. *Circulation*, **58**, 41-47.

Ferguson, R. J., Dupras, G., Poirier, J. F., & Chaitman, B. R. (1981). Ventricular function in supine and upright exercise after coronary bypass surgery. *Medicine and Science in Sports and Exercise* (abstract), **13**, 102.

Ferguson, R. J., Taylor, A. W., Côté, P., Charlebois, J., Dinelle, Y., Péronnet, F., de Champlain, J., & Bourassa, M. G. (1982). Skeletal muscle and cardiac changes with training in patients with angina pectoris. *American Journal of Physiology (Heart and Circulation Physiology)*, **243**, H830-H836.

Ludbrook, G., Koziol, B. J., & O'Rourke, R. A. (1974). Effects of submaximal isometric handgrip on left ventricular size and wall motion. *American Journal of Cardiology*, **33**, 30-36.

Paine, T. D., Dye, L. E., Roitman, D. J., Sheffield, L. T., Rackley, C. E., Russell, R. O., Jr., & Rogers, W. J. (1978). Relation of graded exercise test findings after myocardial infarction to extent of coronary artery disease and left ventricular dysfunction. *American Journal of Cardiology*, **42**, 718-723.

Rerych, S. K., Scholz, P. M., Newman, G. E., Sabiston, D. C., & Jones, R. H. (1978). Cardiac function at rest and during exercise in normals and in patients with coronary disease. Evaluation by radionuclide angiography. *Annals of Surgery*, **187**, 449-463.

Slutsky, R., Karliner, J., Ricci, D., Schuler, G., Pfisterer, M., Peterson, K., & Ashburn, W. (1979). Response of left ventricular volume to exercise in man assessed by radionuclide equilibrium angiography. *Circulation*, **60**, 565-571.

Taylor, A. W., Ferguson, R. J., Côté, P., Gauthier, P., & Bourassa, M. G. (1976). Skeletal muscle adaptation with training in patients with angina pectoris. *Circulation* (abstract), **53-54** (Suppl. 2), 206.

Taylor, A. W., Lavoie, S., Lemieux, G., Dufresne, C., Skinner, J. S., & Vallee, J. (1978). Effects of endurance training on the fibre area and enzyme activities of skeletal muscle of French Canadians. In F. Landry & W. A. R. Orban (Eds.), *Third Annual Symposium of Biochemistry of Exercise* (pp. 267-278). Miami: Symposia Specialists.

The Physiological Basis for Cardiac Rehabilitation

Ronald J. Ferguson

Exercise conditioning has been shown to improve the maximal exercise capacity of coronary artery disease (CAD) patients with angina pectoris (Clausen, 1976; Ferguson, Côté, Gauthier, & Bourassa, 1978), after myocardial infarction (Detry, Rousseau, & Brasseur, 1975), and following aortocoronary bypass surgery (Oldridge, Nagle, Balke, Corliss, & Kahn, 1978). By what mechanisms does this natural therapy improve exercise tolerance? The hypotheses can be grouped within four interdependent lines of investigation: (a) a possible increase in myocardial oxygen delivery in peak exercise; (b) an improved ventricular function; (c) peripheral adaptations in trained skeletal muscle; and (d) a decreased myocardial oxygen.

Increase in Myocardial Oxygen Delivery

An improvement in myocardial perfusion of CAD patients with training was postulated by Eckstein (1957), who found increases in retrograde flow of dog arteries in which partial obstructions had been created. Other earlier animal studies (Burt & Jackson, 1965; Kaplinsky, Hood, McCarthy, McCombs, & Lown, 1968) failed to find evidence of increased collateral circulation with training in completely obstructed or normal arteries. Repeat coronary cine-arteriography studies in CAD patients before and after 1 year of physical conditioning failed to demonstrate collateral development specific to training (Ferguson et al., 1974). Other studies have followed, and we can conclude that there is no change in the extent of collateralization on the arteriograms that is specific to the physical conditioning program, that collateralization is secondary to severe obstruction, and that exercise capacity can be significantly increased without the presence of new collateral vessels.

A major criticism of coronary arteriographic studies is that they are performed at rest and are not measures of coronary artery flow. Several animal studies have used radioactive microspheres to measure coronary flow in dogs. Cohen, Yipintsoi, Malhotra, Penpargkul, and Scheuer (1978) found no difference in collateral flow or regional flow between trained and untrained dogs when aortic pressure was elevated. However, Laughlin, Diana, and Tipton (1978) found a larger coronary reactive hyperemia and a greater endo-to-epicardial flow ratio during isoproterenol infusion in trained

Table 1 Changes in Coronary Hemodynamics Before and After Physical Conditioning in Patients With Exertional Angina Pectoris (Ferguson et al., 1982)

Testing variables	Before conditioning	After conditioning
Work load at angina (kgm/min)	470 ± 30	665 ± 35 ***
Coronary sinus blood flow (ml/min)	192 ± 10	208 ± 9 *
Left ventricular oxygen consumption (ml/min)	23.2 ± 1.5	25.8 ± 1.6*
Arteriocoronary venous oxygen difference (ml/l)	122 ± 5	126 ± 4 ***
Heart rate (beats/min)	130 ± 4	132 ± 4 ***
Systolic blood pressure (mmHg)	182 ± 4	186 ± 4 ***
RPP^a × 10^{-3}	237 ± 9	246 ± 7 ***

Note. From "Skeletal Muscle and Cardiac Changes with Training in Patients with Angina Pectoris" by R.J. Ferguson et al., 1982, *American Journal of Physiology (Heart and Circulation Physiology)*, **243**, H834. Reprinted with permission.
^{a}RPP = heart rate × systolic blood pressure.
*$p < .05$. ***$p < .001$.

as compared to untrained dogs, and Heaton, Marr, Capurro, Goldstein, and Epstein (1978) found significantly higher regional flow to a collateral-dependent zone of the myocardium only in trained dogs. Finally, Wyatt and Mitchell (1978) produced significant increases in circumflex coronary artery diameter in dogs after 12 weeks of conditioning, changes that were reversed after 6 weeks of deconditioning.

Many studies of humans have been carried out in patients with exertional angina pectoris, because the onset of chest pain can provide a reasonably reproducible end point for the termination of exercise (Robinson, 1967). A possible increase in myocardial oxygen delivery had been suggested by studies in which the maximal rate-pressure product at the onset of angina was higher following physical conditioning (Redwood, Rosing, & Epstein, 1972). We have argued that this may relate more to the exercise protocol employed than to a physiologic adaptation, because it occurs when progressive multistage protocols are used but not when a constant work load of approximately 5-min duration is employed to induce angina (Ferguson et al., 1978).

We determined coronary sinus blood flow and left ventricular oxygen consumption by the thermodilution technique at the onset of angina during upright exercise before and after 6 months of physical conditioning in 29 patients (Ferguson et al., 1982) (Table 1). Despite an increase of 40%

in the symptom-limited maximal work load, coronary sinus blood flow and left ventricular oxygen consumption only increased slightly (8% and 11%, respectively). These increases were barely greater than the error of measurement (e.g., 14 ml for coronary sinus blood flow) and were not accompanied by significant increases in the RPP (heart rate × systolic blood pressure). RPP does not reflect ventricular volume changes, and it is possible that some patients exercised to a greater degree of left ventricular dysfunction after conditioning and thus to larger systolic and diastolic volumes. This may account for the small increases in MVO_2 with no significant change in RPP. It appears that any increase in maximal myocardial oxygen delivery could only account for a very small portion of the observed increase in exercise capacity with training.

Improved Ventricular Function

It has been suggested that physical conditioning may improve ventricular function by producing hypertrophy or by increasing contractility (Clausen, 1976). However, in healthy young individuals there is little or no change in ventricular wall thickness with training (Péronnet, Ferguson, Perrault, Ricci, & Lajoie, 1981). In contradiction to earlier reports, conditioning does not increase the myofibrillar adenosine triphosphatase (ATPase) activity of rat hearts (Tibbits, Koziol, Roberts, Baldwin, & Barnard, 1978) or dog hearts (Cohen et al., 1978), although there is some evidence that calcium ion (CA^{++}) availability may be enhanced with training (Tibbits et al., 1978). Although the exercise-induced drop in stroke volume still occurs in patients after conditioning, it does so at a higher work load (Detry, Rousseau, & Brasseur, 1975). Similarly, Jensen et al. (1980) report a higher ejection fraction for a fixed submaximal work load following conditioning in coronary artery disease patients. Physical training may delay the onset of left ventricular ischemia and thus ventricular dysfunction.

Adaptations in Trained Skeletal Muscle

Detry et al. (1971) suggested that the increased maximal arteriovenous oxygen difference in CAD patients following physical conditioning could be due to an enhanced oxidative capacity within trained skeletal muscle. We have documented such things with conditioning in CAD patients (Ferguson et al., 1982; Taylor, Ferguson, Côté, Gauthier, & Bourassa, 1976). Six months of physical conditioning resulted in significant increases in skeletal muscle succinate dehydrogenase (SDH) activity (1.75 ± 0.24 to 3.31 ± 0.24 I.U.) and in the areas of Type I (43.6 ± 3.3 to 54.4 ± 3.3 m.10^2) and of Type II fibers (43.9 ± 2.4 to 57.2 ± 5.1 m.10^2). PFK activity and fiber distribution were unchanged with conditioning. These changes in size and oxidative capacity of skeletal muscle may explain the increase in maximal arteriovenous oxygen difference and thus part of the increased exercise tolerance found after conditioning in CAD patients.

Decreased Myocardial Oxygen Requirement

Despite all other mechanisms by which physical conditioning may improve exercise tolerance in the coronary patient, the most convincing evidence suggests that conditioning reduces the ratio of myocardial oxygen consumption to total body oxygen consumption (MVO_2/VO_2) during exercise. In other words, the heart uses less oxygen for any given work load after a conditioning program. This is similar to the goal of most antianginal drug therapies (nitroglycerin, beta blockers, and slow channel calcium blockers).

Coronary sinus blood flow, left ventricular oxygen consumption, and RPP are reduced during submaximal upright exercise (400 and 500 kgm/min) after conditioning in angina patients (Ferguson et al., 1978) (Table 2). Whereas an average work load of 500 kgm/min induced angina before conditioning, this did not occur after conditioning until a work load of 700 kgm/min. The reduction in the myocardial oxygen requirement of submaximal exercise gave the patient a reserve and permitted him or her to work at a higher work load before reaching the critical limit of oxygen supply and demand.

These coronary hemodynamic changes with conditioning are related to reductions in sympathetic drive with corresponding decreases in heart rate, systolic blood pressure, and total plasma catecholamines (Cousineau et al., 1977; Ferguson et al., 1982). This reduced sympathetic drive following physical conditioning has been attributed to less stimulation from higher nervous centers, termed *central command*, or to a decreased afferent feedback to cardiovascular control centers from trained skeletal muscle (Clausen, 1976). Support for this hypothesis comes from data showing that the training-induced exercise bradycardia is more pronounced when exercise is performed with trained versus untrained muscle groups (Clausen, 1976; Saltin et al., 1976). This could be brought about by cellular adaptations that result in a lesser stimulation of skeletal muscle mechano- or chemoreceptors after training.

However, the relative importance of the skeletal muscle adaptations to training previously mentioned is not clear at the present time. No significant correlations were found between the increases in skeletal muscle oxidative capacity (SDH activity) or in fiber size and the reduced heart rate at a fixed submaximal work load or the increased symptom-limited exercise capacity in angina patients after conditioning (Ferguson et al., 1982). Also, in normal subjects training-induced increases in skeletal muscle oxidative capacity have not been shown to be highly correlated to indices of training, including higher $\dot{V}O_2$max (Henriksson & Reitman, 1977), submaximal heart rate, maximal work load, or skeletal muscle capillary development (Andersen & Henriksson, 1977).

Conclusion

At this time one could conclude that physical conditioning improves the exercise tolerance of CAD patients mainly by reducing myocardial oxygen

Table 2   Changes in Coronary Hemodynamics for a Given Exercise Workload Before and After Physical Conditioning in Angina Patients (Ferguson et al., 1978)

Testing variables	M = 400 kgm/min		M = 500 kgm/min	
	Before conditioning	After conditioning	Before conditioning[a]	After conditioning
Left ventricular oxygen consumption (ml/min)	20.1 ± 5.2	17.3 ± 3.6*	25.2 ± 5.3	18.6 ± 3.6*
Coronary sinus blood flow (ml/min)	163 ± 36	135 ± 21	200 ± 56	145 ± 24 *
Arteriocoronary venous oxygen difference (ml/l)	123 ± 21	127 ± 16	130 ± 18	129 ± 18
Heart rate (beats/min)	120 ± 14	103 ± 11 **	132 ± 18	114 ± 20 **
Systolic blood pressure (mmHg)	180 ± 25	168 ± 30 *	183 ± 26	176 ± 31

Note. From "Skeletal Muscle and Cardiac Changes with Training in Patients with Angina Pectoris" by R.J. Ferguson et al., 1982, *American Journal of Physiology (Heart and Circulation Physiology),* **243,** H835. Reprinted with permission.
[a]Average exercise intensity inducing angina before the physical conditioning program.
*$p < .05$. **$p < .01$.

demands during exercise. This would delay the onset of electrocardio-graphic abnormalities, angina pectoris, and left ventricular dysfunction to a higher work load. The reduced MVO_2 is related to diminished sympathetic activity because heart rate, systolic blood pressure, and plasma catecholamines are lowered. This reduced sympathetic activity may be due to reduced "central command" or afferent feedback when trained muscles are employed. An increase in the oxidative capacity of skeletal muscle may improve exercise capacity in some patients by increasing the maximum arteriovenous oxygen difference. Finally, small increases in maximal coronary blood flow would account for only a small portion of the training-induced increase in the exercise capacity of coronary artery disease patients.

References

Andersen, P., & Henriksson, J. (1977). Capillary supply of the quadriceps femoris muscle in man. Adaptive response to exercise. *Journal of Physiology*, 270, 677-690.

Burt, J. J., & Jackson, R. (1965). The effect of physical exercise on the coronary collateral circulation of dogs. *Journal of Sports Medicine and Physical Fitness*, 5, 203-206.

Clausen, J. P. (1976). Circulatory adjustments to dynamic exercise and effect of physical training in normal subjects and patients with coronary artery disease. *Progress in Cardiovascular Disease*, 18, 459-495.

Cohen, M. V., Yipintsoi, T., Malhotra, A., Penpargkul, S., & Scheuer, J. (1978). Effect of exercise on collateral development in dogs with normal coronary arteries. *Journal of Applied Physiology*, 45, 797-805.

Cousineau, D., Ferguson, R. J., de Champlain, J., Gauthier, P., Côté, P., & Bourassa, M. (1977). Catecholamines in coronary sinus during exercise in man before and after training. *Journal of Applied Physiology: Respiratory, Environmental, Exercise Physiology*, 43, 801-806.

Detry, J. M. R., Rousseau, M. T., & Brasseur, L. A. (1975). Early hemo-dynamic adaptations to physical training in patients with healed myocardial infarction. *European Journal of Cardiology*, 2, 307-313.

Detry, J. M. R., Rousseau, M., Vandenbrouke, F., Kasumi, F., Brasseur, L. A., & Bruce, R. A. (1971). Increased arteriovenous oxygen difference after physical training in coronary disease. *Circulation*, 44, 109-118.

Eckstein, R. W. (1957). Effect of exercise and coronary artery narrowing on coronary collateral circulation. *Circulation Research*, 5, 230-235.

Ferguson, R. J., Côté, P., Gauthier, P., & Bourassa, M. G. (1978). Changes in exercise coronary sinus blood flow with training in patients with angina pectoris. *Circulation*, 58, 41-47.

Ferguson, R. J., Petitclerc, R., Choquette, G., Chaniotis, L., Gauthier, P., Huot, R., Allard, C., Jankowski, L., & Campeau, L. (1974). Effect of physical training on treadmill exercise capacity, collateral circulation and progression of coronary disease. *American Journal of Cardiology*, **34**, 764-769.

Ferguson, R. J., Taylor, A. W., Côté, P., Charlebois, J., Dinelle, Y., Péronnet, F., de Champlain, J., & Bourassa, M. (1982). Skeletal muscle and cardiac changes with training in patients with angina pectoris. *American Journal of Physiology (Heart and Circulation Physiology)*, **243**, H830-H836.

Heaton, W. H., Marr, K. C., Capurro, N. L., Goldstein, R. E., & Epstein, S. E. (1978). Beneficial effect of physical training on blood flow to myocardium perfused by chronic collaterals in the exercising dog. *Circulation*, **57**, 575-581.

Henriksson, J., & Reitman, J. S. (1977). Time course of activity changes in human skeletal muscle succinate dehydrogenase and cytochrome oxidase activities and maximal oxygen uptake with physical activity and inactivity. *Acta Physiologica Scandinavica*, **98**, 91-97.

Jensen, D., Atwood, E., Froelicher, V., McKirnan, D. M., Battler, A., Ashburn, W., & Ross, J. (1980). Improvement in ventricular function during exercise studied with radionuclide ventriculography after cardiac rehabilitation. *American Journal of Cardiology*, **46**, 770-777.

Kaplinsky, E., Hood, W. B., McCarthy, B., Jr., McCombs, L., & Lown, B. (1968). Effects of physical training in dogs with coronary artery ligation. *Circulation*, **37**, 556-565.

Laughlin, M. H., Diana, J. N., & Tipton, C. M. (1978). Effects of exercise training on coronary reactive hyperemia and blood flow in the dog. *Journal of Applied Physiology*, **45**, 604-610.

Oldridge, N. B., Nagle, F. J., Balke, B., Corliss, R. J., & Kahn, D. R. (1978). Aortocoronary bypass surgery: Effects of surgery and 32 months of physical conditioning on treadmill performance. *Archives of Physical Medicine and Rehabilitation*, **59**, 268-275.

Péronnet, F., Ferguson, R. J., Perrault, H., Ricci, G., & Lajoie, D. (1981). Echocardiography and the athlete's heart. *The Physician and Sports Medicine*, **9**, 103-112.

Redwood, D. R., Rosing, D. R., & Epstein, S. E. (1972). Circulatory and symptomatic effects of physical training in patients with coronary artery disease and angina pectoris. *New England Journal of Medicine*, **286**, 959-965.

Robinson, B. F. (1967). Relationship of heart rate and systolic blood pressure to the onset of pain in angina pectoris. *Circulation*, **35**, 1073-1083.

Saltin, B., Nazar, K., Costill, D. L., Stein, E., Jansson, E., Essén, B., & Gollnick, P. D. (1976). The nature of the training response; peripheral and central adaptations to one-legged exercise. *Acta Physiologica Scandinavica*, **96**, 289-305.

Taylor, A. W., Ferguson, R. J., Côté, P., Gauthier, P., & Bourassa, M. G. (1976). Skeletal muscle adaptation with training in patients with angina pectoris. *Circulation* (abstract), **53-54** (Suppl. 2), 206.

Tibbits, G., Koziol, B. J., Roberts, N. K., Baldwin, K. M., & Barnard, R. J. (1978). Adaptation of the rat myocardium to endurance training. *Journal of Applied Physiology, 44*, 85-89.

Wyatt, H. L., & Mitchell, J. E. (1978). Influences of physical conditioning and deconditioning on coronary vasculature of dogs. *Journal of Applied Physiology, 45*, 619-625.

Relaxation Counseling and Multiple Sclerosis: Cardiac Stress and Physiological Changes

Clermont P. Simard
Jean Jobin
Nicole Morissette

In addition to living with an important pathology, persons afflicted with multiple sclerosis (MS) endure considerable stress on the psychophysiological level. Parallel to the above factors, these persons are often tired and lack a sufficient level of physical activity needed to maintain an efficient level of the principal physiological functions.

Because the Cardiac Tension Index (CTI: SAT $\times$ CF $\times$ 10^{-2}) is highly correlated to the myocardial oxygen consumption and the general state of stress of the person, we used this variable as an indicator of tension in the person suffering from multiple sclerosis (Feinberg, Katz, & Boyd, 1962; Herd, 1984; Katz & Feinberg, 1958; Sarnoff et al., 1958). It is possible to use different approaches to improve the human condition of this group by reducing the stress rate at rest or in a less-than-maximum exertion (Burish, Handrix, & Frost, 1981; Rice & Blanchard, 1982). Some respiratory parameters were taken as factors associated with the physical condition of MS sufferers. Cardiac frequency and arterial tension were the other measurements taken.

Our hypothesis is that the relaxation counseling technique reduces the stress level of persons suffering from MS without affecting the respiratory parameters.

Methodology

All subjects signed a letter of consent informing them about their involvement in this project. Eighteen multiple sclerosis sufferers were divided at random into a test group and a control group.

The treatment was provided by a psychologist for a period of 12 weeks. Each 90-min lesson was offered twice a week, with a 60-min period for exercises and a 30-min period for counseling. The relaxation was achieved with a harmonious mixture of yoga, autogenous training, and progressive relaxation. The counseling period consisted of a process of sharing

Table 1   Changes in Cardiac Parameters in Control and Test Groups Before and After Treatment

Group	Cardiac frequency (CF)	Systolic arterial tension (SAT)	Double product (CF × SAT × 10^{-2}) (DP)
Control group			
Pre	72.7 ± 2.3	116.9 ± 3.5	84.6 ± 2.0
Post	81.2 ± 6.6	111.9 ± 3.9	89.8 ± 6.1
Test group			
Pre	77.7 ± 3.1	114.2 ± 3.9	88.7 ± 4.7
Post	71.5 ± 2.7	106.0 ± 3.3	75.6 ± 3.2

and interaction between participants and the monitor, starting from experiences each had lived through. Most of the time, background music was used. Each subject had a mattress available; sessions took place in an atmosphere conducive to relaxation.

The exertion tests were conducted on an adaptable manual cyclergometer. The tests lasted about 8 min, and cardiac frequency was recorded for each subject with the same work load in pre- and posttesting. The measurements of the cardiac frequency (CF) and of the systolic arterial tension (SAT) were taken after 10 min of rest in pre- and posttesting. The Collin's spirometer allowed us to take various respiratory measurements: vital capacity (VC), maximum expiratory breathing capacity in 1 s (MEBCS), the median maximal expiratory output (MMEO), and the maximum respiratory capacity (MRC). Averages were calculated for our different data, and the significance of differences between these parameters was verified by use of the Student t test.

Results

The data on the cardiac frequency (CF), the systolic arterial tensions (SAT), and the double product (DP) of the test and control groups are presented in Table 1. At the beginning, the DP remained similar between the test group and the control group and in the control group before and after the experiment. The DP decreased significantly ($p \leqslant .01$) in the test group at the end of the experiment, and this decrease was also significant ($p \leqslant .01$) in relation to the posttest data of the control group.

In the test group, the DP went from 88.7 ± 4.7 to 75.6 ± 3.2; in the control group it was 89.8 ± 6.1.

The various respiratory parameters remained similar in the two groups before and after the experiment, except for the vital capacity (VC). This

Table 2 Changes in Respiratory Parameters in Control and Test Groups Before and After Treatment

Group	Vital capacity (l)	Maximum expiratory breathing capacity (sec/l)	MEBC/VC[a] (%)	Maximum median expiratory output (l/sec)	Maximum respiratory capacity (l/min)
Control group					
Pre	3.24 ± 0.44	2.56 ± 0.32	81.6 ± 5.5	3.07 ± 0.62	89.1 ± 11.3
Post	2.91 ± 0.40	2.43 ± 0.29	86.2 ± 5.5	3.14 ± 0.59	84.5 ± 10.2
Test group					
Pre	3.02 ± 0.28	2.42 ± 0.20	80.6 ± 3.4	2.80 ± 0.24	84.1 ± 7.0
Post	2.91 ± 0.26	2.42 ± 0.19	83.3 ± 3.0	2.98 ± 0.27	84.2 ± 6.8

[a]MEBC = maximum expiratory breathing capacity, and VC = vital capacity.

decreased significantly ($p \leqslant .05$) in both groups. It went from 3.24 l to 2.91 l in the control group and from 3.02 l to 2.91 l in the test group. The data on the respiratory parameters are presented in Table 2.

Discussion

The data for the respiratory parameters remained quite similar. The decreases of 10% and 4% in pre- and posttesting in the control and test groups are significant because our values are paired and because we found a slight decrease among different subjects. The insignificant change in the control and test groups of the MEBCS/VC, which increased slightly in both groups, is due to a decrease in the VC. The other parameters, the MMEO and the MRC, remained the same.

The effects of the treatment on the level of the DP are interesting. They show the influence of our program and indicate that persons suffering from multiple sclerosis may block secondary components of this pathology.

In the test group, the DP decreased by 15% ($p \leqslant .01$) after treatment. This decrease is linked to a change in both the CF level and in the SAT. However, the values obtained are at a very acceptable level; this is linked to the fairly low SAT.

The increase of the DP in the control group is explained by an increase of the CF, but we also observed a slight decrease of the SAT. It is obvious that these persons often become upset emotionally.

It is shown that cardiac stress is related to DP (Herd, 1984; Katz & Feinberg, 1958) and that these cardiovascular changes are related to the level of anxiety of a person (Goodwin & Guze, 1979). It was of interest for us to know whether our intervention techniques influence this level of stress. In addition, several biofeedback studies were carried out to determine whether certain parameters, such as the CF, could be used to reduce anxiety levels in individuals. Gatchel (1977) showed that using the CF for biofeedback has a positive effect on human behavior.

It would be interesting to develop an appropriate service for MS sufferers in times of difficulty that we could add to our relaxation counseling—a biofeedback service based on the CF and the SAT. While admitting the importance of medical research in this field, it is of interest to note that, with appropriate programs, we could improve the living conditions of this group by reducing the negative effects of certain features of this pathology.

References

Burish, T., Handrix, E. M., & Frost, R. O. (1981). Comparison of frontal EMG biofeedback and several types of relaxation instructions in reducing multiple indice of arousal. *Psychophysiology*, **18**, 594-599.

Feinberg, H., Katz, L. N., & Boyd, E. (1962). Determinants of coronary flow and myocardial oxygen consumption. *American Journal of Physiology*, **202**, 45-52.

Gatchel, R. J. (1977). Therapeutic effectiveness of voluntary heart control in reducing anxiety. *Journal of Consulting and Clinical Psychology*, **45**, 689-691.

Goodwin, D. W., & Guze, S. B. (1979). *Psychiatric diagnosis*. New York: Oxford University Press.

Herd, J. A. (1984). Cardiovascular response to stress in man. *Annual Review of Physiology*, **46**, 177-185.

Katz, L. N., & Feinberg, H. (1958). The relation of cardiac effort to myocardial oxygen consumption and coronary flow. *Clinical Research*, **6**, 656-669.

Rice, K. M., & Blanchard, E. B. (1982). Biofeedback in the treatment of anxiety disorders. *Clinical Psychological Review*, **2**, 557-577.

Sarnoff, S. J., Brunwald, E., Welch, G. H., Case, R. B., Stainsby, W.N., & Macruz, R. (1958). Hemodynamic determinants of oxygen consumption of the heart with special reference to tension-time index. *American Journal of Physiology*, **192**, 148-156.

The Benefits of a Postoperative Exercise Program for Children With Congenital Heart Disease

Patricia E. Longmuir
Richard D. Rowe
Peter M. Olley
Robert C. Goode

Many children with congenital heart disease have a low level of physical activity, which is determined by both physical and psychological factors. After corrective surgery, low preoperative fitness levels often persist despite anatomically excellent results (Goldberg, Adams, & Hurwitz, 1967; Goldberg, Weiss, & Adams, 1966; Irving & Godman, 1980; James et al., 1976; Mathews et al., 1983; Mocellin, Bastanier, Hofacker, & Buhlmeyer, 1976). James et al. (1976) suggest that the decreased physical work capacity is due to restricted physical activity during the developmental years and perhaps a lack of cardiac rehabilitation after surgery. Activity restrictions during development may result in the loss of ability to learn basic motor skills and may isolate the child from normal social contacts with healthy peers (Shephard, 1983; Strauzenberg, 1982).

Postoperative training programs involving sophisticated equipment and trained personnel can improve the fitness of children with congenital heart disease (Goldberg et al., 1981; Ruttenberg, Adams, Orsmond, Conlee, & Fischer, 1983). The purpose of our study was to evaluate the effect in children with heart disease of a simple home program administered early in the postoperative period.

Methods

The subjects were all patients undergoing cardiac surgery at the Hospital for Sick Children, Toronto, between March 1982 and September 1983. The study included all types of heart defects, with the exception of the following:

- Patients less than 5 years of age at the time of surgery
- Patients with arrhythmias
- Patients with persistent congestive heart failure

- Patients with disabilities other than heart disease
- Patients who developed postpericardiotomy syndrome
- Patients not followed at the hospital after surgery

Sixty subjects completed the study, 31 controls and 29 in the experimental group. Patients were assigned to the experimental group if they lived within the metropolitan Toronto area, so that they could be retested on completion of the program. Patients living outside Toronto were placed in the control group. All patients were seen by their cardiologist and retested 6 months after surgery.

Exercise Program and Testing

Each subject was evaluated before and after surgery. The initial assessment took place when the child was admitted to the hospital for surgery. Members of the experimental group received an exercise program based on their preoperative results, whereas the controls did not receive any instruction. Members of the experimental group were retested when the exercise program had been completed and then were allowed to determine their own level of activity. Testing 6 months after surgery evaluated the carry-over of the program to the daily level of activity of the subjects.

Study subjects and a group of healthy children were assessed with seven tests designed to measure cardiovascular endurance, strength, flexibility, and coordination. Most of the tests are based on the Canada Fitness Award (Measurement and Evaluation Committee, 1980), which has the advantages of being familiar to children and having good reproducibility (Johnson & Nelson, 1969). The shuttle run was used to assess agility and coordination. Cardiovascular endurance was estimated using the distance jog, in which the subject is required to jog until there is a sudden increase in breathlessness that limits conversation. The numbers of sit-ups and push-ups successfully completed were used as measures of strength. Three tests of flexibility were chosen from a fitness study involving healthy schoolchildren (Gluppe, 1977). The tests included back, shoulder, and hamstring measurements.

A standard program of mobilization was followed by each member of the experimental group, beginning when the child returned to the ward from the intensive care unit and continuing after discharge until the child returned to school. This was followed by the 6-week individualized home exercise program.

Written guidelines for the program activities were explained and demonstrated to the child and parents before discharge from hospital. The families were contacted every 2 weeks after discharge to clarify problems and to monitor the child's progress. The relatively short duration of the program allowed most children to complete it successfully. However, the motivation of each child varied, and some dropouts occurred.

Table 1 Study Group Profile

Variables	Compliant group	Noncompliant group	Control group
Number of subjects	20	9	31
Age	9.2 ± 3.2	9.8 ± 4.5	8.6 ± 3.9
Sex ratio:			
Female	10	3	14
Male	10	6	17
Cyanotic	2	3	6
Acyanotic	18	6	25
History of congestive heart failure	3	1	10

Scoring and Statistical Analysis

Each subject was scored and programmed separately for strength, endurance, flexibility, and coordination. Each area was scored out of 5 points, for a maximum score of 20 points. One point was awarded for a score below the 20th percentile, 2 for the 21st to 40th percentile, up to 5 for a score above the 80th percentile.

Areas that scored 5 points were not included in the exercise program. A 4-point score received a 4-week program. Activities scored in levels 1, 2, or 3 were included in the 6-week exercise program.

The children were expected to return at least to the preoperative level without intervention. Significant postoperative improvement of the experimental group above the controls should indicate a beneficial effect of the program. The pre- and postoperative scores of the experimental and control groups were compared using an analysis of variance. The benefits of the exercise program and the maintenance of these benefits after the program was completed were assessed at 6 months.

Results

At the end of the study, the experimental group was divided into compliant ($n = 20$) and noncompliant ($n = 9$) subgroups. Compliant individuals were those who completed the exercise program at least twice a week for 6 weeks.

The groups were analyzed by age, sex, diagnosis, and history of congestive heart failure (Table 1). There was no significant difference in the age, sex, or diagnosis (cyanotic vs. acyanotic) of the experimental and control

PRE-PROGRAM SCORES:

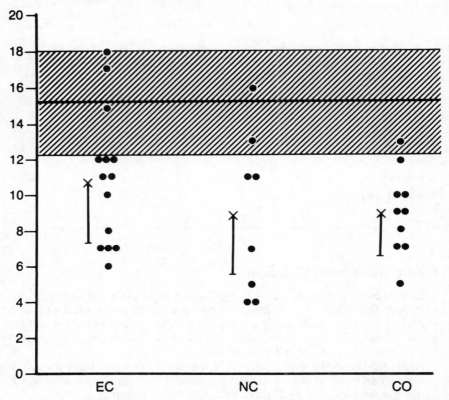

Figure 1 Pre-exercise program scores. In this and other figures, EC = compliant group, NC = noncompliant, CO = controls. Hatched area represents mean ± *SD* of test scores for 27 healthy children.

groups. The control group appears to have more subjects with a history of congestive heart failure.

Results of the initial preoperative assessment (Figure 1) showed no significant difference among the three patient groups. The scores of the healthy children were significantly higher than the means of all the patient groups ($p < .01$). The healthy children ($n = 27$) were tested as part of the pilot study.

The experimental subjects were retested 3 months after surgery, when the home exercise program had been completed. The compliant group scores were significantly higher than the initial scores ($p < .01$) and were not significantly different than the scores of the healthy children (Figure 2). The scores of the noncompliant group remained below the normal values ($p < .01$).

All of the study subjects were retested 6 months after surgery (Figure 3). The scores of all the patient groups had improved since the preopera-

END OF PROGRAM SCORES

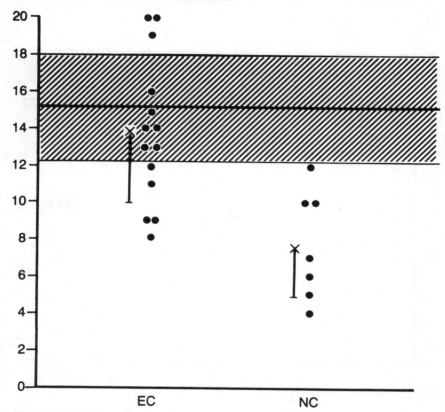

Figure 2   End of program scores.

tive test. There was no significant difference between the healthy and compliant groups. The scores of the noncompliant and control groups remained significantly lower than the compliant group and healthy children ($p < .01$).

Discussion

Recent attempts to provide exercise training for children with congenital heart disease have shown the benefits of an exercise program (Goldberg et al., 1981; Ruttenberg et al., 1983). Ruttenberg et al. studied children who had undergone surgical correction at least 1 year prior to the exercise test. The subjects were compared to healthy controls and were given a maximal treadmill exercise test before and after a jogging program. They found that all subjects improved their level of fitness with training. Goldberg

FINAL TEST SCORES:

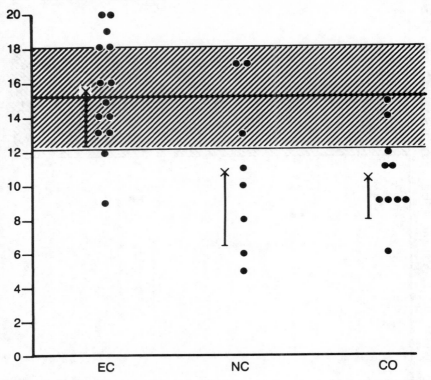

Figure 3 Final test scores.

et al. tested children following repair of tetralogy of Fallot or ventricular septal defect. The subjects were assessed with maximum and submaximal protocols on a cycle ergometer. After a 6-week training program on a cycle ergometer, the subjects were able to complete similar work loads with a lower heart rate and reduced oxygen consumption.

The emphasis of our program was simplicity coupled with application as soon after surgery as possible. The tests and exercises were selected to avoid the use of complex equipment and highly trained personnel.

Preoperatively there were no significant differences between the study groups. The exercise rehabilitation began immediately after surgery and continued for 3 months. The compliant children significantly improved their fitness by the end of the program. This improvement was maintained until the 6-month assessment without a further specific program. This would seem to indicate that the program effectively encouraged the children to adopt a more active life-style. Further follow-up should determine whether these benefits are maintained over a longer period.

The fitness scores of the noncompliant group at the end of the exercise program were not significantly different than their preoperative scores.

The explanation for noncompliance given by the parents was that they felt that the child was normally active and, therefore, that the program was unnecessary. After 6 months, the noncompliant and control groups had significantly improved their scores ($p < .01$) but remained below the compliant and healthy subjects ($p < .01$). These results indicate that although the children had recovered from their surgery and their fitness levels had improved, they still fell short of their potential for improvement.

The scores of the healthy children were significantly better than the preoperative scores of the children with heart disease. The postoperative scores of the noncompliant and control groups remained significantly lower than those of the healthy children. However, the compliant group increased their fitness scores to the level of their healthy peers. Presumably this would allow these children to participate in the normal activities of their peer group.

The duration of follow-up in this study was relatively short, and possibly the benefits obtained by the compliant group may also be short-term. It is possible that over a longer period of time the compliant group will return to the activity level of the control group.

A second possible explanation of the difference would be the noncomparability of the study groups. This seems unlikely, as there was no difference when the groups were analyzed for age, sex, or type of heart lesion. The area that appears to show some difference is the positive history of congestive heart failure. Thirty percent of the control group had a history of failure compared to 15% of the compliant group and 11% of the noncompliant subjects. None of the subjects had signs of heart failure during the study. Most often the failure had occurred during infancy, before the heart lesion was diagnosed. Possibly the occurrence of failure heightens parental anxiety resulting in greater overprotection during childhood. It is unlikely that this affected the exercise scores because the group with the fewest children with a history of failure (noncompliant group) had the lowest initial mean exercise score, although the difference was not significant.

The relative contributions of exercise and counseling to the changes observed in the compliant group is unknown. The smaller improvement in the noncompliant group suggests that it was the performance of the exercise program rather than counseling that provided the greatest benefit.

The graph of the preoperative scores (Figure 1) suggests that the noncompliant group may represent a particularly unfit subsection of the cardiac population. The mean initial score is lower, although not significantly, than the initial scores of the compliant and control groups. This suggests that the noncompliant group may be children who have a more severely restricted level of physical activity.

Conclusion

Previous research indicates that the fitness levels of children with congenital heart disease are low and that these low levels persist after corrective procedures. Our study suggests that a simple home program can enhance the postoperative improvement in physical fitness of children undergoing heart surgery. The program was designed to improve fitness for everyday recreational activities, not maximal endurance. The children were evaluated with physical performance tests in the areas of endurance, flexibility, strength, and coordination. Test and program activities were simplified so that a minimum of skill and equipment was required. By using basic tests, it was hoped that the program would receive greater support from patients, their families, and staff. Because such a simple, inexpensive program appears to be effective, the necessity of a more complex approach is questionable (Goldberg et al., 1981; Ruttenberg et al., 1983).

Acknowledgment

This research was supported by a Grant-in-Aid from the Physicians Services Incorporated.

References

Gluppe, G. (1977). *Fitness norms for North York Junior High School students.* Toronto: North York Board of Education.

Goldberg, B., Fripp, R. R., Lister, G., Loke, J., Nicholas, J. A., & Talner, N. S. (1981). Effect of physical training on exercise performance of children following surgical repair of congenital heart disease. *Pediatrics,* 68(5), 691-699.

Goldberg, S. J., Adams, F. H., & Hurwitz, R. A. (1967). Effect of cardiac surgery on exercise performance. *Journal of Pediatrics, 71,* 192-197.

Goldberg, S. J., Weiss, R., & Adams, E. H. (1966). A comparison of the maximal endurance of normal children and patients with congenital heart disease. *Journal of Pediatrics,* 69(1), 46-55.

Irving, J. B., & Godman, M. J. (1980). Exercise testing and ambulatory electrocardiographic monitoring following surgical repair of Tetralogy of Fallot. *European Heart Journal,* 1(2), 117-121.

James, F. W., Kaplan, S., Schwartz, D. C., Chou, T. C., Sandker, M. J., & Naylor, V. (1976). Response to exercise in patients after total surgical correction of Tetralogy of Fallot. *Circulation,* 54(4), 671-679.

Johnson, B. L., & Nelson, J. K. (1969). *Practical measurements for evaluation in physical education.* Minneapolis, MN: Burgess.

Mathews, R. A., Fricker, S. J., Beerman, L. B., Stephenson, R. J., Fischer, D. R., Neches, W. H., Park, S. C., Lenox, C. C., & Zuberbuhler, J. R. (1983). Exercise studies after the mustard operation in transposition of the great arteries. *American Journal of Cardiology,* 51(9), 1526-1529.

Measurement and Evaluation Committee. (1980). *Canada fitness award.* Ottawa: Canadian Association for Health, Physical Education, and Recreation.

Mocellin, R., Bastanier, C., Hofacker, W., & Buhlmeyer, K. (1976). Exercise performance in children and adolescents after surgical repair of Tetralogy of Fallot. *European Journal of Cardiology,* **4**(3), 367-374.

Ruttenberg, H. D., Adams, T. D., Orsmond, G. S., Conlee, R. K., & Fischer, A. G. (1983). Effects of exercise training on aerobic fitness in children after open heart surgery. *Pediatric Cardiology,* **4**(1), 19-24.

Shephard, R. J. (1983). Physical activity and the healthy mind. *Canadian Medical Association Journal,* **128**(5), 525-530.

Strauzenberg, S. E. (Chair). (1982). Recommendations for physical activity and sports in children with heart disease [Editorial]. *Journal of Sports Medicine and Physical Fitness,* **22**(4), 401-406.

PART IV

Programming for the Handicapped

A Process Toward the Integration of Mentally Handicapped Students Into Community Learn-To-Swim Programs

Shirley Johannsen

> Whatever the educational situation we should seek to give children the joys and excitement of physical activity and play in some form. We should use this natural childhood activity to give handicapped children as much opportunity as possible for independence and acceptance by other children. (Groves, 1979, p. 3)

Physical education has an important part to play in the development of children's physical, social, and emotional growth. In play many early and valuable social experiences take place. Awareness and feelings of self-confidence are closely linked with bodily experiences. Many authors have stressed the value of successful physical experiences in total development (Groves, 1979). Few authors, however, have emphasized the consequences of failure in physical activity, which can have detrimental long-term effects.

It has been well demonstrated through numerous studies that mentally handicapped children have difficulties in play (Carr, 1970; Watkinson & Wall, 1982). Lacking not only in the prerequisite physical skills, they may also not understand the rules of play (Keeran, Grove, & Zachofsky, 1969; Wall, 1976). This leaves mentally handicapped children in jeopardy in that they do not have the skills required for play nor the social skills to partake in group activities, which may lead to social rejection from their normal peers. Additionally, mentally handicapped children sometimes display unusual social behaviors or lack simple accepted social skills, causing them to stand out in a peer group, resulting often in ridicule by or isolation from peers.

The answer to this problem is not to withdraw children from play nor to protect them from possible failure or rejection by others; rather, it becomes increasingly important for teachers and parents to assist mentally handicapped children to improve their social and motor skills so that they may join in activities with nonhandicapped children. Evidence has demonstrated that physical fitness and motor skills of mentally handicapped children can be improved with effective instruction (Auxter, 1982; Ersing, Loovis, & Ryan, 1982; Wall, 1976). Groves (1979) has suggested that those children whose motor skills improve may also demonstrate improvements in social and behavioral skills.

109

Teachers and specialists must remember, however, that the degree to which handicapped children can eventually participate with nonhandicapped children will vary, depending on the skills of the handicapped individual. One cannot expect integration to be successful for all mentally handicapped students. Some students will lack the physical or social skills required in integrated settings even after programs of intensive instruction. The responsibility of educators, then, is to assist students to develop their skills to the best of their abilities. Achievement of these skills will facilitate their entry into integrated activities.

Swimming is an activity that provides an individual with an opportunity for a lifelong recreational outlet with peers and family. It can assist individuals in achieving some degree of physical fitness if engaged in on a regular basis. Initially easy to learn, swimming engenders feelings of success. Opportunities for participation are available in most communities across Canada. Thus the mentally handicapped can benefit greatly from programs that prepare them to be integrated into this activity.

Various researchers have suggested that as people in the community become more aware of the potential for integration of individuals who are handicapped, they begin to seek information on how to develop their programs (Hutchison & Lord, 1979). A model, or continuum, for the development of recreational programs can assist people who are mentally handicapped to progress step by step toward their potential. With effective instruction in upgrading programs, mentally handicapped individuals can improve their performance on instructed skills.

However, unless individuals have been taught to generalize acquired skills, the probability of performing these skills in a new setting (e.g., in a community program) is highly unlikely (Stokes & Baer, 1977; Wehman, Abramson, & Norman, 1977). If children are expected to be able to perform acquired skills in other settings, with family and in the presence of nonhandicapped peers, they need first of all to be taught to generalize their skills. Since generalization of skills is a key determinant of the success of the integration of mentally handicapped students, models toward integration must be developed that include deliberate training for generalization.

Purpose of the Study

The purpose of this study was to develop and evaluate a process toward integration into community learn-to-swim programs that are based on a combination of skill upgrading, generalization training, and systematic introduction to community swim programs. This process followed a sequence of phases, each one bringing the student closer toward self-sufficient integration.

Progress through the phases was dependent upon students' ability to generalize their acquired swim and social skills in coping with the demands in a pool environment. In order for students to progress successfully through subsequent phases, they were required to reach a certain degree of competence in both swim and social skills. Criteria were established as requirements for entry into each phase of the process. Success in each phase was determined by continued progress on these skills.

In order to evaluate the success of this process toward integration the following questions were answered:

- Can minimal competencies in swim and social skills be described as criteria for entrance into each phase of the process?
- Did subjects with required swim and social skills progress satisfactorily through sucessive phases? (Satisfactory progress was operationally defined as continued skill maintenance in the new instructional phase.)
- Did progress through this process result in successful integration into community learn-to-swim programs?

Instructional Model

The focus of this study was to develop a process toward integration of mentally handicapped students into community learn-to-swim programs. Utilizing swimming as the skill through which to evaluate a process toward integration, seven phases were developed and tested illustrating a systematic process toward integration.

Phase 1: Skill Acquisition and Upgrading

The first phase was designed to take place in a segregated physical activity class. Participation in this setting offered familiarity and security for the mentally handicapped student. A direct, criterion-referenced model of instruction was utilized to teach beginning swimming skills. In addition to the acquisition of physical skills, the program focused on the development of appropriate social, self-help, and safety skills that are prerequisites to participation in community swim programs (Lister-Piercy, 1985).

The model of instruction utilized, based on the PREP model of instruction (Watkinson & Hall, 1982), utilized a prompting continuum during instructional episodes. This resulted in progressive decreasing of instructor assistance as a student's independence increased and skill level improved.

This individualized instructional model (adapted for swim skill instruction) was characterized by the following six processes:

1. Observational assessment of students' swim skill proficiency demonstrated during free swim
2. Individual detailed criterion-referenced assessment of each student's level of skill performance on identified target skills
3. Selection of two target skills for instruction (based on range and degree of proficiency)
4. Identification of response level at which the student performed prescribed skill

5. Individualized instruction on prescribed task
6. Monitoring of student's progress during instruction, with an ongoing progress evaluation over time

Phase 2: Skill Upgrading and Generalization Training

In the second phase of the process instruction was continued in the same manner as in Phase 1. In addition, systematic attempts were made to facilitate the generalization of skills to new stimulus conditions.

When acquiring a skill, a student must learn to perform it for different instructors and in different settings. Stokes and Baer (1977) concluded that if one wishes to program the generalized performance of responses across various settings, conditions, or persons, training should occur across a sufficient number of setting conditions and with various persons.

In order to train generalization sequentially and systematically, it was determined that first and most importantly the students should learn to perform their skills for a variety of people. Thus, generalization training to other instructors was the first step of Phase 2. Once students' levels of performance on their swim and social skills met the preestablished criteria (Lister-Piercy, 1985), instruction in different settings was employed to train generalization across settings.

Hill, Wehman, and Horst (1980) successfully utilized an alternating treatment whereby on alternate sessions students received instruction in a community setting. Students' performances in the new setting could then be compared to performances in the regular, segregated setting. The above method of alternating treatments was utilized to train students to generalize their skill learning to different settings.

Similarly, in the second part of this phase, instruction in two different settings took place. On alternate days instruction took place in an unknown pool rather than in the known one.

Phase 3: Consciously Simulated Integrated Program With Required Supports

Phase 3 of the process was comprised of a program of reverse integration. This phase provided an intermediate step between segregated and totally normative community-based programs for handicapped individuals. The step between Phase 2 of a specialized program in a new setting and an integrated program is simply too large for a student to be expected to continue to demonstrate improvement. The intermediate step thus permitted handicapped students to become accustomed to the presence of small numbers of nonhandicapped peers before being immersed in an integrated program where the ratio of handicapped to nonhandicapped individuals would be reversed.

Phase 4: Integrated Recreational Activity Program With Known Peers/Family

By the time mentally handicapped students reach adolescence, parents' hopes may already be diminished for the probability of their child's integration into community activity programs (Wehman & Hill, 1980). If, however, parents are made aware of the goals of the program and how to assist their children in the water, they will be more likely to take the opportunity to participate in recreational swims with their children. This phase constituted an opportunity for parents to become involved with their children in the instructional swim program. They were then better prepared to work with them during community recreation swim sessions. Phase 4, then, constituted recreational involvement with family or known peers in a community swim program.

Phase 5: Integrated Instructional Program With Continuous Support

The goal of this phase was to provide an opportunity for mentally handicapped students to participate in integrated swim instructional programs in the community.

In this phase, students participated in public learn-to-swim classes accompanied by a familiar instructor. Instruction in this phase was provided on a group basis, with approximately six to eight students to one instructor. Students were assessed and instructed through the Standardized Red Cross model of swim instructional levels. A known instructor (volunteer from the previous phases) accompanied the student in the class setting. The role of this instructor was varied as needed. Instructors assisted in changing and in finding the correct pool, as well as by providing additional instructions for the student to understand and by providing encouragement as the student attempted new skills.

From Phase 5 onward, parental support was necessary to assist a student to bring appropriate clothing and to provide or arrange transportation to and from the recreational facility. If parents were unable to provide the required assistance, then students were unable to participate in this and subsequent phases.

Phase 6: Integrated Instructional Program With Minimal Support

In Phase 6, students continued to participate in public learn-to-swim classes accompanied by a familiar swim instructor. In this phase, however, an instructor's support was provided only on a verbal level. Instructors did not enter the water, providing additional verbal instructions only when necessary to assist the students' understanding of directions. Thus interaction was provided on a minimal basis when needed for assistance on instructions, practice, or changing clothing. Students were aware that their instructors were present to assist them if they needed help.

Phase 7: Integrated Instructional Program With No Support

Once students had performed consistently at the levels on swim and social skills that were established as criteria for entry into this phase, they were ready to participate self-sufficiently in an integrated community learn-to-swim program. Community swim instructors were sensitized to the presence of handicapped students in the class so that they were able to cope with problems that might arise. However, students would participate self-sufficiently on a daily basis in the program.

For some individuals, the continuum offers an opportunity to develop skills and confidence that promote independent involvement in community recreational programs. Participation at this level emphasizes normative participation by mentally handicapped students whereby appropriate social, self-help, and safety skills can be displayed both in and around the pool and facility. However, achievement of this level by mentally handicapped individuals requires the commitment of many individuals over time to assist students' acquisition of necessary physical and social skills (Arsenault & Wall, 1979).

Discussion

The purpose of this study was to develop and evaluate a process toward the integration of mentally handicapped students into community learn-to-swim programs. The process followed a sequence of phases, each one bringing students closer to self-sufficient integration.

Progress through the phases was dependent upon subjects' ability to successfully generalize their swim skills and social maturity in each learning environment. In order for students to progress to successive phases, they were required to demonstrate a certain degree of competence on both swim and social skills as determined by a sequence of preestablished criteria. Success of each phase was determined through students' ability to maintain or demonstrate an improvement in their performance on both swim and social skills as they entered a new phase of the process.

Fourteen students initially began Phase 1 of the process. All students were assessed on their swim skill level. Based on this assessment, two or three swim skills were prescribed for instruction, which was carried out in an individualized manner according to the PREP model of instruction (Watkinson & Wall, 1982).

When students' swim and social skills met the required criteria, they progressed to the following phase of the process, which consisted of generalization training across instructors and settings. Seven students' skills met the preestablished criteria, and thus they entered Phase 2 of the process.

These seven students maintained or demonstrated improvement on their skills in Phase 2. All seven students' skill performances eventually met the preestablished criteria for progress to Phase 3. Phase 3 consisted of a consciously simulated integrated instructional program whereby the ratio of handicapped individuals to nonhandicapped was approximately the same. All seven students who entered Phase 3 were successful in meeting the criteria and were eligible to enter Phase 4 of the process. Phase 4 consisted of recreational participation with known peers and family. Due to diverse family reasons, only four of the seven students were able to participate with their families during scheduled times. All of these students were successful in meeting the criteria to progress to Phase 5, participating in an integrated program with the support of a known instructor. One student was required to terminate participation in the program after the third lesson due to family reasons. However, the other three students did continue in the integration program, with excellent results. They all demonstrated an improvement in the level of their swim skill performance and social skill competencies. In the program, no negative interactions were observed between handicapped and nonhandicapped students.

The study was formally terminated after Phase 5 of the process. However, two students were informally monitored as they entered the next session of the swim program. Information from all sources (support instructor, parents, and regular swim instructor) suggested that the students were participating successfully and continuing to demonstrate improvement on their swim skills.

A single-subject changing criterion design facilitated illustration of each changing phase that students participated in. When a student met the criteria required for completion of Phase 1, he or she was promoted to Phase 2 of the process. Students' swim skills were analyzed visually for changes in trends, levels, or stability over time. Success of each phase was defined as maintenance or improvement on acquired skills over time.

All students in the program maintained or improved their skill performance levels as they progressed through each phase of the process. Thus, according to the definition for success, the minimal competencies on swim and social skills described for progress through the phases adequately screened the readiness of each subject for entry into a subsequent phase of the process. The purpose of this study was thus achieved, as the process toward integration into community learn-to-swim programs was a successful experience for all students regardless of where they were on the continuum.

Conclusions

The development and evaluation of this process toward the integration of mentally handicapped students into regular community learn-to-swim classes provide support for the following conclusions:

1. Individualized instruction and progress through each of the phases facilitated successful experiences for each student in the program.
2. With adequate preparation, utilizing two exemplars, students were successful in generalizing acquired skills across instructors and settings. Generally, students appeared to be more sensitive to people rather than settings when placed in a new learning environment.

3. The preestablished criteria levels on swim and social skills were adequate in screening subjects' performance levels on swim and social skills to facilitate successful experiences in subsequent phases of instruction.
4. Continued progress of a student beyond Phase 3 of the process required a strong commitment from a student's parents to ensure that the child would be transported regularly, on time, to swim lessons. Some students were unable to progress beyond Phase 3 of the process due to lack of support from their parents.
5. With adequate preparation through a systematic, progressive continuum, adequate screening of students on physical and social skills, and adequate preparation of a community swim instructor and support staff, some students can be successfully integrated into regular community learn-to-swim programs.

References

Arsenault, D., & Wall, A. E. (1979). *Service continuum for recreation*. Unpublished manuscript, University of Alberta, Edmonton.

Auxter, D. (1982). Physical fitness and adapted physical education. *Exceptional Education Quarterly*, **3**(1), 54-63.

Carr, J. (1970). Mental and motor development in young mongol children. *Journal of Mental Deficiency Research*, **14**, 204-220.

Ersing, W. F., Loovis, E. M., & Ryan, T. M. (1982). On the nature of motor development in special populations. *Exceptional Education Quarterly*, **3**(1), 64-72.

Groves, L. (1979). Physical education as part of the total education of handicapped children. In L. Groves (Ed.), *Physical education for special needs* (pp. 3-18). London: Cambridge University Press.

Hill, J. W., Wehman, P., & Horst, G. (1980). Acquisition and generalization of leisure skills in severely and profoundly handicapped youth: Use of a pinball machine. In P. Wehman & J. W. Hill (Eds.), *Instructional programming for severely handicapped youth* (pp. 43-62). Richmond, VA: Virginia Commonwealth University.

Hutchison, P., & Lord, J. (1979). *Recreation integration*. Ottawa: Leisurability Publications.

Keeran, C. V., Grove, F. A., & Zachofsky, T. (1969). Assessing the playground skills of the severely retarded. *Mental Retardation*, **7**(3), 29-32.

Lister-Piercy, S. (1985). *A process of the integration of mentally handicapped students into community learn-to-swim programs*. Unpublished master's thesis, University of Alberta, Edmonton.

Stokes, T., & Baer, D. (1977). An implicit technology of generalization. *Journal of Applied Behavior Analysis*, **10**(2), 349-367.

Wall, A. E. (1976). The motor performance of the mentally retarded. *McGill Journal of Education, 4*, 74-82.

Watkinson, E. J., & Wall, A. E. (1982). *PREP. The PREP play program: Play skill instruction for mentally handicapped children.* Ottawa: Canadian Association of Health, Physical Education, and Recreation.

Wehman, P., Abramson, M., & Norman, C. (1977). Transfer of training in behavior analysis programs: An evaluative review. *Journal of Special Education, 11*(2), 217-231.

Wehman, P., & Hill, J. W. (1980). Preparing severely and profoundly handicapped youth to enter less restrictive environments. In P. Wehman & J. W. Hill (Eds.), *Instructional programming for severely handicapped youth* (pp. 1-23). Richmond, VA: Virginia Commonwealth University.

The Effects of Training Selected Psychomotor Skills and the Relationship to Adaptive Behavior

Jeffrey A. McCubbin
Paul Jansma

Deinstitutionalization and *normalization* are two terms that connote a current trend in society to provide community living opportunities for handicapped adults in a more normal or less restrictive environment. However, recent literature relating to client adaptation following community placement indicates that deinstitutionalization is not living up to expectations (Cohen, Conroy, Frazer, Snelbecker, & Spreat, 1977; Conroy, 1977). Of particular relevance to this article, Gollay, Freedman, Wyngarden, and Kurtz (1978) discuss the importance of preparing mentally retarded persons for such placement. In this regard, increased attention has been given to the potential value of exercise programs for the mentally retarded. Two reasons identified by Moon and Renzaglia (1982) for such increased attention are a general trend of the population to recognize the value of improving health through exercise and the potential benefits of exercise to various psychological variables. Most of the past research in this area has concentrated on the mildly and moderately retarded school-aged population (Campbell, 1978; Johnson & Londeree, 1976; Rarick & Dobbins, 1972). Only recently have researchers begun to look at the effects of physical and psychological variables on severely and profoundly retarded adults (Jansma, Ersing, & McCubbin, 1986; Tomporowski & Ellis, 1984; Tomporowski & Jameson, 1985).

This particular study, entitled Project TRANSITION, evaluated the effects of an age-appropriate, health-related physical fitness training program on the fitness performance and adaptive behavior of moderately, severely, and profoundly retarded institutionalized adults. The dependent variables were the treatment effects of three different health-related training programs. Two critical questions needed to be answered: What would be the effect of each of three different 14-week health-related training programs on the physical fitness performance of institutionalized mentally retarded adults? and What effects would these training programs have on the subjects' Adaptive Behavior Scale (Nihira, Foster, Shellhaas, & Leland, 1974) score, a test purportedly used in the deinstitutionalization process?

Method

Subjects

Eighty-eight mentally retarded male and female subjects were selected to be involved in the research. Common characteristics of the subjects included no gross neurological impairment, ability to walk, parental/guardian permission, and medical clearance to participate. Due to attrition for a variety of valid reasons, 17 subjects were eliminated. The data reported herein reflect the 71 subjects (40 males, 31 females) that completed the program.

The mean age of the subjects was 33 years (range 16 to 55). Using guidelines developed by the State of Ohio Department of Mental Retardation/Developmental Disabilities, the Mental Retardation Level and the Adaptive Behavior Level of the subjects ranged from moderate to profound, with a mean score indicating the severe range in both categories. These subjects all resided in a large, state-operated developmental center.

The subjects were randomized to one of four experimental groups based on a stratified randomization technique. The two criteria in the stratification were living unit and participation in these researchers' pilot study (1/84 to 6/84). The living units were generally divided by functional abilities of the clients. Stratification was used to approximate representation from the wide range of abilities of the subjects. Accurate data on the length of residence in the institution serving as the research site were not available.

Procedure

The subjects participated in a 14-week treatment program of varying combinations, of health-related training. The training groups included Group 1, fitness four times per week; Group 2, personal hygiene training four times per week; Group 3, a combination of 2 days of fitness and 2 days of hygiene training per week; and Group 4, control group with no additional training. Each training session lasted approximately 45 min. The experimental treatment was the implementation of a validated and reliable series of curriculum-embedded tests developed for the research. The fitness skills included abdominal endurance (flexed knee sit-up), upper body strength/endurance (modified bench press), cardiorespiratory endurance (300-yd run/walk), lower back and hamstring flexibility (modified sit and reach), and grip strenth (bilateral). The personal hygiene skills included hand washing, toothbrushing, face washing, deodorant use, and personal appearance (grooming). These skills were chosen as being both health-related and of functional value to the subjects.

The instructor/subject teaching ratio was individualized to meet the needs of subject. Reinforcers consisted of age-appropriate social reinforcers, with delayed tangible reinforcers made available following each daily session. The reinforcement schedules were individualized with efforts made to fade. The instructors were graduate students highly trained in implementing the curriculum.

Data collected on these measures were based on the actual performance score (e.g., pounds lifted, seconds timed) and two scores that measured the subjects' independent ability to perform each skill. These scores were the *percent task score* and *average independence score*. The percent task score was the percent of task-analyzed steps for each skill that the subject could perform with only an initial verbal prompt to initiate movement. The average independence score was a percentage score that reflected the amount and type of the prompt needed to complete each skill.

The five physical fitness skills were tested on a pretest/posttest basis. The performance scores measured were: number of sit-ups in 60 s, pounds lifted in the modified bench press, centimeters reached in the modified sit and reach, seconds to complete a 300-yd run/walk, and pressure of grip strength (measured in kPa) for each hand. Two scores on each dependent variable were collected during both the pretest and the posttest. A mean score was used in the analyses. As indicated, each dependent variable had three scores, including performance score, percent task score, and average independence score. These data were all analyzed separately.

The Adaptive Behavior Scale scores were also collected on a pretest/posttest basis. Direct care staff who were familiar with the subjects were interviewed by trained administrators of the test. Raw scores were used in the analyses. Seven subscales were identified as being most pertinent to this research. These included independent functioning, physical development, socialization, vocational activity, hyperactivity, antisocial behavior, and violent/destructive behavior.

Results

A multivariate analysis of variance technique was used on all pre- to posttest difference scores (SAS Institute, 1985). The overall group effect was analyzed, and an $F = 3.45$ was found with a significance of $p < .05$. Subsequent univariate analysis of variance found significant group performance score differences on four of the five fitness skills. Only the grip strength showed no significant group differences following training. Table 1 contains the group mean difference scores in performance for all four experimental groups and the specific corresponding alpha levels.

Table 2 contains follow-up Tukey post hoc comparisons on the four fitness skills with significant group performance score differences at the .05 level of confidence.

No significant group differences were found following multivariate analysis of variance on the two measures of independence (percent task score and average independence score). However, subsequent univariate analysis indicated a significant group difference in the sit-up average independence score ($F = 4.25$, $p < .05$) and percent task score ($F = 2.94$, $p < .05$). The follow-up Tukey indicated the significant differences were between Group 1 (Fitness) and Group 4 (Control) and also between Group

Table 1 Fitness Performance Group Mean Difference Scores

Fitness skill	Fitness (n = 18)	Hygiene (n = 18)	Combined (n = 17)	Control (n = 18)
Sit-ups (reps) $p = .0001$	8.11	3.63	7.58	1.58
Bench press (lbs) $p = .0001$	25.86	5.61	26.67	8.97
Back and hamstring flexibility (cms) $p = .0173$	7.58	2.72	5.76	1.86
300-yd run/walk (s) $p = .0204$	−74.50	−16.33	−44.82	−20.91
Grip strength—right (kPa) $p = .3502$	3.22	0.50	6.20	−1.08
Grip strength—left (kPa) $p = .2825$	3.44	1.83	4.61	−1.97

3 (Combined) and Group 4 (Control). No significant post hoc comparisons were evident with percent task score.

No significant differences were found on the multivariate analyses of the seven Adaptive Behavior Scale subscales used in the analyses. Univariate analysis of variance used for each subscale also found no significant differences.

Discussion

The physical fitness data generated from Project TRANSITION indicate that the level of the subjects' fitness was significantly improved following the 14-week training program. The fitness group, which trained four times per week in only fitness tasks, appeared to make the largest gains. Supporting this finding, the American College of Sports Medicine (1980) advocates that exercising three times per week is necessary to improve fitness levels. The combined group, which trained only twice per week in fitness tasks, also made significant gains. Positive change following twice-a-week training is likely due to the very low level of fitness of most of the subjects at the outset.

The significant group changes in physical fitness performance warrant the use of the Project TRANSITION curriculum materials. Unquestionably, improving skills in health-related fitness areas is a positive step in any subject's rehabilitative programming geared toward deinstitutionalization.

The lack of significant group changes in most of the independence measures as they related to physical fitness training may have occurred

Table 2   Significant Tukey Post Hoc Comparisons of Fitness Performance Scores

Fitness skill	Group	
	Greater mean score	Smaller mean score
Sit-ups	Fitness	Hygiene
	Fitness	Control
	Combined	Control
Bench press	Fitness	Hygiene
	Fitness	Control
	Combined	Hygiene
	Combined	Control
Back and hamstring flexibility	Fitness	Control
300-yd run/walk	Fitness	Hygiene
	Fitness	Control

for one of two reasons: An inadequate period of time was spent in training for the more profoundly retarded subjects, and a possible dependence developed for the verbal prompting that was more readily available in the training sessions but not during testing. The lack of statistical significance does not mean that the process of measuring independent abilities is not valuable. By keeping daily records of the independent abilities of the performers, the instructor has valuable information that can assist in program evaluation.

No statistical significance in adaptive behavior in this research project concurs with recent research by Tomporowski and Ellis (1984). There are two factors that may have contributed here: The length of the study may have been too short to cause any measurable changes in the subjects' adaptive behavior, and the Adaptive Behavior Scale may not have been sensitive enough to discriminate discrete behavioral changes. It is important to note, however, that the Adaptive Behavior Scale has been found to be a reliable and valid instrument frequently used in decisions related to the deinstitutionalization process (Spreat, 1982). Its value may best be utilized when making decisions on an individual basis, when individual scores are not subjected to group data analyses.

It is hoped that the data collected in this research and the curriculum materials developed as an integral part of it will be valuable to professionals interested in improving the physical fitness of moderately, severely, and profoundly retarded individuals. More research relative to Project TRANSITION, which extends the limited literature in this little-researched area, is unquestionably warranted.

Acknowledgments

Funding for this project was from the Office of Special Education and Rehabilitative Services (OSERS), U.S. Department of Education, project number G008300001. The contents of this article are those of the authors and do not necessarily reflect the position or policy of OSERS, and no official endorsement by OSERS should be inferred.

The principal investigators for this project were Paul Jansma and Walter Ersing. The project coordinator was Jeffrey McCubbin. The hard work of the project staff during this principal study deserves recognition. They included C. Sue Combs, James Decker, Roslyn Jackson, Janet Rogers, and Susan Long. The authors are grateful to the staff at the Columbus Developmental Center, Columbus, Ohio, for their support of the project.

References

American College of Sports Medicine. (1980). *Guidelines for graded exercise testing and exercise prescription* (2nd ed.). Philadelphia: Lea & Febiger.

Campbell, J. (1978). Evaluation of physical fitness programs for retarded boys. *Journal of Special Education of the Mentally Retarded, 14*, 78-82.

Cohen, H., Conroy, T., Frazer, U., Snelbecker, G., & Spreat, S. (1977). Behavioral effect of interinstitutional relocation of mentally retarded residents. *American Journal of Mental Deficiency, 82*, 12-18.

Conroy, J. (1977). Trends in deinstitutionalization of the mentally retarded. *Mental Retardation, 15*, 44-46.

Gollay, E., Freedman, R., Wyngarden, M., & Kurtz, N. (1978). *Coming back: The deinstitutionalization of mentally retarded people*. Cambridge, MA: Abt Books.

Jansma, P., Ersing, W., & McCubbin, J. (1986). *The effects of physical fitness and personal hygiene training on the preparation for community placement of institutionalized mentally retarded adults*. (Project TRANSITION Final Project Report, U.S. Department of Education Grant No. G008300001). Columbus: Ohio State University.

Johnson, L., & Londeree, B. (1976). *Motor fitness testing manual for the moderately mentally retarded*. Washington, DC: American Association for Health, Physical Education, and Recreation.

Moon, M. S., & Renzaglia, A. (1982). Physical fitness and the mentally retarded: A critical review of the literature. *The Journal of Special Education, 16*, 269-287.

Nihira, K., Foster, R., Shellhaas, M., & Leland, H. (1974). *AAMD Adaptive Behavior Scale*. Washington, DC: American Association on Mental Deficiency.

Rarick, G. L., & Dobbins, D. A. (1972). *Basic components in the motor performance of educable mentally retarded chilren* (Report No. 142714). Washington, DC: Bureau of Education for the Handicapped, U.S. Office of Education.

SAS Institute. (1985). *SAS user's guide: Basics, version 5 edition*. Cary, NC: SAS Institute.

Spreat, S. (1982). The AAMD Adaptive Behavior Scale: A psychometric review. *The Journal of School Psychology, 20*, 45-56.

Tomporowski, P., & Ellis, N. (1984). Effects of exercise on the physical fitness, intelligence and adaptive behavior of institutionalized mentally retarded adults. *Applied Research in Mental Retardation, 5*, 329-337.

Tomporowski, P., & Jameson, L. D. (1985). Effects of a physical fitness training program on the exercise behavior of institutionalized mentally retarded adults. *Adapted Physical Activity Quarterly, 2*, 197-205.

Exercise Capacity of Children With Cystic Fibrosis

Patricia E. Longmuir

J.A. Peter Turner

Peter M. Olley

In recent years, considerable interest has been focused on the exercise capacity of cystic fibrosis patients. Exercise testing has involved both maximal and submaximal stress testing on the treadmill or cycle ergometer. Results of the exercise tests have been correlated with measures of pulmonary function, severity of chest X-ray changes, and the Schwachman score (Cerny, Pullano, & Cropp, 1982; Coates, Boyce, Shaw, Godfrey, & Mearns, 1981; Godfrey & Mearns, 1971; Orenstein, Henke, & Cerny, 1983; Orenstein et al., 1981). Not surprisingly, as the severity of disease increases, maximal exercise capacity decreases.

It is generally accepted that children with cystic fibrosis who have the best prognosis are those who are most physically active. However, it is not certain whether the extent of disease is the cause or the result of the level of physical activity. Several reports have shown that the physical fitness of children with cystic fibrosis can improve through participation in an exercise program (Keens et al., 1977; Orenstein et al., 1981; Orenstein et al., 1983; Zach, Oberwaldner, & Häusler, 1982; Zach, Purrer, & Oberwaldner, 1981). Whether cystic fibrosis patients have a "normal" exercise capacity has not been investigated, as it has been assumed that their lung disease would decrease fitness levels (Clément, Jankowski, & Beaudry, 1979).

The purpose of this research study was to evaluate the fitness of children with cystic fibrosis. It appeared unlikely that all patients would necessarily have a low level of physical fitness. Exercise evaluation was completed using standardized tests with published norms for children. It is recognized that the clinical status of cystic fibrosis patients decreases with increasing age. Presumably physical fitness scores would decrease correspondingly.

Methods

Subject Selection

Study subjects were selected from children between 6 and 17 years of age attending the Cystic Fibrosis Clinic at the Hospital for Sick Children,

Toronto. Patients with health problems other than cystic fibrosis and those receiving treatment for an acute exacerbation of their disease were excluded from the study.

Exercise Assessment

Children were evaluated using the Canada Fitness Test (Measurement and Evaluation Committee, 1980). This includes six test items designed to measure cardiovascular endurance, strength, and agility. The norms for each test item are published for males and females between 6 and 17 years of age inclusive. Initial assessment was completed between March 1982 and August 1983. Following the initial test, subjects who scored below the 40th percentile on any test item were provided with a home exercise program. All subjects, both those who did and did not receive training programs, were retested during their two subsequent clinic appointments.

The home exercise program required a maximum of 15 min per day for 12 to 14 weeks and included the lowest scoring test items. Subjects who received a home exercise program completed their training between the first and second test sessions. The second and third evaluations were carried out in those subjects without further home training. The control group was assessed using the same exercise testing procedures at the same time intervals in the absence of any home training.

Evaluation of Results

The Student t test (Garrett, 1962) was used to determine the existence of significant differences between the study groups. The initial test results were compared to the norms for children of the same age and sex. This allowed evaluation of the level of physical fitness of children with cystic fibrosis relative to their healthy peers. Without a home program, the fitness scores would not be expected to change over the duration of the study. Comparison of the first and second test results assessed the effectiveness of the home exercise program. The carry-over effect of training was evaluated through changes between the second and third test sessions.

Results

One hundred and sixty subjects completed the initial test session. The initial Canada Fitness Test scores of all subjects were compared to the published norms. There was no significant difference between the scores of the study subjects and the healthy norms, with the exception of the 6-year-old females ($p < .01$), 16-year-old males ($p < .05$), and 17-year-old females ($p < .01$), who were all significantly lower.

The pulmonary function scores (FEV_1) of the study subjects and published norms for children of the same age were compared (Weng & Levison, 1969). The pulmonary function scores were significantly lower

Table 1 Profile of Study Subjects by Age and Sex

Subjects	Age	Males (n)	Females (n)
Compliant	9.76 ± 2.95	20	22
Noncompliant	10.04 ± 2.78	20	7
Control	10.00 ± 3.34	16	11

than the healthy norms ($p < .01$), with the exception of 11-year-old females and 11- and 12-year-old males, who were not significantly different.

The initial exercise scores of all of the study subjects were compared to the Modified Schwachman, radiographic, and pulmonary function scores. There was no correlation between the scores of clinical status and the exercise score except at the extreme ends of performance. Subjects with an exercise score below the 20th percentile (15 out of 75 points) also had Schwachman, radiographic, FEV_1, forced vital capacity (FVC), and forced expiratory flow (FEF) scores that were significantly lower ($p < .01$) than subjects with exercise scores above the 20th percentile. Subjects with a perfect Modified Schwachman score, an X-ray score above 20 points, or an FVC or FEV_1 above 80% of that predicted for a normal subject of the same size, age, and sex, had exercise scores that were significantly higher than the exercise scores of subjects with lower Schwachman, X-ray, and pulmonary function scores ($p < .01$).

Sixty-four subjects refused or were unable to complete the study protocol. Of 96 subjects who successfully completed the study, 27 subjects scored sufficiently well that they could be assigned to the control group and did not, therefore, receive a home exercise program. Sixty-nine subjects were assigned to the experimental group. At the end of the study, the experimental group was further divided between compliant ($n = 42$) and noncompliant ($n = 27$) subjects.

The study groups were analyzed for age and sex distribution (see Table 1). There was no significant difference among the mean ages of the three groups. The proportion of males and females in the experimental and control groups was not significantly different. However, there was a difference in the proportion of males and females in the noncompliant group, with 50% of the males being noncompliant but only 25% of the females.

The initial fitness scores of the control group were significantly higher than those in the experimental group ($p < .01$). Within the experimental group, the scores of the noncompliant subjects were initially significantly higher than the compliant ones ($p < .05$).

At the time of the second test, following the home exercise program, the compliant subjects were sufficiently improved so that there was no significant difference between the compliant and noncompliant groups.

The control group scores remained significantly higher than those in the experimental group ($p < .05$). Results remained unchanged after the final test.

Discussion

In general, the fitness scores of cystic fibrosis patients were not significantly different from the healthy norms. There was no correlation between the measures of clinical status (Modified Schwachman, X-ray, and pulmonary function scores) and the physical performance tests used in this study. Individual exercise scores related more closely to the motivation of the subject rather than the clinical status of the disease.

The exceptions were the groups at the extremes of the fitness scale. Subjects with a normal clinical status (defined as a perfect Schwachman score and pulmonary function scores above the 80th percentile) had exercise scores that were significantly higher than those subjects with abnormal clinical findings. Similarly, subjects whose exercise scores fell below the 20th percentile had clinical scores significantly below those subjects whose exercise scores were within the normal range.

Cystic fibrosis is a highly variable disease. Each patient exhibits a unique pattern of symptoms and disease severity, which makes interindividual comparisons and long-term projections of clinical status difficult. As a result, investigation of the cause and effect relationship between clinical status and physical activity would be difficult, if not impossible. Until the answer to this problem is obtained, patients should be encouraged to remain as active as possible. Physical activity is a necessary part of the normal growth and development of children. When unnecessary activity restrictions are applied, the child may suffer physically, psychologically, emotionally, and socially (Thoren, 1978). Because motivation appears to be the most important factor in determining a patient's level of physical activity, parents, the physician, and teachers should encourage participation in all types of physical activity. The results of this study indicate that children with cystic fibrosis should be expected to participate fully in peer activities.

The experimental group comprised 40 males and 29 females. Of these, 20 males and 7 females were noncompliant. This may reflect the fact that the boys saw themselves as being quite physically fit and that, therefore, a home program was unnecessary. Males may be more rebellious than females, making it more difficult for parents to maintain compliance. A third possible explanation relates to the different prognosis for males and females with cystic fibrosis. The prognosis for females declines much more rapidly during the teenage years, a fact that is widely recognized. Knowledge of this difference perhaps provided motivation to the girls and their families to make a positive effort in any program that might be beneficial.

After completion of the home exercise program, the fitness scores of the compliant group had increased and were not significantly different from the noncompliant group, indicating the benefits of the exercise program.

By contrast, the fitness scores of the noncompliant and control groups did not change over the study period.

Conclusion

The findings of this study suggest that physical performance tests are not a reliable indicator of the clinical status of most children with cystic fibrosis. With the exception of the very mild and very severe groups, the exercise performance reflects the amount of motivation rather than the status of the disease. Cystic fibrosis should not be an excuse for a sedentary life-style. Although it is unknown whether an active life-style can improve the prognosis of a patient, children who are not physically active may be targets for physical and psychological problems. Exercise testing does differentiate the children at the extremes of disease severity. However, the clinical status of these children is obvious to those involved in their care, and confirmation of clinical findings by an exercise test appears redundant.

The compliant subjects improved their exercise scores after a home exercise program. The noncompliant subjects, with a large proportion of males, had a higher initial level of fitness. In general, individuals with cystic fibrosis have fitness levels within the normal range. Those levels depend largely on motivation.

Acknowledgment

This research was supported by a Grant-in-Aid from the Physicians Services Incorporated.

References

Cerny, F. J., Pullano, T. P., & Cropp, G. J. (1982). Cardiorespiratory adaptations to exercise in cystic fibrosis. *American Review of Respiratory Disease, 126*(2), 217-220.

Clément, M., Jankowski, L. W., & Beaudry, P. H. (1979). Prone immersion physical exercise therapy in three children with cystic fibrosis. *Nursing Research, 28*(6), 325-329.

Coates, A. L., Boyce, P., Shaw, D. G., Godfrey, S., & Mearns, M. (1981). Relationship between chest radiograph, regional lung function studies, exercise tolerance, and clinical condition in cystic fibrosis. *Archives of Diseases of Childhood, 56*(2), 106-111.

Garrett, H. E. (1962). *Elementary statistics* (2nd ed.). New York: David McKay.

Godfrey, S., & Mearns, M. (1971, April). Pulmonary function and response to exercise in cystic fibrosis. *Archives of Diseases of Childhood*, **46**, 144-151.

Keens, T. F., Krastins, I., Wannamaker, E. M., Levison, H., Crozier, D. N., & Bryan, A. C. (1977). Ventilatory muscle endurance training in normal subjects and patients with cystic fibrosis. *American Review of Respiratory Disease*, **116**(5), 853-860.

Measurement and Evaluation Committee. (1980). *Canada Fitness Award*. Ottawa: Canadian Association for Health, Physical Education, and Recreation.

Orenstein, D. M., Franklin, B. A., Doershuk, C. F., Hellerstein, H. K., Germann, K. J., Horowitz, J. G., & Stern, R. C. (1981). Exercise conditioning and cardiopulmonary fitness in cystic fibrosis. *Chest*, **80**(4), 392-398.

Orenstein, D. M., Henke, K. G., & Cerny, F. J. (1983). Exercise and cystic fibrosis. *The Physician and Sportsmedicine*, **11**(1), 57-63.

Thoren, C. (1978). Exercise testing in children. *Paediatrician*, **7**, 100.

Weng, T. R., & Levinson, H. (1969). Standards of pulmonary function in children. *American Review of Respiratory Disease*, **99**(6), 879-894.

Zach, M., Oberwaldner, B., & Häusler, F. (1982). Cystic fibrosis: Physical exercise versus chest physiotherapy. *Archives of Diseases of Childhood*, **57**(8), 587-589.

Zach, M., Purrer, B., & Oberwaldner, B. (1981). Effect of swimming on forced expiration and sputum clearance in cystic fibrosis. *Lancet*, **2**, 1201-1203.

PART V

Diagnosis and Physical Activity Prescription in Psychiatric Disorders

The Interaction Between Mood and Movement Pattern

Leon Sloman
Mavis E. Berridge

Although physical educators are already making an impact on the promotion of mental health, it is our contention that it is possible for them to make a much greater contribution. Furthermore, the psychiatric profession itself needs to recognize the role that physical education can play.

Some psychiatrists advise their depressed patients to do a physical activity like swimming or jogging. This is because there is well-documented evidence that regular physical activity can have a positive impact on mood (Kavanagh, Shephard, & Tuck, 1975; Leer, 1980), self-image (Heinzelmann & Baggley, 1970; Shepherd, 1981), and well-being and intellectual alertness (Shephard, 1982). Because of these beneficial effects, more attention is being paid to physical fitness.

How much one moves is important. Yet we would argue that insufficient attention has been paid to *how* one moves. Certainly those who teach sports like tennis, swimming, and so forth train their pupils to move with style and efficiency. Many health practitioners focus on teaching poise or proper movement, like teachers of the Alexander technique (Maisel, 1974) or dance therapists. A whole range of techniques is based on often overlapping hypotheses about specific movement patterns that are more desirable.

One reason why psychiatrists often overlook the importance of studying the way their patients move is that there has been little research in the area, and this is partly due to the difficulty of measuring movement and personality variables. Another reason is the influence of Freud, who treated his patients reclining while he himself was seated. The focus on the patients' inner fantasies inevitably led to a defocusing on the patients' patterns of movements. Finally, the thrust of a good deal of current research has been in the area of biochemistry of psychiatric disorder. One natural outcome has been a lessening of interest in observing the whole individual, which includes studying the way he or she moves.

However, positive developments are happening. New techniques have been developed to measure and record movement patterns with greater precision and economy of effort. Furthermore, many mental health professionals have drawn attention to the importance of studying their patients' movement patterns, and some mental health schools devote much time to physical exercises (Gendlin, 1975).

Movement Patterns and Psychological State

It is often assumed that postural patterns develop as a result of the way one feels. However, the contrary, namely that postural patterns determine the way one feels, has been proposed by Lange and James (1922). Bull (1951) subsequently took an intermediate position by suggesting that the relationship between feelings and movement patterns is a reciprocal one. Schilder (1951), who was a psychoanalyst, took a similar stance, stating "there is so close an interrelation between the muscular sequence and the psychic attitude that not only does the psychic attitude connect up with the muscular state but also every sequence of tension and relaxation provokes a specific attitude" (p. 208).

Three different perspectives on the relation between psychological state and movement patterns can be distinguished. First, there is the psychoanalytic point of view, which focuses on patients' fantasies acted out by their movement patterns (Deutsch, 1949). Second, the view of "body psychotherapists" concentrates on changing movement patterns to effect changes in "feelings," which includes gestalt therapy, orthodox Reichian therapy (Reich, 1949), and bioenergetics (Lowen, 1967). These schools have in common the belief that natural life energy and its ease of flow through the musculature constitute the biological foundation of higher psychological and personal evolution. Practitioners in the third group do not consider feelings or interpersonal processes. They focus on concepts like body awareness or developing refined movement patterns or body alignments. This group includes physical education (Brown & Sommer, 1967), Jacobson's progressive muscular relaxation (Jacobson, 1970), the Alexander technique (Maisel, 1974), the Feldenkrais method (Feldenkrais, 1972), and dance therapy.

Implicit in all the above approaches is the notion of improving movement pattern, though the psychoanalyst would see this as a by-product rather than the primary goal. If improved movement patterns are one criterion of successful therapy, there arises the question of whether there is any consensus among these schools about what constitutes improvement. Physical educators have defined "good movement" as movement that displays naturalness, ease of motion, and rhythm (Brown & Sommer, 1967), but these criteria are not easy to quantify for the purpose of measuring improvement.

Several investigators have hypothesized that the performance criterion governing human motion is the minimization of energy expended (Hardt, 1978; Hatze, 1976). Pierrynowski, Winter, and Norman (1980) and, recently, Williams and Cavanagh (1983) have shown that efficient movement patterns demonstrate an abundance of mechanical energy transfer from one body segment to another and a transfer from potential to kinetic energy within each body segment. However, because of the marked variation in techniques for measuring the efficiency of human movement, the concept of desirable movement patterns remains a controversial issue.

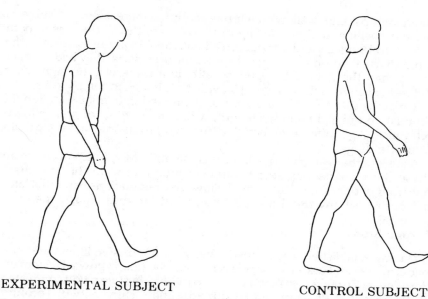

EXPERIMENTAL SUBJECT   CONTROL SUBJECT

Figure 1   Locomotor patterns of depressed and normal subjects.

Studies of Gait and Depression

Although many are convinced of the close interrelationship between movement patterns and the psyche, there is a need for scientific study, which is why we conducted our research. We decided to study gait patterns first because walking is a simple, everyday activity and second because there had been no previous study comparing mood state and movement patterns. There has been little in the literature to suggest that there is an optimal way of walking. However, many centuries ago Aristotle (Kietz, 1952) commented that the person who walks with short and slow steps starts his business sluggishly and does not pursue a goal.

First Study

The purpose of our first study (Sloman, Berridge, Homatidis, Hunter, & Duck, 1982) was to differentiate the gait patterns of patients with depressive illness from those of normal control subjects and to determine whether the gait patterns of these patients changed on recovery from acute depressive episodes. Although we had clear ideas about what we wanted to measure, we were initially far from clear as to how to proceed. We used cinematography and the lengthy process known as frame-by-frame digitization.

Our findings in this study suggested that depressive illness is accompanied by a measurable difference in locomotor patterns. Specifically, depressed patients walk with a lifting motion, whereas normal subjects use a propelling motion (see Figure 1). This was clearly the case in both our control subjects and our depressed patients. As a consequence of the more effective propulsion shown by the control subjects, they had a longer stride than the depressed patients, although there was no significant difference between the two groups in the time it took to complete a stride.

It may be that the measurement of depressed patients' stride length (in relation to height and leg length) will turn out to be of great clinical relevance. Age differences between the two groups did not contribute to our findings.

As to whether gait patterns of recovered patients begin to approximate those of normal people, despite our best efforts we were able to contact only four of our original subjects. Follow-up examinations 6 months later did not reveal any trend toward "normality" in these four patients.

Second Study

Having established a relationship between depressive illness and gait pattern, we embarked on our second study (Pierrynowski, Sloman, Berridge, & Tupling, 1984), which was part of a life-style study conducted at the School of Physical and Health Education, University of Toronto. It explored whether mood and gait pattern were also related and hypothesized that there would be a correlation between the subject's mood and the ground reaction forces.

There were 87 subjects. Each was required to indicate the mood he or she was in on the day of testing using a Visual Analog Scale (VAS) (Aitken, 1969). This measurement device ranges from 0 (most depressed) to 100 (most happy). This self-administered test is highly correlated with objective measures of mood (Aitken & Zealley, 1970).

All subjects were then required to walk at their own natural pace across a force plate designed to measure three-dimensional forces during a single step of the gait cycle. Data from five walks were collected for analysis. The findings were graphically recorded in a printout of ground reaction forces (newtons) in the anterior-posterior (Fx), upward (Fy), sideways (Fz) directions and the rotary force (torque) about the vertical axis (My).

As all subjects were required to attend for a reevaluation about 1 year later, it was decided on the basis of the earlier findings to add the Beck Mood Scale (Beck, Ward, Mendelson, Mock, & Erbaugh, 1961) to the post-test measures. This is a 21-question inventory completed by the subjects that provides a quantitative assessment of the intensity of depression, and it has been widely used for research purposes. Compared with the pretest group of 87, there were 53 subjects at the time of posttesting, and 47 of them completed the Beck Mood Scale in addition to the VAS. Subjects, as before, walked across the force plate five times.

In the pretest data (Pierrynowski et al., 1984), analysis of variance revealed that the low-mood group on the VAS exhibited a smaller push-off force both in the posterior and downward directions that was significant at greater than the .5 level.

In the analysis of posttest data, each of the ground force reaction parameters was correlated with the Beck score using the Pearson Product Moment correlation coefficient. The correlation between the forward force on the plate during weight acceptance (F1) and the Beck score was significant ($p < .07$). The significant findings were consistent with the hypothesis that a propelling gait was negatively correlated with mood. The correlation between the Beck score and the VAS posttest was significant ($p < .0005$).

The results obtained in this study were in accordance with our hypothesis that those who were less depressed had a more propelling gait. The conclusion is that those who are more unhappy or depressed have more of a lifting gait than others. Furthermore, the use of a more refined instrument to measure depressive mood, namely the Beck scale, appreciably increased the magnitude of the correlations between mood and gait patterns.

Gait Modification as a Psychological Intervention

The findings about the characteristic gait of depressed patients have led Sloman to use gait modification as a method of intervention in working with younger depressed patients. He has used it with six patients. Though these patients appear to have done well, the small number of patients and absence of controls have prevented, so far, the drawing of any definitive conclusions.

When the propelling gait is taught, the subject is asked to focus on stretching at the hip and, a number of strides later, to focus on stretching the knee of the same leg. The subject is then asked to repeat the procedure on the opposite side. The therapist comments on his or her observations in order to promote change. The subject is then asked to concentrate on achieving a greater push-off with the rear foot. Though the instructions are simple, even subjects who cooperate have difficulty in following them, particularly when they feel down. When the subject has mastered the new pattern, the therapist gives instructions to practice it for 1 hr a day. The therapist will, at a later stage, help the subject to relax the shoulders and arms while walking with a propelling gait.

If the relationship that we have found turns out to be a consistent finding, an examination of gait pattern might facilitate an early recognition of the onset of depressive illness and an early diagnosis of relapses in those with a history of affective disorder. This could be very useful in the primary prevention of teenage suicide, which is a leading cause of death in young people, and also in the reduction of treatment cost for all age groups through early diagnosis.

Conclusion

Over the last few years, there has been an explosion of interest in various forms of movement therapy. When one compares these therapies,

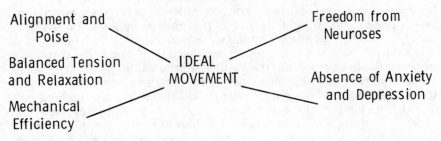

Figure 2 A model of positive health.

one finds that in spite of their differences they have in common a focus on increasing body awareness, promoting relaxation in movement, and helping movements become easier and more pleasurable. Furthermore, grace, poise, and efficiency might in the final analysis be very similar. For example, Winter (1978), in his discussion of gait, states that "efficient" energy exchanges are characterized by smooth-looking movements. He goes on to say that a ballet dancer and a high jumper might execute smooth movements for a different reason, one for artistic purposes, the other for "efficiency."

The absence of an agreed-upon definition of what constitutes good movement underlies the need for objective yardsticks by means of which movement can be judged. Such objective criteria could contribute to a delineation of a concept of positive health. Although this is speculative, positive health might be represented by the kind of model illustrated in Figure 2.

Clearly, more research is required before drawing any final conclusions about the issues of optimal or depressed gaits. Based on our research, we believe that further study of these issues will be highly rewarding.

Acknowledgments

We would like to express our thanks to the numerous collaborators without whom these studies would not have been possible—in particular, Michael Pierrynowski and Soula Homatidis of the University of Toronto and Tom Duck of York University.

References

Aitken, R. C. B. (1969). Measurement of feelings using visual analogue scales. *Proceedings of the Royal Society of Medicine*, **62**, 989.

Aitken, R. C. B., & Zealley, A. K. (1970). Measurement of moods. *British Journal of Hospital Medicine, 3,* 215.

Beck, A. T., Ward, C. H., Mendelson, M., Mock, J., & Erbaugh, J. (1961). An inventory for measuring depression. *Archives of General Psychiatry, 4,* 561-571.

Brown, M. A., & Sommer, B. K. (1967). *Movement education: Its evolution and a modern approach.* Reading, MA: Addison-Wesley.

Bull, N. (1951). *The attitude theory of emotion.* New York: Johnson Reprint.

Deutsch, F. L. (1949). Analysis of postural behaviour. *Psychoanalytic Quarterly, 16,* 195.

Feldenkrais, M. (1972). *Awareness through movement.* New York: Harper and Row.

Gendlin, E. T. (1975). The body psychotherapies. In D. Freedman & J. E. Dyrud (Eds.), *American handbook of psychiatry* (2nd ed.). New York: Basic Books.

Hardt, D. E. (1978). Determining muscle forces in the leg during normal human walking—An application and evaluation of optimization methods. *Journal of Biomechanical Engineering, 100,* 72-78.

Hatze, H. (1976). The complete optimization of human motion. *Mathematical Biosciences, 28,* 99-135.

Heinzelmann, F., & Baggley, R. (1970). Response to physical activity programs and their effects on health behavior. *Public Health Report, 85,* 905-911.

Jacobson, E. (1970). *Modern treatment of tense patients.* Springfield, IL: C. C. Thomas.

Kavanagh, J., Shephard, R. J., & Tuck, J. A. (1975). Depression after myocardial infarction. *Canadian Medical Association Journal, 113,* 23-27.

Kietz, G. (1952). *Der Ausdrucksgehalt des menschlichen Ganges* [The expressional form of human gait]. Leipzig: J. A. Barth.

Lange, C. G., & James, W. (1922). *The emotions.* Baltimore, MD: Williams and Wilkins.

Leer, F. (1980). Running as an adjunct to psychotherapy. *Social Work, 37,* 20-25.

Lowen, A. (1967). *The betrayal of the body.* New York: Collier-Macmillan.

Maisel, E. (Ed.). (1974). *F. Matthias Alexander. The resurrection of the body.* New York: Delta Books.

Pierrynowski, M. R., Sloman, L., Berridge, M. E., & Tupling, S. (1984, August). *The relationship of mood and ground reaction forces in a random sample of elderly adults.* Paper presented at the Human Locomotion III Conference, Winnipeg.

Pierrynowski, M. R., Winter, D. A., & Norman, R. W. (1980). Transfers of mechanical energy within the total body and mechanical efficiency during treadmill walking. *Ergonomics, 23,* 147-156.

Reich, W. (1949). *Character analysis.* New York: Farrar, Straus & Giroux, The Noonday Press.

Schilder, P. (1951). *The image and appearance of the human body.* New York: John Wiley.

Shephard, R. J. (1981). *Physical activity and growth.* Chicago: Year Book.

Shephard, R. J. (1982, May). *Physical activity and the healthy mind.* Paper presented at the annual meeting of the American Psychiatric Association, Toronto.

Sloman, L., Berridge, M. E., Homatidis, S., Hunter, D., & Duck, T. (1982). Gait patterns of depressed patients and normal subjects. *American Journal of Psychiatry, 139,* 94-97.

Williams, K. R., & Cavanagh, P. R. (1983). A model for the calculation of mechanical power during distance running. *Journal of Biomechanics, 16,* 115-128.

Winter, D. A. (1978). Energy assessments in pathological gait. *Physiotherapy Canada, 30,* 185.

The Role of Physical Activity in the Management of Substance Abuse

R. Gordon Bell
Wendy Robinson
Blanche Horsham
Winona Mulligan

The programs at Bellwood Health Services and the clinical operations that preceded them have been based on a stress syndrome orientation to the analysis and management of substance abuse and dependence. Central to all patterns of substance abuse are varying degrees of dependence on harmful quantities of the substances involved. When physiological, psychological, and social adaptation to the repeated intake of stressful quantities combine to expand dependence beyond the range of control, the abnormal state becomes the progressively destructive behavioral cancer known as addiction. The potential role of physical fitness in recovery from all forms of uncontrolled dependence—drugs, alcohol, food, and tobacco—is an important factor in the design and operation of effective recovery programs.

Practically all aspects of current treatment have been developed within the past 50 years. In the 1930s, the two most notable pioneering efforts were the founding of the Fellowship of Alcoholics Anonymous (AA) and the initiation of new research into alcohol problems by the Yale School of Alcohol Studies. AA was the first to demonstrate that the universal pessimism concerning recovery from an uncontrolled dependence on alcohol had no basis in reality. By the 1940s a few new clinics were established, including our own, in an attempt to design a clinical dimension to programs of recovery from dependence on alcohol. In our case, the definition of health by the World Health Organization as a state of "complete physical, mental and social well-being" provided the initial guideline for the new rewarding life-style to replace the one progressively dominated by dependence on alcohol or drugs. Eventually, as an extension of the AA approach to sobriety, we added a spiritual dimension to our interpretation of the World Health Organization definition. Accordingly, improved physical health has been an integral component of our health and recovery programs for almost 40 years. Improvement in physical fitness, balanced nutrition, and ability to relax have provided the cornerstones for the physical health component of our total health plan.

Most medical attention to addictive disorders is limited to recurrent treatment of the related medical, surgical, and psychiatric problems. Although such patients account for at least 20% of the admissions to general hospitals in Canada, rarely is the treatment of related disabilities followed by comparable attention to the dependence itself. Accordingly, recurrent admissions for the care of secondary clinical problems are the norm. The unit of concern for the effective management of secondary medical or surgical problems is the damaged organ or organ system.

Addictive disorders are an extension of the stresses, folkways, and pressures of a particular culture. They represent one of the universal hazards of abundance. Because dependence on one or more chemical comforts originates in each case from a unique complex of personal and social factors, the unit of concern in the interruption, reduction, and inactivation of dependence can be no less than the entire person interacting with a constantly changing physical, biological, and social environment. Treating the whole person becomes difficult for members of the medical profession whose specialized training is focused on repair of damage to smaller and smaller areas of the body. However, comparable difficulties are not experienced by other branches of the clinical professions, nonprofessional personnel, recovering patients, and community volunteers.

Bellwood Health Services' Treatment Program

To find an acceptable compromise to these widely divergent orientations to the clinical management of chemical abuse and dependence, a comprehensive treatment plan was designed utilizing both. The initial examination and treatment of intoxication and related pathology are carried out or supervised by physicians. This is a routine first step to more comprehensive assessment by other professional personnel to introduce a long-term program of recovery from dependence, continuing repair of related damage, and the design of a new life-style based on total health guidelines. Throughout a 5-year period of attention and supervision by a variety of professional and nonprofessional personnel, the physicians remain an available back-up resource whenever needed. The ultimate objective for the addict is to become accustomed to feeling good from a new stable level of general well-being as a welcome alternative to feeling good from the effects of alcohol or drugs.

Our basic nature and needs have not changed significantly in the thousands of years since the norm for our ancestors was a physically active life of communal hunting, gathering, and territorial aggression. The advent of the motorcar in this century has produced the most significant reduction in essential physical activity of all time. It is most interesting that the multicultural vogue of jogging and marathon running represents a return to the identical physical state essential for health and survival by our distant hunting ancestors. Jogging could be considered a form of compensatory physical health activity. Comparable compensatory mental health programs are required to maintain an adequate degree of stimulation and sense of identity, security, and purpose. With the rapid erosion of the traditional social frameworks for interdependent effort—family, occupation, church, and community—new compensatory social frameworks are being provided by such self-help groups as Alcoholics Anonymous and other relationships based on common problems and interests.

It is with these concepts in mind that a review of current literature concerned with the role of physical activity in the management of substance abuse was undertaken. Within the past decade there have been a few published reports of the effects of incorporating a physical fitness component into addiction treatment services.

- David E. Smith (1984) emphasized the benefits of an exercise program in recovery from cocaine dependence.
- Tom Brown and Peter Seraganian said, ''Alcoholics who participated in a fitness program had improved rates of abstinence'' (Sinyor, Brown, Rostant, & Seraganian, 1982, p. 380-385).
- Wojtek J. Chodzko-Zajko said, ''There is increasingly strong support for the hypothesis that exercise is a 'natural medicine' that may mediate favorable emotional changes in both normal and clinical populations'' (Chodzko-Zajko & Ismail, 1984, p. 163-169).
- Vivian Gary and Dixon Guthrie concluded, ''Hospitalized alcoholics who jogged a mile a day for 20 days improved the cardiovascular fitness and their self-esteem and slept better'' (1972, p. 1073-1078).
- Alan Frankel and John Murphy found that ''alcoholics participating in a 12-week physical fitness program had better scores on measures of physical fitness after the program than before, and improved M.M.P.I. [Minnesota Multiphasic Personality Inventory] scores'' (1974, p. 1272-1278).

The experience at Bellwood Health Services is that most addicts have reduced, discontinued, or never engaged in a level of physical activity compatible with optimal health. Our physical health program for clients initially involves 1/2 hr of supervised exercise daily from Monday to Friday for the first 3 to 6 weeks of a long-term program. Thereafter, they are encouraged to continue appropriate exercises on their own as recommended by our physiotherapist. The exercises are designed to promote deep breathing, muscle toning, stretching, improved circulation, good posture, and awareness of back protection. Training in the techniques of progressive relaxation is routine. Additional confirmation of the benefits of a physical activity component to treatment of addiction has been obtained by direct contact with associates at the Addiction Research Foundation and the Donwood Institute in Toronto.

Discussion

The related areas of concern in addictive disorders are assessed by a comprehensive diagnostic tool based on a stress syndrome orientation.

It is referred to as a *nine-part chart*. For example, with alcohol the first three areas of concern are the physical, psychological, and social predisposing factors that combine to initiate and sustain the repeated intake of alcohol in intoxicating or stressful quantities. The middle three areas of concern are the physical, psychological, and social changes from the process of adaptation to the repeated intake of stressor quantities: physical adaptation with the progression from increasing tolerance to withdrawal reactions, psychological adaptation by the progression from habituation to alibi systems, and social adaptation by the progression from social accommodation to social manipulation. The final three areas are concerned with phenomena following the phase of exhaustion in the general adaptation syndrome. Breakdown in tolerance is accompanied by physical, psychological, and social damage. The cumulative effects of intoxication and malnutrition plus the pathological changes from tissue irritation at the sites of entry by ingestion, inhalation, or injection can finally reveal the nature and complexity of a long-standing obscure problem.

The physical factors in recovery are based on permanent interruption of intoxication, compensatory programs in nutrition, physical fitness, rest and relaxation, and specific medical attention as indicated. The physical health and recovery program is graded according to individual needs and serves as one vehicle to focus attention away from former drinking time, to counteract boredom, and to avoid new dependencies. On the positive side, it quickly contributes to an improved sense of well-being and self-image. However, it is important with addicted patients to be sure that the physical health program is kept in balance—to avoid becoming as overinvolved with exercise as they had been with chemicals.

The concurrent recoveries from dependence and the related problems are facilitated by keeping a personal diary. It should "police" the tendency to resume the "stinking thinking" of the alibi system as a precursor to reactivation of the dependence. In it patients should note any changes in emotional control, mood swings, concentration, and tendency to project responsibility for personal problems to others. The diary can greatly facilitate awareness of when to turn for help in the recovery process as well as record adherence to the total health program and exploration of alternative coping techniques. Progress in the repair of damaged relationships and development of new ones should be noted.

Eventually, a new dimension in spiritual health can emerge with new or renewed value systems, sense of social responsibility, and genuine concern for the well-being of others.

Summary

The ultimate goal of the health and recovery program is to acquire a new sense of identity, fulfillment, and purpose as an extension of a balanced state of total well-being. The physical health component is essential because initially it may be the most acceptable area for introduction to the comprehensive health plan. Thus it can open the door to progressive involvement in the other areas. Finally, because improvement in physical health can be experienced quickly, with many addicts this rapid sense of successful response to treatment can facilitate motivation for involvement in the rest of the program.

References

Chodzko-Zajko, W. J., & Ismail, A. H. (1984, January). Relationships in middle-aged males before and after an 8-month fitness program. *Journal of Clinical Psychology, 4*(1), 163-169.

Frankel, A., & Murphy, J. (1974). Physical fitness and personality in alcoholism. *Quarterly Journal of Studies on Alcohol, 35,* 1272-1278.

Gary, V., & Guthrie, D. (1972). The effect of jogging on physical fitness and self-concept in hospitalized alcoholics. *Quarterly Journal of Studies on Alcohol, 33,* 1073-1078.

Sinyor, D., Brown, T., Rostant, L., & Seraganian, P. (1982). The role of a physical fitness program in the treatment of alcoholism. *Journal of Studies on Alcohol, 43*(3), 380-385.

Smith, D. E. (1984). Diagnostic treatment and aftercare approaches to cocaine abuse. *Journal of Substance Abuse Treatment, 1,* 5-9.

The Physical Activity of Mentally Disturbed Finnish Adults

Esko Antero Mälkiä
Matti Joukamaa
Jouni Maatela
Arpo Aromaa
Markku Heliövaara

In an earlier study, the Mini-Finland Health Survey, the relationship between physical activity and mental disturbances was examined. Other findings on this relationship are hard to locate in the literature, but in many studies the decreased physical fitness of people with mental problems has been observed. This relationship has been seen in the aerobic condition and also in muscular performance (Arvidsson, Dencker, & Grimby, 1970; Mälkiä, 1983; Morgan, 1974). The purpose of this study is to determine whether there is any relationship sensitive to different ways of measuring mental disturbances and problems and physical activity at work, in spare time, and on the way to work.

Methods

The population of 8,000 people in the sample studied had been selected to represent the Finnish population aged 30 years and over. Physical activity was measured by the interview method. Results of the sample and of physical activity interview have been reported in another paper (Mälkiä, 1985).

In the Mini-Finland study, psychiatric methods were extensively used in various phases of the study. For the purposes of the present investigation, the following were used: In the initial interview the subjects were asked if they subjectively felt fatigue; in the screening phase they were also asked if they had ever visited a doctor on account of a mental disturbance and were given the 36-item version of the General Health Questionnaire designed by Goldberg (Goldberg, 1972). The comprehensive individual summary of mental health was made using an ADP-based classification program that used all the data concerning mental health that had been gathered in the project. Through this method an assessment of "psychiatric case" and "the need for psychiatric treatment" was made.

Results

The results for men and women were handled separately because in most physical activities there are statistical differences between the sexes (Mälkiä, 1985). The Mini-Finland study observed that people who have visited a doctor owing to mental disturbances worked in physically lighter jobs and were more passive in their spare time than people with no history of mental problems (Mälkiä, 1985). Figures 1 and 2 show the regression between the MET sum of physical activity intensities at work, in spare time, and on the way to work, and the score in the General Health Questionnaire (GHQ). From the figures it can be seen that the larger the score in the GHQ, the smaller is the MET value of the physical activity sum. From Figures 3 and 4 the same kind of regression can be seen between the GHQ and the highest intensity of activity in spare time for both sexes. Figures 5 and 6 show that the MET value of the sum of physical intensities and of the highest intensity of activity in spare time decreases with an increase in the need for psychiatric treatment and with an increase in subjectively felt fatigue. With more severe psychiatric problems and MET values, the same kind of inverse relationship was found for both sexes. The physical intensities of activity on the way to work do not differ between groups with and without mental disturbance. This type of physical activity was the only activity measured in this study where there was no relationship between physical passivity and mental disturbances.

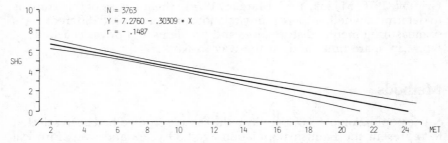

Figure 1   Regression between sum of intensities at work, in spare time, and on way to work, and General Health Questionnaire score for women.

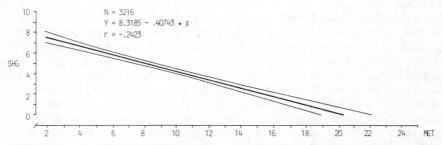

Figure 2   Regression between sum of intensities at work, in spare time, and on way to work, and General Health Questionnaire score for men.

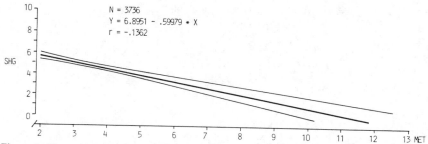

Figure 3   Regression between highest intensity of activity in spare time and General Health Questionnaire score for women.

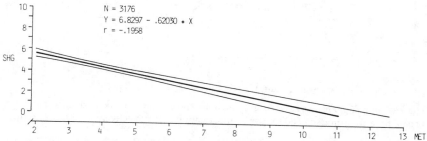

Figure 4   Regression between highest intensity of activity in spare time and General Health Questionnaire score for men.

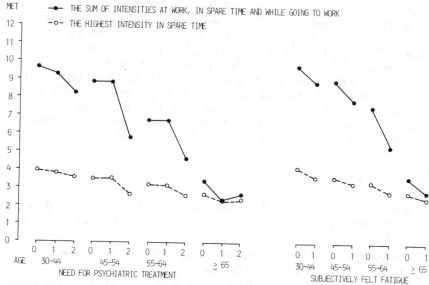

Figure 5   Sum of intensities at work, in spare time, and on way to work, and highest intensity in spare time according to need for psychiatric treatment or subjectively felt fatigue for women.

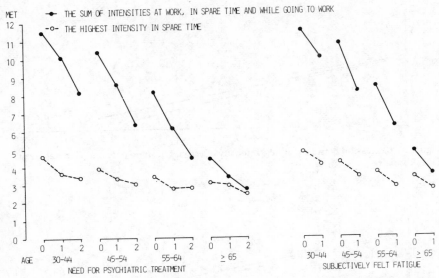

Figure 6 Sum of intensities at work, in spare time, and on way to work, and highest intensity in spare time according to need for psychiatric treatment or subjectively felt fatigue for men.

Discussion

The results show that there is a clear, linear inverse relationship between mental disturbance measured in different ways and the intensity of physical activity at work and in spare time. The same relation holds for men and women and in all age cohorts. Even people with mild mental problems were found to be more passive than people with no mental problems. This cannot be due solely to the use of sedatives, tranquilizers, or other medicines. It is very difficult, however, to determine from this study whether the physically passive way of life comes about before or after the onset of mental disturbances or whether the passivity is connected with other changes attributable to the mental disturbance.

References

Arvidsson, S., Dencker, S. J., & Grimby, G. (1970). Fysisk träning på mentalsjukhus [Physical education in mental hospitals]. *Läkartidningen,* **67**, 58-64.

Goldberg, D. P. (1972). *The detection of psychiatric illness by questionnaire* (Maudsley Monograph No. 21). London: Oxford University Press.

Mälkiä, E. (1983). *Muscular performance as a determinant of physical ability in Finnish adult population* (English summary). (Publications of the Social Insurance Institution AL:23). Turku, Finland: Social Insurance Institution.

Mälkiä, E. (1985, October). *The physical activity of healthy and sick adults in Finland at work, at leisure, and on the way to work*. Paper presented at the Fifth International Symposium on Adapted Physical Activity, Toronto.

Morgan, W. P. (1974). Exercise and mental disorders. In A. J. Ryan & F. L. Allman (Eds.), *Sports medicine*. New York: Academic Press.

Characteristics and Assessment of Disabled Athletes

Psychological Mood Profiles
of Elite Cerebral Palsied Athletes

Maria Y. Canabal
Claudine Sherrill
Wanda Jean Rainbolt

Local, national, and international organizations promoting sports competition of cerebral palsied (CP) athletes have increased sports participation and training opportunities in the last decade (Adams, 1984). Despite a delayed socialization into sports occurring during the early adolescent years (Sherrill, Rainbolt, Montelione, & Pope, 1985), athletic performance of cerebral palsied athletes has continuously and steadfastly improved. Research interest in the biomechanical, physiological, and sociological description of elite cerebral palsied athletes was evident in presentations made at the 1984 Olympic Scientific Congress in Oregon and at the 1985 American Alliance for Health, Physical Education, Recreation, and Dance (AAHPERD) National Convention in Atlanta. Furthermore, interest in training and coaching aspects is also increasing (Bieber, 1985; Jones, 1984).

At the 1984 International Games for the Disabled, cerebral palsied athletes from 25 countries competed in numerous sports. In rank order, Great Britain, United States, Canada, Holland, and France took home the most gold medals. Athletes participated in the CP-ISRA meet held in Belgium in July 1986. Many cerebral palsied athletes are looking toward 1988, the date of the next International Games for the Disabled, which is scheduled for Korea. With competitive opportunities for CP athletes beginning to parallel those of able-bodied athletes, it is important to examine variables that distinguish between international and noninternational qualifiers.

The ideal approach to investigation of predictors of sport elitism is to collect both personality and physiological data in an attempt to explain as much behavioral variance as possible (Fisher, 1984; Silva, Shultz, Haslam, & Murray, 1981). Whereas research on able-bodied athletes has generated hundreds of studies that can be used in evolving psychophysiological models to guide further investigation, virtually no personality research has been conducted on cerebral palsied athletes and almost none on individuals with cerebral palsy. The initiation of a body of knowledge in relation to the psychological characteristics of CP athletes, therefore, seems a first step in extending sport psychology to encompass disabled athletes.

The mental health model espoused by Morgan (1980b) as predictive of success in athletics appears applicable to cerebral palsy sport. In this model, success and positive mental health are viewed as directly proportional. High scores on vigor and low scores on tension, depression, anger, fatigue, and confusion are believed to characterize good mental health and thus to contribute to athletic success. The Profile of Mood States (POMS) is one psychological test that measures these dimensions and is believed to be highly predictive of athletic success (Morgan, 1980a).

Numerous researchers have used POMS in the study of able-bodied athletes. Differences between elite and nonelite able-bodied athletes in terms of psychological variables have been reported by Nagle, Morgan, Hellickson, Serfass, and Alexander (1975), by Silva et al. (1981), and by Morgan and Pollock (1977).

Two studies of disabled athletes have been based on POMS data (Henschen, Horvat, & French, 1984; Mastro, 1985). This research, done with National Wheelchair Athletic Association (NWAA) athletes and blind athletes, respectively, indicated that disabled athletes are similar in mood dimensions to able-bodied athletes.

Purpose of Study

The purpose of this study is to compare the psychological mood profiles of international and noninternational cerebral palsied athletes. Specific hypotheses examined are these: There is no significant difference between genders across the six POMS mood dimensions; there is no significant difference between international and noninternational CP athlete groups across the six POMS mood dimensions; and there are no significant correlations between POMS mood dimensions and the variables of number of years of national competition, gender, and sports classification.

Methods

Subjects

Subjects included in this study were 39 cerebral palsied athletes who represented the United States in the 1984 International Games for the Disabled in New York and 34 CP athletes who competed in the 1983 National Cerebral Palsied/Les Autres Games in Fort Worth, Texas, but who were not selected to represent the United States in international competition. All 73 athletes studied were elite in that they had met qualifying standards for national competition.

Descriptive information for international and noninternational CP athletes is presented in Table 1. Subjects ranged from 16 to 45 years of age. The mean ages of the international and noninternational samples, respectively, were 26.07 and 27.28 years. Slight differences between the two groups existed, however, in distribution of gender, sports class, and schooling. Failure to control for these differences is a weakness in this study. As might be expected, international athletes had considerably more competitive experience than noninternational athletes.

Table 1 Description of Subjects

Variables	International %	Noninternational %
Gender		
Male	51.3	55.9
Female	48.7	44.1
Number of meets		
1-2	41	85.3
3-5	59	14.7
Sports class		
1-4	46.2	41.2
5-8	53.8	58.8
Schooling		
No diploma	12.8	23.5
High school	41	41.2
College	43.6	35.3

Instrument and Data Collection

Data were collected through administration of the Profile of Mood States developed by McNair, Lorr, and Droppleman (1971). The POMS is a self-report instrument of short duration (5-7 min) designed to assess subjective mood data through the rating of 65 adjectives that cluster into six mood dimensions: tension, depression, anger, vigor, fatigue, and confusion. Each mood dimension is rated on a 5-point scale.

Morgan (1980a) states that the POMS has been highly predictive of athletic success in his studies. Internal consistency reliabilities of the six POMS mood dimensions from 350 male and 650 female outpatients, who were administered the POMS when admitted to the Boston University Psychiatric Clinic from 1966 to 1969, ranged from .84 to .95. Factorial validity was also reported as satisfactory from six factor analytic replications during development of the POMS (McNair et al., 1971).

Results

The hypothesis of no significant difference between genders across the six POMS mood dimensions was examined separately for the 39 international athletes and the 34 noninternational athletes. The BMDP3D multivariate computer program (Dixon, 1983) was used in this analysis. No

Table 2 Means, Standard Deviations, Multivariate *t* Comparisons for International and Noninternational CP Samples

Variable	M	SD	t	p
Tension			.87	.39
Int	10.10	7.49		
Nonint	11.47	5.66		
Depression			1.78	.08
Int	8.90	10.00		
Nonint	13.09	10.07		
Anger			1.06	.29
Int	8.31	8.76		
Nonint	10.32	7.33		
Vigor			2.27^a	.03*
Int	22.82	6.61		
Nonint	18.94	7.81		
Fatigue			1.35	.18
Int	7.00	5.83		
Nonint	8.79	5.54		
Confusion			.20^a	.84
Int	6.79	5.45		
Nonint	7.03	4.40		

^{a}The pooled *t* formula, with 71 *df*, was used for all comparisons except vigor and confusion because Levene's test of homogeneity of variance indicated homogeneous variances. Separate *t* formulas, with *df* of 65.1 and 70.6, respectively, were used for vigor and confusion.
*$p < .05$.

significant differences between genders were found in the overall POMS scores: international group, $F(6, 32) = .52$, $p = .79$; noninternational group, $F(6, 27) = 1.47$, $p = .23$. Because no significant gender differences were found, male and female data were combined for further statistical analysis.

The hypothesis of no significant difference between international and noninternational CP athletes across the six POMS mood dimensions was examined using the same BMDP3D multivariate computer program (Dixon, 1983). The genders were combined in this analysis. No significant differences between international and noninternational athletes were found on the overall POMS scores, $F(6, 66) = 1.49$, $p = .19$.

Table 3   Pearson Product Moment Correlation Coefficients Between POMS Mood Dimensions and Selected Variables for International and Noninternational Athletes Combined

POMS mood dimensions	Years of national competition	Gender	Sports class
Tension	−.17	.02	−.07
Depression	−.07	.12	−.16
Anger	−.12	.10	−.27*
Vigor[a]			
Fatigue	.01	.05	.05
Confusion	−.25*	.06	−.08

Note. $n = 73$.

[a]Correlation coefficients for vigor were computed separately for international athletes (.05, .21, and .02) and noninternational athletes (.04, −.29, and −.33) because the two groups were significantly different on this dimension.

*$p < .05$.

Although overall multivariate test results were not significant, a significant univariate difference was revealed between international and noninternational CP athletes in their vigor scores, $t (65.1) = 2.27$, $p = .03$. International CP athletes ($M = 22.8$) had significantly higher vigor scores than noninternational CP athletes ($M = 18.9$). Table 2 presents findings in regard to mean performance of the two groups, variability, and differences.

To examine the hypothesis of no significant correlations between POMS mood dimensions and selected variables, data from international and noninternational athletes were combined except for vigor. Because of the significant difference between groups on vigor, separate correlations were computed for international and noninternational athletes. Table 3 presents the results of the correlation computations. For the combined group, significant correlations were found for confusion and years of national competition (−.25) and anger and sports class (−.27). For the noninternational athletes, the correlations of vigor with gender (−.29) and with sports class (−.33) were significant.

Discussion

Male and female CP athletes did not significantly differ in any of the POMS mood scores. This finding is in agreement with the failure to find significant difference between 340 male and 516 female undergraduate students reported by McNair et al. (1971). As with the college normative sample, male and female CP athletes in the international and noninternational groups had similar POMS profiles.

Vigor scores of international CP athletes were significantly higher than scores of noninternational athletes. This finding is consistent with the related literature for elite able-bodied and disabled athletes. Wrestlers who qualified for international meets had significantly higher scores than those who did not qualify in studies reported by Nagle et al. (1975) and Silva et al. (1981). Mastro (1985) also reported significantly higher vigor scores of elite visually impaired athletes as compared with elite sighted Greco-Roman wrestlers. High vigor scores thus seem essential toward a competitive edge for both elite disabled and able-bodied international competitors.

Another finding in this study is the low but significant correlation ($-.27$) between anger and sports classification. Nonambulatory status was associated with anger. Anger was also high in the mood profiles of wheelchair athletes reported by Henschen et al. (1984). Nonambulatory athletes thus may be readily aroused to and maintain anger as a reaction to everyday frustrations.

CP athletes also evidenced a low but significant correlation ($-.25$) between confusion and years of national competition. High confusion scores were evident in athletes with few years of competition. It might be speculated that increasing participation in equitable sports competition, where ability and not disability is emphasized, may provide a sense of direction and purpose. Anderson (1984) has stated that enrichment and sense of determination to do the best are derived from participation in CP sports.

Among noninternational athletes only, there was a significant but low relationship between being male and having high vigor ($-.29$) and toward being nonambulatory and having high vigor ($-.33$). These findings are unexpected. Gender and mood dimension correlations in the college normative sample (McNair et al., 1971) were low and nonsignificant ($r = .00$, $p < .001$). Nonambulatory athletes have more barriers of abnormal reflex retention, motor incoordination, and communication problems to be overcome than ambulatory peers; perhaps they tend to have more vigor because it is necessary for survival.

Conclusion

Within the limitations of this study, it may be concluded that international and noninternational CP athletes are similar on POMS mood dimensions with one exception, vigor. International athletes score significantly higher on vigor.

References

Adams, C. (1984). The national association of sports for cerebral palsy. *Journal of Physical Education, Recreation, and Dance*, **55**(2), 36-37.

Anderson, N. E. (1984). Golden opportunities. *Palaestra,* **1**(1), 40-41, 48.

Bieber, R. (1985, April-June). Winning is a partnership. *UCPA News,* pp. 31-33.

Dixon, W. J. (Ed.). (1983). *BMDP statistical software.* Berkeley: University of California Press.

Fisher, A. C. (1984). New directions in sport personality research. In J. Silva & R. Weinberg (Eds.), *Psychological foundations of sport* (pp. 70-80). Champaign, IL: Human Kinetics.

Henschen, K., Horvat, M., & French, R. (1984). A visual comparison of psychological profiles between able-bodied and wheelchair athletes. *Adapted Physical Activity Quarterly,* **1**(2), 118-124.

Jones, J. A. (1984). *Training guide to cerebral palsy sports* (2nd ed.). New York: United Cerebral Palsy Assocations.

Mastro, J. V. (1985). *Psychological characteristics of elite male visually impaired and sighted athletes.* Unpublished doctoral dissertation, Texas Woman's University, Denton.

McNair, D., Lorr, M., & Droppleman, L. (1971). *Manual for profile of mood states.* San Diego, CA: Educational and Industrial Testing Service.

Morgan, W. P. (1980a). Test of champions. *Psychology Today,* **14**(2), 92-108.

Morgan, W. P. (1980b). The trait psychology controversy. *Research Quarterly for Exercise and Sport,* **51**(1), 50-76.

Morgan, W. P., & Pollock, M. L. (1977). Psychologic characterization of elite distance runners. *Annals of the New York Academy of Sciences,* **301**, 382-403.

Nagle, F. J., Morgan, W. P., Hellickson, R. O., Serfass, R. C., & Alexander, J. F. (1975). Spotting success traits in Olympic contenders. *The Physician and Sports Medicine,* **13**(3), 31-34.

Sherrill, C., Rainbolt, W., Montelione, T., & Pope, C. (1985). Sports socialization of blind and of cerebral palsied elite athletes. In C. Sherrill (Ed.), *Sport and disabled athletes* (pp. 189-195). Champaign, IL: Human Kinetics.

Silva, J. M., Shultz, B. B., Haslam, R. W., & Murray, D. (1981). A psychophysiological assessment of elite wrestlers. *Research Quarterly for Exercise and Sport,* **52**(3), 348-358.

Characteristics of Adult Blind Athletes, Competition Experience, and Training Practices

Wanda Jean Rainbolt
Claudine Sherrill

Since the formation of the United States Association for Blind Athletes (USABA) in 1976, opportunities for blind persons to compete in organized sport have grown tremendously. USABA offers national competition for both men and women in six sports: goal ball, track, field, pentathlon, swimming, and power lifting; for men only in wrestling; and for women only in gymnastics. Additionally, national winter sports competition is available in alpine skiing, slalom, and cross-country skiing. Any person of any age whose corrected vision is less than 20/200 may compete in the USABA nationals, which are held once each year. The blind competitors do not have to meet preestablished qualifying standards as sighted athletes do in order to achieve eligibility for national level competition. One reason for this is the small number of blind persons who, thus far, have entered USABA competition. Less than 1% of the eligible blind population appears to be competing in sports conducted by USABA. Although percentages are not available, it is believed that participation of blind athletes in sports with sighted athletes is low.

Purpose of Study

The purpose of this study was to investigate the characteristics of adult blind athletes, their participation in national sports competition, and their training practices. Answers to the following questions were sought:

1. What are the personal attributes of adult blind athletes?
2. In how many national USABA meets have adult blind athletes participated?
3. At what age do adult blind athletes first compete in national USABA meets?
4. What influences the adult blind athlete to participate in a national USABA meet?
5. What one USABA sport event does the adult blind athlete perceive as his or her best and most likely to win?

6. What age was the adult blind athlete when he or she first learned of and first competed in his or her best sport event at the local, state or regional, and national meets?
7. To what extent has the adult blind athlete competed in this one best sport with nondisabled persons?
8. What is the training program of an adult blind athlete preparing for a national meet?
9. Was a coach present during the workout, and what was the coach's regular employment?
10. How often do national-level adult blind athletes engage in competition against others during the year and prior to a national meet?

Subjects

The population selected for study consisted of adult athletes ($N = 207$) who competed in the seventh national USABA games. The intent was to interview as many athletes as possible during the 5-day meet. A purposive sampling design (Kerlinger, 1973, p. 129) was used with every effort made to obtain a sample representative of the population in sex, age, and visual classification. The resulting sample ($n = 100$) included 38% of the total population. Table 1 describes the sample in terms of sex, age, visual classification, ethnic group, and onset of blindness and the population with respect to the first three variables, thus showing that the sample met the criterion of representativeness. Population data on the last two variables were not available.

Of these variables, visual classification is considered most important in those sports in which degree of sight might prove advantageous (i.e., all USABA sports except wrestling, power lifting, and goal ball). The visual classifications adopted by USABA in 1982 and used at the time of this study were as follows:

Class B1. No light perception at all in either eye up to light perception, but inability to recognize objects or contours in any directions and at any distance

Class B2. Ability to recognize objects or contours up to a visual acuity of 2/60 and/or a limitation of field of vision of 5 degrees

Class B3. 2/60 to 6/60 (20/200) vision and/or field of vision between 5 and 60 degrees

In USABA sports, athletes compete only against persons with the same visual classification except in goal ball, wrestling, and power lifting. In goal ball, visual ability is equalized by all players wearing blindfolds rather than uniformity within visual classifications (Kearny & Copeland, 1979).

Table 1   Percentage of Blind Athletes Comprising the Population and Sample on Which Study is Based

Variables	% of population (N = 207)	% of sample (n = 100)
Sex		
Male	65.7	62
Female	34.3	38
Age		
17-19 years	36.5	32
20+ years	63.5	68
Visual classification		
B1 (totally blind)	31.1	32
B2 (hand movement to 20/400)	22.8	30
B3 (legally blind)	46.1	38
Ethnic group		
White	—[a]	70
Nonwhite	—	30
Onset of blindness		
Congenital	—	61
Adventitious	—	39

[a]Information for population not available.

Methodology

The Disabled Athlete Sport Inventory (Sherrill, 1983) was the data collection instrument. This inventory includes 82 items categorized under six headings: personal attributes, sport socializing agents, sport socializing settings, sport participation benefits and barriers, physical education and sport training (past and present), and sport competition (past and present). The Disabled Athlete Sport Inventory-Form B (DASI-B) used in this study was a revision of an earlier inventory pilot tested with 133 athletes who competed in the Sixth Annual National Championships of USABA (Sherrill, Pope, & Arnhold, 1986) and reviewed for content validity by the USABA Board of Directors.

Data were collected by having DASI-B read to subjects (i.e., an interview technique) or by permitting subjects with adequate vision for regular print materials (many Class B3 athletes) to complete the inventory in-dependently. The interviewers were three doctoral level graduate students with specialization in adapted physical education.

Resulting data were treated by the frequencies, crosstabs, and analysis of variance programs of the Statistical Package for Social Sciences (SPSS) (SPSS, 1983). Significant differences were determined by means of chi-square and analysis of variance for categorical and numerical data respectively.

Results and Discussion

Personal Attributes

Personal attributes selected for study were age, gender, ethnic group, visual classification, onset of vision impairment, cause of visual impair-ment, status of vision, the birth position, number of brothers and sisters, visual impairment of family members, educational background, living arrangement, and occupation.

The adult blind athletes in this sample ranged in age from 17 to 60 years, with a mean average of 21.32 years. The age distribution of the blind ath-letes was as follows: 17 to 19 years, 32%; 20 to 29 years, 39%; 30 years or older, 29%. With regard to gender distribution of blind athletes, 62% were male and 38% were female.

Ethnic group is considered an important variable in athletic success, with more blacks represented in top-level competition than in the general population. The most recent census figures indicate that 79.6% of the United States population is white, 11.7% is black, 6.5% is Hispanic, and 2.2% encompasses Indians, Orientals, and Eskimos (Population Reference Bureau, 1982, p. 6). Of the 100 adult blind athletes in this study, 70% were white, and 30% were nonwhite, which included black, Hispanic, Oriental, and American Indian. Phillips (1976) reported that approximately 25% of the nation's best track-and-field performers are black, particularly in sprints, hurdles, and long and triple jumps.

With regard to visual classifications, 32% of the sample were totally blind (Class B1), 30% were Class B2, and 38% were legally blind (Class B3). Of the 100 athletes interviewed, onset of visual impairment was congenital for 61% and adventitious for 39%. The major cause of visual impairment was identified as glaucoma, 13.1%. Other causes are optic nerve problems, 11.1%; retrolental fibroplasia, 10.1%; retinosa pigmentosa, 8.1%; macular degeneration, 7.1%; albinism, detached retina, and diabetes, 6.1%; cataracts and injury, 5.1%; cancer, 3.0%; infectious disease, 2.0%; and unknown cause, 17.2%. The present visual condition was described by the adult blind athletes as getting worse, 31%; about the same, 46%; and getting better, 8%.

In the present sample, 3.1% of the adult blind athletes were only chil-dren, and 4.2% were products of twin or multiple births. Birth order was first born, 28.1%; last born, 24%, and in-between, 40.6%. This information was requested because birth order has been shown to be a significant variable in choice of sports (Casher, 1977; Yiannakis, 1976) and in motor performance (Alberts & Landers, 1977). Birth order, rather than family size or socioeconomic background, is significantly related to high-risk sports (e.g., wrestling, skiing, and diving), with later borns seeking more dangerous, exciting activities than first- and second-born children.

Of the 28 adult blind athletes who reported family members who were also blind, 16 (57.1%) had siblings who were visually impaired, 7 (25%) reported the mother was visually impaired, 3 (10.7%) indicated the father was visually impaired, and 2 (7.1%) responded that their children were visually impaired. Seventy-two reported no one else in the immediate family with visual impairment.

Most athletes had brothers and sisters. The number of brothers ranged from 0 to 7, with a mean of 2.1. Seventeen percent of the blind athletes had no brothers. The number of sisters ranged from 0 to 7, with a mean of 2.3. Twenty-seven percent of the blind athletes had no sisters.

Concerning highest educational level achieved, 1.1% of the athletes had opted not to complete high school, 14.9% were still in high school; 29.8% cited a high school diploma, 28.7% had engaged in some university study, and 6% did not respond. Of the athletes reporting college or university work, 12.8% had stopped with the bachelor's degree, 12.8% had continued on in graduate school, and 28.7% were still in college. A large percentage (45.6%) of the adult blind athletes were in school; 14.9% were in high school, 28.7% were in college, and 2% marked "other." Of those athletes who were not students, 61.5% were employed, 13.5% were unemployed, and 25% did not respond.

Asked with whom they live, the adult blind athletes responded as follows: 30.3%, with parents or relatives; 22.2%, with spouse or one other; 21.2%, alone; 15.2%, with spouse and children; and 11.1%, with several housemates. The fact that most athletes lived with parents or relatives may be explained partly by the high percentage (45.6%) who were still students.

Previous National Competition Experience

The adult blind athletes were an experienced group in competition at national USABA meets. The athletes responded that 10% were competing in their first national meet, 23% were competing in their second national meet, 19% were competing in their third national meet, 19% were competing in their fourth national meet, 17% were competing in their fifth national meet, 7% were competing in their sixth national meet, and 5% were competing in their seventh national meet (i.e., they had entered all national meets conducted by USABA).

Concerning the age at which the adult blind athletes first competed in a national meet, the athletes reported a range from 12 to 64 years. The mean, mode, and median respectively were 22.36, 17.00, and 18.00.

To the question, What one factor most influenced your learning about

USABA and started you to compete in USABA meets? the athletes responded as follows: residential schoolteachers and friends, 41%; agencies for the blind, 19%; sports club for blind, 12%; public schoolteachers and friends, 7%; family and relatives, 3%; and others, 18%.

In response to the question, What one sport are you best skilled at and most likely to win? athletes responded as follows: track, 26.5%; goal ball, 22.4%; field, 18.4%; swimming, 12.2%; wrestling, 10.2%; power lifting, 6.1%; gymnastics, 3.1%; and no response, 3%.

The age of the athletes when they first learned their best sport ranged from 2 to 51 years, with a mean of 16.84 years. The blind athletes reported competition in their best sports event at the local level ranged from 7 to 51 years, with a mean of 17.29 years. Competition at the state or regional level ranged from 10 to 51 years, with a mean of 18.55 years. National competition ranged from 12 to 51 years, with a mean of 20.62 years.

To the question, What extent have you competed in your best sport with nondisabled persons? the adult blind athletes responded as follows: a few times, 33.7%; never, 28.6%; almost always, 22.4%; and a lot, 15.3%.

Training

Adult blind athletes reported working out in their favorite sport from 2 to 30 days during the month prior to national competition, with a mean of 19.72 days. The training or workout consisted of jogging, 48%; practice in specific skills, 28.6%; weight training, 12.2%; other activities, 6.1%; and practice in game play, 5.1%.

When asked if a coach was present during most of their workouts, the athletes responded 43.4%, no; 34.3%, yes; and 22.2%, not applicable—I don't have a coach. The regular employment of the coaches of adult blind athletes was physical education teachers, 52.3%; other employment, 26.1%; information not available, 18.2%; and recreation, 3.4%.

Thirty days before the national meet, the athletes reported they had engaged in serious sport competition against others an average of 4.89 days. The range was 1 to 25 days. During the past year the athletes had engaged in serious sport competition against others an average of 19.3 days, with a range from 1 to 99 days.

Summary

The findings of this study indicate that increasing numbers of blind persons are participating in sport, documenting the fact that they are not helpless and that adult blind athletes enjoy the same vigorous physical activities as their sighted peers. The personal attributes of national-level adult blind athletes are similar to sighted peers. The adult blind athletes are a highly educated group with a large percentage in high school and college. The adult blind athletes are an experienced group at national USABA meets. The training practices of the group indicate that these athletes are self-motivated in their sport training schedule, because many of them do not have a coach or train without a coach being present.

References

Alberts, C., & Landers, D. (1977). Birth order, motor performance, and maternal influence. *Research Quarterly*, **48**(4), 661-670.

Casher, B. (1977). Relationship between birth order and participation in dangerous sports. *Research Quarterly*, **48**(1), 33-40.

Kearney, S., & Copeland, R. (1979). Goal ball. *Journal of Physical Education and Recreation*, **50**, 24-26.

Kerlinger, F. (1973). *Foundations of behavioral research* (2nd ed.). New York: Holt, Rinehart, and Winston.

Phillips, J. (1976). Toward an explanation of racial variations in top-level sports participation. *International Review of Sport Sociology*, **11**(3), 39–56.

Population Reference Bureau. (1982). U.S. population: Where we are; where we're going. *Population Bulletin*, **37**(2), 3-15.

Sherrill, C. (1983). *Disabled athletes sports inventory*. Unpublished manuscript, Texas Woman's University, Denton.

Sherrill, C., Pope, C., & Arnhold, R. (1986). Sport socialization of blind athletes: An exploratory study. *Journal of Visual Impairment and Blindness*, **80**(5), 740-744.

Statistical Package for Social Sciences. (1983). *SPSS users guide*. Chicago: McGraw-Hill.

Yiannakis, A. (1976). Birth order and preference for dangerous sports among men. *Research Quarterly*, **47**(1), 62-67.

Blind Athletes Who Compete in the Mainstream

Charles E. Buell

Thousands of times in the past 20 years, blind athletes have defeated sighted opponents. It is reasonable to assume that if blind athletes can successfully participate in regular athletics, blind children can take part meaningfully in regular public school physical education classes (Buell, 1982). Unfortunately, it is estimated that many blind children are being denied this opportunity.

The purpose of this paper is to persuade educators to reexamine their policies on physical education for blind children. There are laws giving blind children the right to enter regular physical education classes, but many educators are not carrying out the laws. Some administrators and teachers are providing blind children regular physical education, but they are in the minority.

Understanding Blindness

First, the majority of educators and the general public do not understand the condition of blindness. This is the greatest obstacle to overcome before blind children can receive the rights given to them by law. There are two misconceptions, widely held, that need to be eliminated. First, it is generally believed that blindness and sightlessness refer to the same condition. This is not true. According to the law, blindness is defined as 20/200, 1/10, or less vision. Using this definition, at least 80% of blind people have some useful vision. An individual who has some useful vision can adjust to sports in many ways not open to a sightless athlete. So it is not nearly as difficult for these blind children to adjust to regular physical education as educators believe. Another misconception widely held is that sightlessness is similar to what one experiences when blindfolded or the lights go out. Under such conditions, the average person with sight is helpless for some time. However, sightless persons have lived with the condition for months and years, and most of them have learned to perform thousands of activities without vision. These activities include participation in regular physical education classes in public schools and many types of athletic competition.

Blind Athletes Compete in the Mainstream

Blind athletes successfully participate in many sports. Only a few outstanding examples will be mentioned in any one sport.

Contact sports.   More blind athletes successfully compete against able-bodied opponents in wrestling than in any other sport. Each year about 5,000 sighted athletes compete against blind wrestlers. Whether a wrestler has vision or not need not have any influence upon the outcome of bouts. In high school, the wrestling rule book gives the blind wrestler the opportunity to start from touch. This requirement does not interfere with the sighted wrestler's style. Breaks are permitted, but wrestlers move forward immediately to secure holds. Thus a bout becomes competitive wrestling and not a series of flying tackles.

How many sports are there in which a sightless athlete can win a state championship? In the past 20 years, over 50 blind wrestlers have won state high school championships. In 1985, Keith West of the School for the Blind won his second Alabama State High School Wrestling Championship. During the previous 2 years, West compiled a record of 66–2. In both 1982 and 1984, sightless Lonzy Jenkins won individual championships in South Carolina State High School Wrestling meets. In addition to state champions, there have been over 100 other blind boys who have placed second, third, fourth, or fifth in state competition.

Hundreds of blind wrestlers have successfully competed in intercollegiate and amateur wrestling. One is James Mastro, who recently earned a doctor's degree at Texas Woman's University in adapted physical education. In 1976, Mastro, 89.8 kg or 198 lb, placed third in the NAAU Greco-Roman competition and was named as an alternate on the regular United States Olympic Wrestling Team.

Other contact sports in which blind individuals successfully compete are judo and karate. The rules in these sports need not be modified for blind participants. In 1980, sightless Anthony Maczynski of Delaware won a black belt in judo. A few years later he placed sixth in a national karate championship.

Power lifting.   Blind power lifters use regular rules to compete in power lifting. At the 1984 Drug Free New Jersey Powerlifting Meet, Lisa Mellea, 46.3 kg or 102 lb, had a total lift of 302.4 kg or 672 lb in the women's division.

Gymnastics.   Blind individuals have won letters in gymnastics on high school and college teams. A few years ago at Weymouth South High School in Massachusetts, sightless Gail Castonquay earned a letter on the gymnastics team. Pita Quintana, with 10% vision, placed second in vaulting and fifth in all-around at the 1979 New Mexico State Girls Gymnastics Meet.

Water sports.   Individuals with as little as 1/30 vision have successfully competed in mainstream swimming. Sightless swimmers are at somewhat of a disadvantage. However, a sightless Swedish swimmer has a time of 1:02.13 in the 100-m freestyle for men.

Trischa Zorn has times of 59.46 for 91.4-m (100-yd) and 2:06.64 for 182.8-m (200-yd) backstroke events. With 1/30 vision, Zorn is one of the top backstrokers in the United States, blind or sighted. As a member of the Mission Viejo, California High School Swim Team, she was selected on the All-America High School Female Swim Team. Upon graduation she was offered a dozen full-time athletic scholarships. She decided to compete for the University of Nebraska, where she has won letters for the past 2 years. In the backstroke, Zorn can see the flags stretched across the pool. Zorn can also see the markings on the bottom of the pool most of the time. After swimming thousands of laps in practice, she is accustomed to making turns. In practice, her teammates tell her the time remaining on the clock.

In June 1985 John Morgan was selected on the All-America Distance Swim Team. In one of his swims, he placed 10th in a field of 135 able-bodied swimmers. This was a 3-mi race in the ocean. Morgan placed third in a field of 50 able-bodied competitors in a 10-mi ocean swim in the summer of 1984. During his distance swims, he is accompanied by a swimmer on a surfboard who gives him directions from time to time. John Morgan, with 1/30 vision, earned a letter in swimming at Golden West College, California, in 1984. In the International Games for the Disabled recently held in New York, Morgan posted a time of 56.2 in the 100-m freestyle. He starts all races in the water, so that his detached retina will not be endangered. Thus, he is losing a second or two to competitors who normally use a diving start; still, he is able to be competitive.

In 1983 Englishmen Gerald Price and Nigel Verbeeck water-skied across the English Channel. The following year sightless Harry Cordellos water-skied 31 mi from Long Beach to Catalina Island in California. Hundreds of blind persons water-ski for recreation, but a few perform outstanding feats. Because successful waterskiing largely depends upon balance, not vision, it is an ideal sport for many blind persons.

Bowling. Perhaps the most popular sport among persons who are blind is bowling. National tournaments in the United States draw over 2,000 blind bowlers. Also, it is a sport based upon handicap scoring, so a blind person can enjoy the sport with his sighted family and acquaintances. Bowlers with low vision or no vision often use a portable guide rail that can be taken to any lane. A bowler runs his fingers along the rail to give him direction before releasing the ball.

In 1979, legally blind John Bleloch of Chicago bowled a game of 298. Two sightless men have posted scores of 256 each.

Golf. In the 1984 Bob Hope Tournament, legally blind Jim Simons placed second to earn a prize of $43,200. One must make very good use of his or her vision to be competitive in golf. Even totally blind golfers sometimes score below 100. A sighted companion gives them assistance from time to time.

Track and field.   Legally blind athletes have earned letters in inter-scholastic and intercollegiate track and field. A person with some vision can see the lane markers on a track and, to some extent, the position of competitors. Flags are placed at the end of take-off boards in jumping events. Also, streamers can be hung on the crossbar in high jumping.

Legally blind Leamon Stansell won letters in track at Santa Monica College, California, for 1983 and 1984. In a meet against Long Beach City College, he ran 5,000 m in 16:03.1. His time for 1,500 m against Pasadena City College was 4:17.6.

At El Camino College, California, Paul Smith, legally blind, had a best time of 10.7 s to earn a letter in track in 1984. This is within 0.8 s of Carl Lewis's best time.

A few years ago at the University of South Carolina, legally blind John Orcutt high jumped 6 ft 10 in. or 2.09 m. At about the same time, Janet Rowley, also legally blind, high jumped 5 ft 1 in. or 1.55 m at Boston University.

For a number of years one of the outstanding performances in World Masters Games has been turned in by a sightless athlete, Fritz Assmy of West Germany. At the 1983 meet in Puerto Rico, he defeated former world-class sprinter Payton Jordan in the 200-m and 400-m runs. Assmy runs in Lane 8 and is guided by a sighted partner. He has now turned 70 years of age, but he still wins races against able-bodied athletes.

Distance running.   In distance runs, sightless and very low-vision ath-letes are guided by sighted athletes. Some blind runners prefer to tie a short tether to the wrist of a guide, while others prefer to touch arms and elbows from time to time.

Runners with as little as 1/50 vision can perform without partners. Legally blind Carlos Talbert of Florida has run the Boston Marathon in 2 hr and 23 min, whereas sightless Harry Cordellos, 47 years of age, posted a time of 2 hr and 57 min in this well-known event in 1975. Whether there are hundreds or thousands of runners in the field, the San Franciscan finishes in the top third or higher in marathon runs. Cordellos and Talbert have also performed well in triathlons (Cordellos, 1981).

Sightless New Zealander John Stratford ran from Wellington to Auck-land, New Zealand, a distance of 675.4 km or 420 mi in an elapsed time of 61.5 hr. This is an outstanding run for anyone, blind or sighted.

Football.   A number of legally blind players have earned letters in high school and college football. Kevin Szott, who is legally blind, played offen-sive center for St. Lawrence University. He sees well enough to carry out blocking assignments. Szott played on a St. Lawrence team that went to the finals in Division III and was selected as a member of the All-America Team of that division.

Skating.   Thousands of sightless and low-vision persons roller-skate and ice-skate. Those with no vision or very little skate with sighted part-ners. Persons with as little as 1/10 vision can compete in ice skating. An example is Elwin Kelsey of California. In 1964 Kelsey and his partner placed fifth in the National Junior Pairs competition. He became a professional with an Ice Follies show.

Cycling. There have been many outstanding bicycling performances by blind persons. However, most visually impaired cyclists participate in the sport for fun. Those with little or no vision usually ride on tandem bicycles with sighted partners. One of these is Tom Dickey. At 71 years of age, he bicycled coast to coast across the United States to attend the 50th reunion of his class at Amherst College in Massachusetts. The end of the trip was featured on television in 1982.

Hiking. Blind hikers usually walk with a sighted partner. A feat by very few blind or sighted persons is the crossing from the south to the north rims of the Grand Canyon. This was accomplished by two different groups of blind hikers. Although most hikers participate in the sport for fun, some seek challenges and turn in outstanding performances.

Mountain climbing. There have been some exciting mountain climbs made by blind persons under the guidance of experienced guides. In most every case, the blind climbers wanted to show their sighted peers that it could be done by persons without sight.

In July 1981 five blind climbers, an amputee, an epileptic, and two deaf hikers reached the 4,392-m or 14,410-ft peak of Mount Rainier in the state of Washington. The climb received worldwide media coverage.

Sailing. Sightless and low-vision people participate in sailing. Sightless sailors perform duties that do not require vision. Some of them have competed in races, whereas a few have accepted more daring challenges.

The distance between San Francisco and Honolulu is 3,862 km or 2,400 mi. Legally blind Hank Decker sailed this distance alone in 23 days. He used braille charts, a braille compass, a "talking clock," and a navigational system that read his position aloud. He had the misfortune of his radio going dead shortly after the beginning of the trip in August 1983. He had no warning of a tropical storm that overturned his boat for 20 min. When the accident occurred, Decker was in the cabin, not in the water. Fortunately the waves uprighted the boat and Decker completed his trip.

Skydiving. Blind persons participate in skydiving. With the assistance of a sighted companion who is on the ground, the blind person is able to accomplish his or her goal. They communicate by two-way radio. Of course, it is most important that the blind diver be informed of the altitude.

In 1983 sightless Mike May of California parachuted from a plane at 914 m or 3,000 ft. He was in the air 12 min before he landed safely in a rice field. He feels that skydiving is no more difficult for him than it is for anyone else. I was present during the dive and the 4 hr of training that preceded it.

Conclusion

The purpose of this chapter is to persuade educators to reexamine their policies on physical education for blind students in public schools. Those who are not giving blind children opportunities to participate in regular physical education classes should read the foregoing examples of determination and capabilities. It is unfortunate that educators offering realistic physical education programs in the public schools are in the minority. I hope that this condition will be remedied soon.

References

Buell, C. (1982). *Physical education and recreation for the visually handicapped* (rev. ed.). Reston, VA: The American Alliance for Health, Physical Education, Recreation, and Dance.

Cordellos, H. (1981). *Breaking through*. Mountain View, CA: Anderson World.

A Trial Evaluation of a Motor Aptitude Scale for Mentally Deficient Persons

Jean-Claude de Potter

Numerous studies have shown different levels of motor aptitude between normal and mentally deficient children (Danan, 1971). These studies have been based on standard testing of normal children without any particular adaptation to the needs of the special population. These tests evaluate very limited motor aspects with wide-ranging results. In fact, these results are influenced by different characteristics of the mentally deficient population: absent-mindedness, motivation, understanding, motor difficulties, and secondary handicaps (Levarlet-Joye & Ribauville, 1981). Elsewhere I have shown the important correlation between the state of alertness of mentally retarded adolescents and results obtained in psychomotor testing (de Potter, 1981).

Because of the importance of variations in response obtained from different testing, I have also stressed the difficulty in evaluating the motor quotient of mentally deficient persons. The more the method of evaluation deviates from a universality of response, the more the coefficient of variation seems to increase (de Potter, 1983). Likewise, other authors have shown important links between IQ and fragmented, poorly motivating laboratory testing. Thus it seems that objective methods of evaluating motor aptitudes must be based on measurements taken under the most ordinary possible conditions.

Experiment

In order to evaluate the physical aptitude of a broad population of mentally deficient persons and to orient their classification into games, meets, or sports competitions, this study used four classic events spread over a broad population (Conseil de l'Europe, 1983; Hebbelinck & Borms, 1969). These four events were chosen because subjects could understand them easily and could carry them out quickly. These were the standing long jump, 25-m running race, basketball throwing, and static balance. These events appear to encompass fundamental qualities of relaxation, speed, coordination, and neuromuscular control.

The sample was composed of 750 boys and 385 girls chronologically aged 16 to 35. No intellectual or developmental quotient was retained for the eventual categorization of the groups. In this way, I removed from

Table 1   Results of Events

	Range of results	M	Variance	SD
Boys				
Jump	10 - 222 cm	130.8290	2,536.68	50.3655
Race	3.8 - 12.2 s	6.0017	375.36	19.3742
Throwing	111 - 1,949 cm	928.8840	17,234.90	415.1490
Girls				
Jump	10 - 189 cm	99.4185	1,596.66	39.9582
Race	4.8 - 14 s	7.1430	527.71	22.9719
Throwing	100 - 1,100 cm	549.3450	48,151.90	219.4350

the evaluation all prejudice based on extraneous notions of fundamental physical aptitude.

Results

Results of these tests for the first three events are presented in Table 1. For static balance, three stages of increasing difficulty were proposed:

A = 30 points   A + B = 60 points
B = 30 points   B + C = 60 points   A + B + C = 100 points
C = 60 points   A + C = 100 points

The results of these tests were added up to determine three categories:

Category 1:   noncompetitive (NC)   0 to 150 points
Category 2:   semicompetitive (SC)   151 to 250 points
Category 3:   competitive (C)   251 to 400 points

These categories were established solely on the basis of the test results. However, it is obvious that persons with severe physical handicaps were not taken into consideration.

Placing handicapped persons into one of these categories was designed to orient them toward either adapted games where there would be no competitive spirit (Category 1) or toward participation in 4 of the 19 proposed events in the Belgian Special Olympics (Category 3). It seemed very presumptuous, in this first try, to orient with authority all the participants toward either the games or the competition without consulting the instructors

Table 2 Comparison of Results

Events	n	M		NC		SC				C	
			Total	Above M	Total	Above M	Below M	Total	Above M	Below M
100-m race	92	17.3 s	18	1	44	22	22	30	27	3
400-m race	86	1.12.6 min	3	0	23	18	5	60	30	30
Long jump	185	2.434 m	37	3	94	56	38	54	49	5
Weights	101	5.719	17	1	52	31	21	32	19	13

in charge. In addition, in some cases it was difficult to decide that a person should be excluded from all meets when his or her results obtained in the orientation test were average. Therefore, we let instructors decide the classification of persons in the middle category of semicompetitive.

Analysis of the Results

Of 1,135 persons evaluated, 212 were classified as noncompetitive, 334 were classified as semicompetitive, and 589 were classified as competitive. The results and the categories were communicated to instructors, who were nevertheless absolutely free to enroll the participants whatever the assigned orientation. In 99% of the cases, the results were not discussed.

At the end of the Special Olympics of 1985, the results obtained were analyzed in relation to the assigned orientations. Only a sample of the results was retained (see Table 2); the complete analysis is presently under way.

Discussion

Choice of Orientation Tests

Given that persons could participate in several different events requiring different motor abilities, the aim of this study was to evaluate their overall aptitude to participate in meets and to draw up an orientation scale. However, certain mentally deficient persons, even if they can obtain a modest score in their average for the events, are likely to show proficiency in a single discipline; the tests must, therefore, be both complete and selective. Also, the motivation produced by participation in a competition as opposed to a selection test often leads to a clear improvement in results; the choice of events should, therefore, be conditioned by this motivation.

Confirmation or Invalidation of the Assigned Orientation

On the whole, the orientation resulting from the preliminary tests allowed the instructors to improve their judgment. In the vast majority of cases, they respected the given instructions. It appeared that persons classified as noncompetitive could not obtain an average score when assigned to meets. In the orientation, a little too much caution was observed. In fact, the semicompetitive participants obtained results that were about average, and therefore requirements probably need to be raised. A good number of these persons could have been classified as competitive.

Conclusions

It seems that this method of orientation allows an overall evaluation of the motor abilities of mentally deficient persons. However, the results obtained can in no way be used to predict the performance to be achieved. If participation in several events continues, it is advisable to better determine the semicompetitive category by raising performance requirements and to increase the motivation of participants in the preliminary tests.

References

Conseil de l'Europe. (1983). *Evaluation de l'aptitude physique* (Eurofit) [Physical aptitude evaluation]. Strasbourg, France: Author.

Danan, L. (1971). Des athlètes pas comme les autres [Athletes unlike others]. *Tribune de l'enfance*, **8**, 49-52.

de Potter, J.-C. (1981). Vigilance et rapidité motrice d'adolescents arriérés mentaux [Motor vigilance and rapidity of mentally retarded adolescents]. In J.-C. de Potter (Ed.), *Adapted physical activities* (pp. 43-50). Brussels: Brussels University.

de Potter, J.-C. (1983). Evaluation des compétences motrices de déficients mentaux [Evaluation of motor competence in mentally deficient persons]. In R. L. Eason, T. L. Smith, & F. Caron (Eds.), *Adapted physical activity* (pp. 281-286). Champaign, IL: Human Kinetics.

Hebbelinck, M., & Borms, J. (1969). *Tests et échelles de normes de capacité de performance physique* [Tests and standards scales of physical performance capacity]. Belgium: ADEPS.

Levarlet-Joye, H., & Ribauville, A. (1981). Les aptitudes sportives et les possibilités motrices des handicapés mentaux de 12 à 13 ans [The athletic aptitude and motor possibilities of 12- to 13-year-old mentally handicapped youth]. In J.-C. de Potter (Ed.), *Adapted physical activities* (pp. 51-57). Brussels: Brussels University.

A Physical Fitness Assessment of British Columbia Special Olympic Athletes

Anne D. Tilley
R. E. Mosher
G. D. Sinclair

This chapter is concerned with a project undertaken in conjunction with British Columbia Special Olympics (BCSO). The question of whether individuals with Down's syndrome should be regarded as a particular group has been addressed in the literature. Growth studies have documented distinct physical differences (Rarick & Seefeldt, 1974; Thelander & Pryor, 1966) and a separate study of their characteristics has been advised (Sherrill, 1981). The *Canada Fitness Award Manual: Adapted for Use by Trainable Mentally Handicapped Youth* (1983) makes a distinction between Down's syndrome and non–Down's syndrome youth in its level of achievement scores in all but the endurance run. Test appropriateness was a concern during its development and the six motor fitness performance items were task analyzed and simplified. For the flexed arm hang and the sit-ups, three performance levels of increasing difficulty have been introduced. Motivation given throughout the test session is expected, and more than one tester is required to administer the test (Findlay et al., 1984). The adapted Canada Fitness Award is an incentive program and as such it was used in this project.

The original purpose of the project was to provide a year-round fitness profile of BCSO athletes in the lower mainland of British Columbia and to attempt to determine whether BCSO programs could contribute to the development of fitness in their athletes. Athletes were classified as "active" or "semiactive" depending upon their program involvement, but because of the complexities involved in gathering comprehensive data on the physical activity patterns of athletes it was not possible to determine whether higher levels of fitness could be attributed to increased program demands. It became clear that athletes were engaged in a range of activities and that our background knowledge of the athletes was incomplete. After the second of four assessments, it was decided to gather additional data on activity patterns and data relating to the medical, social, and educational background of the athletes. In addition, the project undertook the development of a computer program that would provide an on-site test profile of each athlete over the course of a year.

Procedures

The original requirements for the selection of athletes were that they be engaged regularly in BCSO programs in the lower mainland of British Columbia during a 12-month period and that they be between 16 and 26 years of age. In addition to the standard BCSO athlete, parent, or guardian release form, consent to take part in all phases of the project was obtained. This consent was given by the adult athlete or by the parent/guardian or group home supervisor. Because the intent of the project was to offer an incentive to local programs, no athletes appearing for the first assessment were screened out due to age. The first trial attracted 40 athletes ranging in age from 11 to 53 years. After the second trial, a preliminary analysis of the results was conducted based on the performance of 30 athletes who attended both sessions. Twenty of the original 40 athletes attended all four trials. Of these athletes, 18 postadolescent athletes were selected for study. Eleven males, including 2 with Down's syndrome, ranged in age from 17 to 30 (M = 22.8), and 7 females, including 2 with Down's syndrome, ranged in age from 17 to 31 (M = 23.8).

The *Canada Fitness Award Manual: Adapted for Use by Trainable Mentally Handicapped Youth* (1983) was used to assess the motor fitness of athletes. All trials were conducted indoors, with the first four tests (the flexed arm hang, the shuttle run, sit-ups, and the standing long jump) being administered concurrently. Whereas the 50-m run was conducted on a straight course, the endurance run utilized a 30 × 20-m course requiring 20 laps to complete the 2,000 m. The testing was conducted by graduate students in physical education, most of whom had some experience with moderately retarded individuals. Physical education undergraduate students served as "buddies," and on a one-to-one basis they escorted the athletes through the assessment process. A stringent attempt was made to standardize all test procedures and, in particular, the nature and the amount of encouragement given to athletes. However, there were the usual limitations to consistent test administration. Familiarity with a test brought small but improved practices (Edwards, 1984). Some changes in test personnel were inevitable as student commitments changed. Refusals to take part in a test were very few. On the fourth trial, athletes with Down's syndrome without a medical release for atlantoaxial instability did not take part in the sit-ups.

All test results were entered into the RAST microcomputer program, and an on-site individual profile of results was given to each athlete. A questionnaire relating to activity patterns was circulated to athletes, parents, or group home supervisors at the beginning of the project. Later during the project, a BCSO volunteer and the principal investigator met with small groups of parents to administer a second questionnaire. Additional data on activity patterns and data on the medical, social, and educational background of the athletes were collected from 41 athletes. The data from all trials on the fitness test and the responses to the second questionnaire were categorized by sex and the presence of Down's syndrome, yielding four groups: male non–Down's syndrome (MNDS), female non–Down's syndrome (FNDS), male Down's syndrome (MDS), and female Down's syndrome (FDS).

Results and Discussion

Shuttle run. The overall mean scores for the four groups were FNDS (n = 5) 15.03 s, MDS (n = 2) 15.38 s, MNDS (n = 9) 15.74 s, and FDS (n = 2) 18.18 s. Figure 1 shows the mean performance curves over four trials.

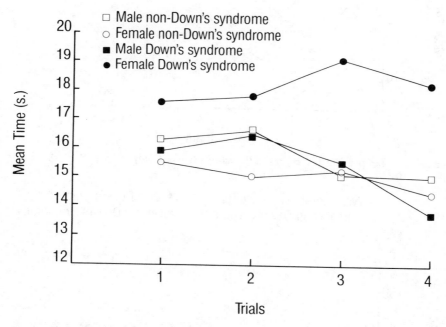

Figure 1 Mean performance curves in the shuttle run.

Sit-ups. The overall mean scores for the groups over three trials were MNDS 31, FNDS 28, FDS 24, and MDS 18. Figure 2 shows the mean performance curves of Down's syndrome athletes over three trials and non–Down's syndrome athletes on four trials.

Standing long jump. The overall mean scores were MNDS 162 cm, FNDS 142 cm, MDS 119 cm, and FDS 108 cm. The mean performance curves over four trials are shown in Figure 3.

50-m run. Athletes ran in pairs over a straight course. The overall mean scores were MNDS 9.11 s, MDS 9.35 s, FNDS 9.64 s, and FDS 12.05 s. The mean performance curves over four trials are shown in Figure 4.

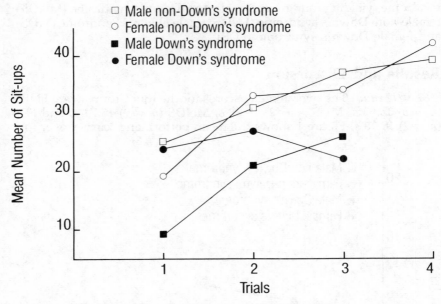

Figure 2 Mean performance curves in the sit-ups (Level 1 only).

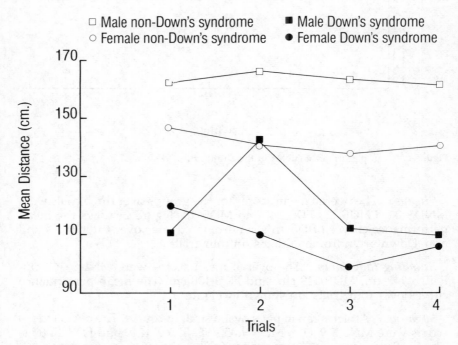

Figure 3 Mean performance curves in the standing long jump.

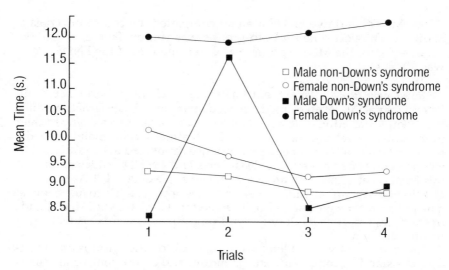

Figure 4 Mean performance curves in the 50-m run.

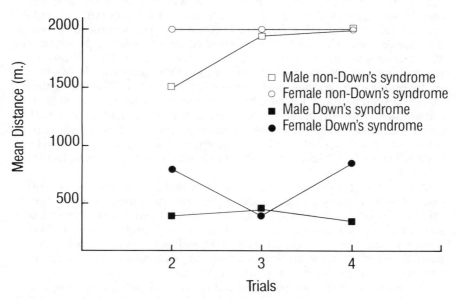

Figure 5 Mean performance curves for distance in the endurance run.

Endurance run. The results of the first trial were discarded due to un-controllable factors during the assessment. The overall mean scores for distance were FNDS 2,000 m, MNDS 1,826 m, FDS 683 m, and MDS 400 m. Figure 5 shows the mean performance curves for distance over three trials.

Five MNDS and five FNDS athletes completed the course on Trials 2, 3, and 4. The best time for both groups was run on Trial 2, where the mean score for the MNDS group was 9.24 s and that of the FNDS group was 13.64 s.

Flexed arm hang.   This event has three levels of performance, with Level 1 (bar at eye level) being the most demanding. Analysis of the results was complex as athletes tested at all levels and 12 athletes changed their performance level during the trials. For 6 athletes who maintained the same level over all trials, peak performances appeared to be random. Fifteen athletes tested at Level 1 at least once, and 4 MNDS athletes tested at this level on all trials with an overall mean score of 30.44 s. As noted by Hayden (1964) and Edwards (1984), athletes appeared not to like being at a height above the ground. Also, it seemed that athletes with small hands or short fingers, such as Down's syndrome athletes, were disadvantaged in this test item.

The scores of MNDS athletes were superior to other groups on the sit-ups, the standing long jump, the 50-m run, and on the completion times for the endurance run. Where no steady improvement occurred, their mean scores showed little variation. The FNDS athletes outperformed both MDS and FDS athletes in all but the 50-m run, where the MDS athletes ranked second. Like the MNDS group, the FNDS mean scores showed considerable consistency. The MDS athletes showed an inconsistent performance. While improving trends were seen in the shuttle run and the sit-ups, fluctuating mean scores occurred in the standing long jump and the 50-m run. In the endurance run their performance was consistent. The performance of FDS athletes differed noticeably on the shuttle run and the 50-m run, where they were surpassed by the other groups on all trials. Unlike other groups, no continually improving trends were present. Peak performances occurred on either Trial 1 or Trial 2 except for the endurance run, where they achieved their highest score on the final trial, outperforming the MDS athletes.

Many interacting genetic and environmental factors could have influenced the performance of the athletes. For example, the physique of male athletes probably conferred advantages on items such as the flexed arm hang. Female Down's syndrome athletes were thought to be doubly disadvantaged by physical characteristics in addition to a variety of environmental factors. Consequently, tentative suggestions are made to account for changes in performance made during the project.

Familiarity with the test situation did not of itself bring about improved scores for FDS athletes in particular. New insights into a test item could account for improved scores in the shuttle run, where athletes understood that there were two beanbags to be collected. Heightened motivation could have influenced performance on any item, and athletes were seen to compete in closely contested 50-m runs.

Speakman (1977) has drawn attention to the need for good rapport in the test environment. In this project the undergraduate buddy was an integral part of the test procedure and when it was necessary to change buddies some athletes were disconcerted for a while after the change. Such a change may have influenced motivation to perform.

Specific practice on the sit-ups was thought to account for higher scores for all groups. Some athletes were known to engage in distance running. Variation in both distance covered and time taken seemed to be influenced by general health factors as well as training effects.

The endurance run raises particular concerns. The medical status of athletes needs regular monitoring. This is most necessary for Down's syndrome athletes, where concerns for atlantoaxial instability and congenital heart disorders (thought to have an incidence of 40 to 62%, Johnson, 1978) are well known. While an overprotective attitude can be counterproductive, an up-to-date medical clearance can allow coaches to increase program demands more confidently.

The relationship between physical activity patterns and the fitness level of athletes was not determined, but their performance scores suggest an active life-style. The context in which this life-style factor arose is described in part by the second questionnaire.

An analysis was made of all responses ($n = 41$) and those of the selected athletes ($n = 18$). This second analysis showed that 11 of 18 athletes (61%) were regarded as having no handicap other than a mental handicap. Four non–Down's syndrome athletes (22%) had other handicaps and were taking medication regularly. Sixteen athletes (85%) were living at home, and 2 non–Down's syndrome athletes (11%) lived independently in an apartment or suite. Fifty percent of athletes traveled to their programs unescorted. (When all responses were considered, 64% of male athletes and 38% of female athletes were independent travelers.) At some point in their education, 32% of athletes had been placed in a special class or regular class, and 68% had attended only special schools. Ten athletes (56%) were youngest children. An attempt was made to determine whether the athlete's family engaged regularly in physical activity. Although this was not easy to assess, 66% of athletes had families who were active regularly. (This picture changed when all responses were analyzed. Only 50% of families in all four subgroups were considered to be active regularly.) An analysis of the activity patterns showed that male athletes participated in 11 activities, the most common being bowling, track and field, soccer, and swimming. Female athletes took part in nine activities headed by fitness, soccer, bowling, and swimming. Four non–Down's syndrome athletes with other handicaps and taking medication achieved Level 1 on the flexed arm hang at least three times, completed the endurance run at least twice, and were engaged in five or more activities during the year.

No attempt has been made to account for the four-trial attendance of the selected 18 athletes compared to the 22 other athletes who also began the project but who withdrew or who were unable to attend all trials. Several factors, including family vacations and missed transportation, influenced attendance.

Future studies will further investigate the athletes' activity preferences and the role of families in the socialization of this population into physical activities.

Acknowledgments

This project was supported by funds from the Canadian Special Olympics Inc. and the British Columbia Special Olympics.

References

Canada Fitness Award manual: Adapted for use by trainable mentally handicapped youth. (1983). Ottawa: Fitness and Amateur Sport.

Edwards, L. (1984). *Report of a fitness assessment of B.C.S.O. participants*. Unpublished manuscript, University of British Columbia, Vancouver.

Findlay, H. A., Watkinson, E. J., Dahlgren, W. J., Evans, J., Lafreniere-Joannette, L., & Bothwell-Meyers, C. (1984). Canada Fitness Award: How to use it: How to change it. *Canadian Association for Health, Physical Education and Recreation Journal*, **50**, 10-16, 23-25.

Hayden, F. J. (1964). *Physical fitness for the mentally retarded*. Toronto: Metropolitan Toronto Association for Retarded Children.

Johnson, A. M. (1978). The management of cardiac disease in Down's syndrome. *Development Medicine and Child Neurology*, **20**, 220-223.

Rarick, G. L., & Seefeldt, V. (1974). Observations from longitudinal data on growth in stature and sitting height of children with Down's's Syndrome. *Journal of Mental Deficiency Research*, **18**, 63-78.

Sherrill, C. (1981). *Adapted physical education and recreation* (2nd ed.). Dubuque, IA: W. C. Brown.

Speakman, H. G. B. (1977). Physical fitness of the mentally retarded: A brief survey of the literature. *Canadian Journal of Applied Sport Sciences*, **2**, 171-176.

Thelander, H. E., & Pryor, H. B. (1966). Abnormal patterns of growth and development in mongolism. An anthropometric study. *Clinical Pediatrics*, **5**, 493-501.

PART VII

Sport and Recreation for the Disabled

Science, Research, and Special Populations: The View From Biomechanics

Colin Higgs

Any symposium address, if it is to be successful, should both inform the audience and stimulate critical thought. If one aspect, information or stimulation, is to be pursued more thoroughly at the expense of the other, it is my belief that emphasis should be on stimulating conference participants to think critically about their own work and the research results presented to them.

I was asked by the conference organizers to present some of my own research findings. This I intend to do but not in the usual form of a literature review. Rather my intention is to show that there are significant problems associated with applying the scientific method to research with special populations. My research will be used to highlight those problems.

The Nature of the Problem

At the heart of the scientific method are the samples used and the statistics that enable us to speak with some confidence about our results. We use samples of our population because, in general, there are too many individuals for us to test them all. The important question then arises—when we have a sample to test or measure—of what is it a sample? To illustrate, let us consider the work done with racing wheelchairs (Higgs, 1983).

At the 1980 Olympic Games for the Disabled at Arnham, Holland, I photographed numerous wheelchairs. Some were high technology innovations used by the most successful "wheelers" at the games, while others were the ill-designed and poorly constructed chairs used by individuals who were pleased simply to have made it to the competition.

My sample consisted of 49 chairs and the athletes who used them. There were chairs used by males and females of every age, athletic ability, and disability. If this was my sample, what was my population? In the strict code of research, my population was no more than those wheelchairs used by the athletes who had been selected to represent their countries during the Olympic celebrations of June and July 1980. My findings of statistical differences between the chairs used by the most and least successful athletes (and between the chairs used in sprint and distance events) implied only that there were differences in chair construction between the chairs of the most and least successful athletes who were at those specific games for those two weeks in 1980. By inference I (and others) have implied that these differences in chair construction are real and that the lessons learned can be applied to other chairs for other athletes at different times and at different levels of competition. This is an act of faith and intuition entirely unfounded in the methods of science. It is an act of faith made in varying degrees by all of us as we interpret our own and other people's research findings.

Other problems were associated with the analysis of the data that I had collected. Several approaches to the analysis of chair design data were possible. I was interested in finding out whether or not there were any differences in the layout of the major chair components between those chairs used with greater or lesser success. In addition, I wanted to know if chairs used in distance events were designed differently from those used in the sprints. I also wanted to know if there were differences between the chairs used by males and females and among those used by athletes who had been placed in different disability categories. Last but not least, I wanted to understand the relationship between chair design and the anthropometric measurements of the athlete using the chair (but only for those who were successful). So much for what I wanted.

The reality is that most research efforts are more closely confined by problems of samples and populations than we care to admit, and as researchers we are more often concerned with the significance of differences rather than the degree to which differences are meaningful. An example might clarify this point. No doubt we all remember our statistics instructors insisting that we needed a large N, or sample size. The reason was, of course, that the larger the samples, the greater the chance of detecting differences among them. The logical extension of this is that with an infinite sample (or the whole population) infinitesimal differences become significant statistically even if they are not meaningful. The converse is also true. With small samples, large and meaningful differences will be shown to be not significant statistically.

In the real-life world of research involving special populations, too small samples are a much more frequent problem than too large. Thus for the analysis of racing wheelchairs I was faced with a major decision. Should I perform a three-way analysis of variance (level of success × sex of athlete × disability classification), or should I clump all of the classifications of disabled athletes of both sexes together and perform a one-way analysis based on success achieved? The trade-offs were interesting. Levin (1975) has shown the relationship between sample size and the likelihood of detecting meaningful differences of various magnitudes. From this work it became clear to me that for the sample size possible in the three-way analysis of variance model, only gigantic differences would be shown to be significant. Even with the one-way analysis model, small, real differences would not be detected as significant.

Using one-way analysis of variance as the method of investigating how differences in chair design varied with level of success had the obvious advantage of making the detection of significant differences more likely.

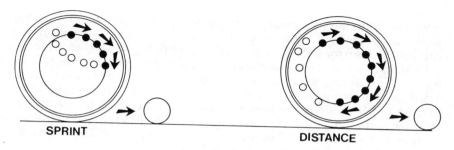

Figure 1 Difference between sprint and distance wheelchair propulsion techniques. Filled circles represent the propulsive phase, open circles, recovery. Arrows show direction of movement.

It also had another positive aspect. In an analysis in which individuals are categorized by level of success, sex, and disability, there is an assumption that each person is analyzed as a sample of that specific population. Now while this is theoretically advantageous, it has some practical limitations. If, in the best of all possible worlds, we could analyze 50 chairs/individuals in each success group, of both sexes, and for each disability classification, we would be able to describe with great accuracy the variations in chair design important within each subpopulation. We would also need 3,500 subjects. Given the much lower number of subjects that were (and usually are) available for research, I was faced with the problem of collapsing groupings in order to get meaningful numbers of measurements in each cell for my analysis. The advantage of this is that any differences that can be shown to be significant can be described as broadly significant. That is, they are important across individual disability groupings—the results apply to everyone.

What then of the results? They showed (Higgs, 1983) that the chairs used by the most successful racers had the seat placed lower and more toward the rear than their less successful counterparts, while overall their chairs were shorter and narrower. The handrims on the chairs used with most success were considerably smaller in diameter than were the others.

When the chairs were analyzed with respect to the distance over which they were raced, a similar pattern emerged. Distance chairs were built with lower and more rearward seats as well as longer and narrower frames. Analysis of the wheeling actions of selected Olympic athletes, both distance and sprint (Higgs, 1986), showed that sprint and distance athletes used significantly different patterns of hand movement in propelling their chairs. The typical hand pattern of the sprinter was characterized by a shuttle motion, while the distance racers used more of a circular action (Figure 1).

It is interesting to speculate on the possible reasons for these differences, but it is likely that they represent a trade-off between power output and efficiency. The sprinters, with their higher and more forward seats, are able to apply considerable force to a restricted segment of the handrim and probably pay a heavy metabolic price in the return of the hand (and upper body) to the start position for the next propulsive phase. Thus the power output is high but is coupled with low efficiency—a situation that can be tolerated for only a short period of time. For the distance racers, the situation is reversed. In distance races, efficiency in converting chemical energy to forward motion becomes crucial. The lower and more rearward seat position provides the athlete with access to a greater proportion of the handrim without the need to adjust upper body position and thus cuts down on movements that do not directly contribute to the forward motion of the wheelchair. This pattern, while not permitting such a high power output, seems more suited to distance racing.

The question of chair length is less clear. It had been my working hypothesis that chairs optimized for sprinting would have a long wheelbase. This long wheelbase, something like the design of a "dragster" car, was thought to provide directional stability and thus would allow the athlete to concentrate on generating propulsive force rather than on applying steering corrections. I was wrong.

The data indicated that the wheelchairs of sprinters were shorter, rather than longer, than those used by the distance racers. One possible explanation of this is that directional stability is proportional to the time it takes to change direction. The sprinter in a long, highly stable chair would be at an advantage as long as he or she was heading in the right direction. Once a change in direction became necessary, it would, however, take a long time to produce, time that is unavailable during a short race. The shorter chair, more responsive to directional change, apparently allows the athlete to get back to straight line propulsion as quickly as possible.

Another, related hypothesis is also tenable and can be expressed as follows. Changes in the direction of a wheelchair can be produced either by a steering mechanism (proscribed by sporting regulations) or by a differential application of force to the two handrims. To turn to the right, the athlete must either apply additional force to the left handrim or apply a force in the opposite direction (i.e., a braking force). If we assume that in a sprint race the athlete is applying maximum driving force to the handrim, it follows that the only method of instigating a corrective turn is to apply a submaximal force to the appropriate handrim. This means that a corrective turn must, of necessity, be associated with a loss of speed, such a loss being difficult if not impossible to regain in a short race. It is also true that the magnitude of the difference in force applied to each handrim to achieve a turn will be proportional to the length of the chair.

For the distance racers, the situation is very different. Because the normal mode of propulsion in distance events is submaximal, the athlete has the choice of either applying a greater force to one handrim or a lesser force to the other as a correction is made. Thus, the corrective action can be accompanied by a useful acceleration or a detrimental braking effect depending on whether the athlete decides to apply a harder propulsive force to the handrim on the inside of the curve or a braking force to the handrim on the outside of the curve. Given this ability to make corrections without a necessary loss of velocity, the distance athlete can afford the luxury of a more directionally stable chair. The sprinter, on the other

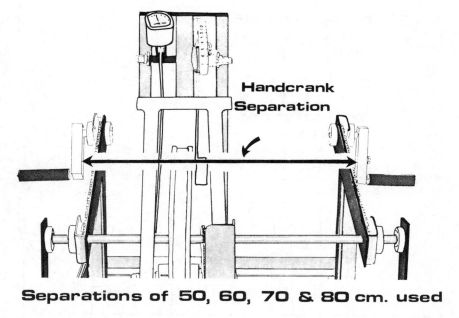

Handcrank Separation

Separations of 50, 60, 70 & 80 cm. used

Figure 2   Front view of wheelchair ergometer showing adjustable width between handcranks.

hand, must pay for his or her ability to change direction with minimal loss of velocity with constant vigilance over the direction of a less stable chair. To the best of my knowledge no empirical data are available to support either of these hypotheses—only time and film analysis will tell.

Laboratory or Track?

The application of the scientific method to work with special populations also runs into the problems associated with internal and external validity. The laboratory, with its emphasis on replication, control, and protocol, provides us with an accuracy of findings that it is difficult, if not impossible, to obtain in the real world. This high internal validity allows us to have confidence in the results we obtain, but it presents difficulties in interpretation and extrapolation to real life situations. An example from my own laboratory may make the problem clearer.

With a grant from the Canadian government's International Year of the Disabled Special Projects fund, Memorial University of Newfoundland built a special ergometer. It was called a wheelchair ergometer, but in reality it was a handcrank ergometer with the handcranks placed in the same position as the handrims on a typical wheelchair. The position of the ergometer seat was adjustable in the anterior-posterior plane, and the distance between the handcranks (analogous to the width of the wheelchair) was also adjustable (see Figure 2). A photoelectric device was

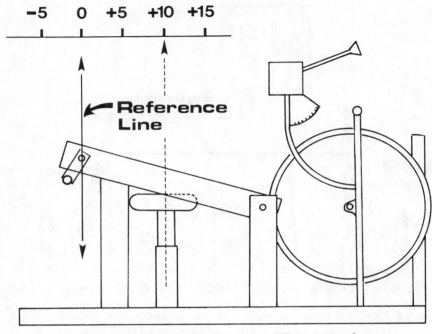

Seat Positions Tested

Seat shown in + 10 cm. Position.

Figure 3 Side view of wheelchair ergometer showing adjustable anterior-posterior seat position.

connected to three lights through a series of relays such that when the experimental subject cranked at 72 revolutions per min (plus or minus one half a revolution) the middle light was illuminated. The other lights indicated a rate of cranking that was either faster or slower. The handcranks were connected through a series of chains and cogs and made to drive a cut-down Monark bicycle ergometer (Higgs, 1982).

Respiratory gas analysis was used in conjunction with the mechanical measurement of work output to calculate the relative efficiency of cranking. Measurements were made on 10 subjects at each of five positions of anterior or posterior seat placement (see Figure 3). In a separate series of experiments, a single anterior or posterior seat position was used with four different handcrank separation widths (distance between handcranks). Figures 4 and 5 show the results of the two experiments, which indicated that gross efficiency decreased with increasing handcrank separation and that efficiency was at its highest when the seat center was positioned 5 cm to 10 cm behind the reference line through the center of the handcrank. What does this research tell us?

It tells us that if we want to build an efficient handcrank ergometer, we should build it as narrow as possible with the seat placed behind the

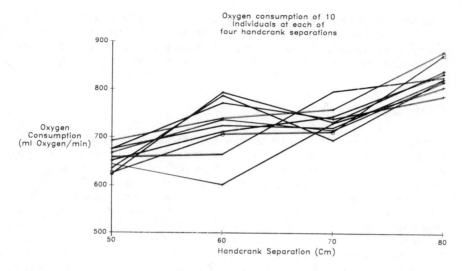

Figure 4 Oxygen consumption versus handcrank separation for 10 subjects.

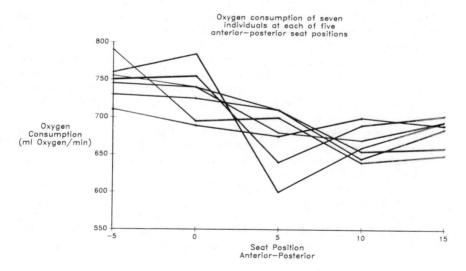

Figure 5 Oxygen consumption versus anterior-posterior seat position for 10 subjects.

midline of the cranks. In reality it tells us nothing about how to design or build efficient wheelchairs. It provides clues to be sure, but with all its high internal validity, its low external validity means that we can apply the results to only the narrowest range of circumstances. It should, however, be noted that when such laboratory results support the data from field research, our confidence in both sets of data is considerably enhanced.

In contrast, the analysis of film taken outside the laboratory gains in veracity what is lost through lack of control. It tells a story of what is, not of what is manipulated. Its internal validity can never approach that of the experimental situation, but its external validity is beyond reproach.

Conclusion

In the application of the scientific method to research with special populations, several problems must be addressed. Should we strive for high internal validity under the controlled conditions of the laboratory, or should we go out into the real world and collect "messy" data with all its imperfections—but data, nonetheless, that can be relied upon to reflect what is real? Should we observe low numbers of each type and category of disability in the sure knowledge that "real" and important knowledge is going to be lost in a deluge of nonsignificant findings, or should we lump categories together to give us the numbers we need to identify moderate but meaningful statistical differences—differences that by the nature of the lumping process are probably more robust and generally applicable than those identified through intense observation of subcategories?

For a clear picture of our subject matter it is obvious that both real world and laboratory investigations are required. They tell different but complementary stories about the world in which we operate. When the stories agree, we have greater faith in our research; when they disagree, we are led to new avenues of approach, new lines of thought, or new techniques for investigation. Both broadly and narrowly focused investigations are required. No one study or line of studies can possibly hope to answer all of the questions.

The danger, however, is that individuals or groups will see different approaches to research only through the window of their own background. The laboratory researcher often sees only the lack of controls exercised in the real world; the observer often notes only the artificial constraints imposed upon laboratory research.

The world is more complex than most of us care to believe. Therefore, in the spirit of true scientists, let us all be critical (in the nonperjorative sense of the word) of the limitations of those studies presented to us, but also let us accept the contribution each can uniquely make to the total understanding of our field.

References

Higgs, C. (1982). *Report on the construction and use of an adjustable wheelchair ergometer with emphasis on oxygen consumption at various chair configurations for a fixed workload* (Final Report, Grant Number 1098). Ottawa: Fitness and Amateur Sport.

Higgs, C. (1983). An analysis of racing wheelchairs used at the 1980 Olympic Games for the Disabled. *Research Quarterly for Exercise and Sport*, **54**(3), 229-233.

Higgs, C. (1986). Propulsion of racing wheelchairs. In C. Sherrill (Ed.), *Sport and disabled athletes* (The 1984 Olympic Scientific Congress Proceedings, Vol. 9, pp. 165-172). Champaign, IL: Human Kinetics.

Levin, J. R. (1975). Determining sample size for planned and post-hoc analysis of variance comparisons. *Journal of Educational Measurement*, **12**(2), 99-109.

Motor Soccer and the Wheelchair Bumper

Lloyd W. Cowin
Michael D. O'Riain
Jacques Sibille
Gilbert Layeux

Leisure is becoming more and more important as people adapt to living in a rapidly changing society. Unemployment, job sharing, and part-time jobs are all on the rise. Together with greater automation in the home, these factors have given people much more free time. These societal changes affect many—young and old, male and female, able-bodied and disabled individuals.

In the last decade we have seen a great increase in the variety of activities with which people become involved in their leisure time. This is especially true in the case of sports for physically disabled individuals. However, for those individuals who are so physically challenged that they require the use of an electric wheelchair, there are not as many options. The few recreational activities in which they can become involved are sedentary and may not meet their needs if excitement and action are what they desire. Competition and high-action leisure pursuits are missing for them. Given that nearly all people are faced with the challenges of a changing society, this lack of leisure opportunities for the most physically disabled can be of substantial consequence. Participation by people who use electric wheelchairs in a team sport such as motor soccer can meet some of these very important needs.

Development of Motor Soccer

Motor soccer was developed simultaneously but independently by the British Columbia division of the Canadian Wheelchair Sports Association. Motor soccer, in its developed form, is described by Cowin, Sibille, and O'Riain (1984). The object of the game is to push the ball across the opposing team's goal line. In Ottawa the sport was initially played with some adaptations from Ringette (a sport for women similar to ice hockey). A basketball court was divided into zones with certain players restricted to particular zones on the court. However, the zones made the sport fairly slow and as a result a number of recommendations were made by the participants. They felt a free-flowing game would be more exciting. They were looking for more action in the sport. The restrictive zones were eliminated, and all players were given access to the entire court. This greatly increased speed and action in the game but brought about some new problems. Collisions became more frequent and more severe. Implementing a "no charging" rule greatly reduced the number and severity of collisions, but some accidental contact still occurred. The greatest danger was injury to the feet of the players. Another difficulty was the irreparable damage to the ball during collisions. A beach ball was initially used because of its light weight. However, because of the fragile skin, balls were being destroyed quickly. More durable but smaller balls were used, but these often rolled under the wheelchair's footrests, causing the wheelchair to tip backward.

An investigation to find a suitable ball for the sport was undertaken. After a lengthy search, the "Gymnastik" ball (60 cm in diameter) was purchased because of its light weight, durable skin, and large size. This ball allows for easier passing, withstands collisions, and is large enough not to become lodged under the wheelchair.

To overcome the foot injury problem, the Rehabilitation Engineering Department at the Royal Ottawa Regional Rehabilitation Centre was approached to design some mode of foot protection. A wheelchair bumper, which is described in detail in Sibille, Layeux, and O'Riain (1984), was designed to fit on almost any wheelchair and safeguard the user's feet in a collision. Because of its design, the bumper is also useful for pushing the ball.

In designing the bumper, four requirements were set down: The bumper should fit on virtually all wheelchairs without modification; height and width should be such that the user's feet are protected in a collision with another wheelchair; the bumper should not shatter on impact; and the attachment to the wheelchair should be rigid and strong enough so that the bumper will not be twisted or torn away in a collision.

Figure 1 shows a bumper designed to meet all of the above criteria. The main part was vacuum-formed from 4.75-mm (3/16-in.) high-density polyethylene (1). The bumper is fixed to the footrest of the wheelchair (2) by three tubes (3 and 4) attached together by the sliding block (5). Tube 3 is fixed to the bumper itself while the other two tubes (4) are fixed to the sliding block (5) and to the wheelchair footrest (2). Unscrewing the thumbscrews (6) unlocks the sliding blocks from tube 3 for the adjustment of the distance between the other two tubes (4) as well as the angle of the bumper (1). When adjusted, the thumbscrews are tightened and the whole assembly locks together.

The bumper is shaped so that it will envelop the feet as much as possible without restricting transfers to and from the wheelchair (Figure 2). To connect the bumper to a wheelchair, one has only to remove the small rubber tips from the footrests, slide on the bumper, and fix it to the wheelchair by the same metal screws that hold the rubber tips. Since the bumper is 15 cm (6 in.) high, a 10-cm (4-in.) height difference between two bumpers will still protect the users in a head-on collision.

The bumper was designed to withstand a 5-m/s impact when attached to a 150-kg electric wheelchair ridden by an 80-kg user. Impact tests were

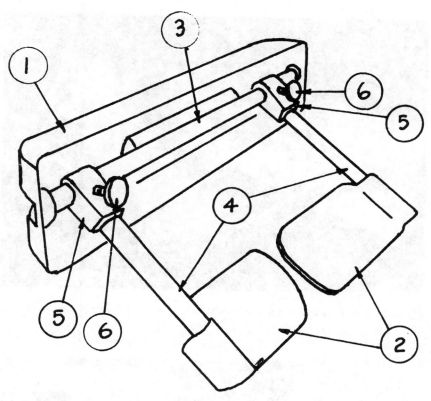

Figure 1   Diagram of a bumper.

carried out using a standard wheelchair loaded with sandbags to simulate the appropriate weight. The wheelchair was driven into a concrete wall at a clocked velocity of 5 m/s. There was no damage to the bumper other than scratches on the plastic surface, although the wheelchair suffered some structural damage. Thus the users must be aware that the impact resistance of their wheelchairs may be less than that of the bumper.

Description of Motor Soccer

Motor soccer, which is shown being played in Figure 3, is a team sport for men and women of all ages. It is played on a basketball court with four members from each team playing at any one time. As mentioned in the previous section, the object of the game is to use the wheelchair to propel the ball over the opponents' goal line, which is 3 m wide.

The game is made up of two 30-min halves with a 10-min halftime break. A coin toss determines which team is to start play with the ball at center court. When a goal is scored (Figure 4) the opposing team resumes play

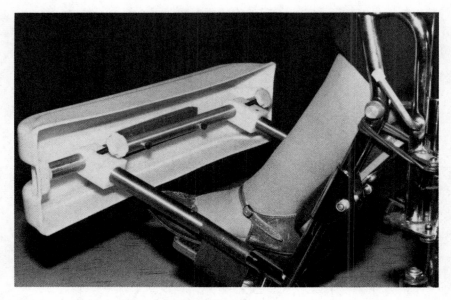

Figure 2 A bumper attached to a wheelchair.

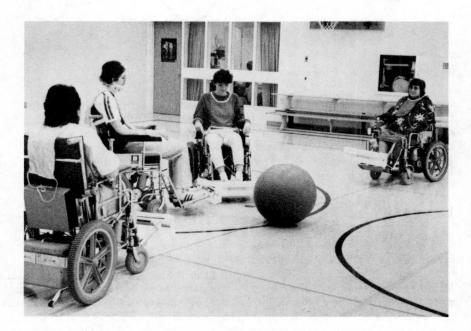

Figure 3 The sport of motor soccer being played.

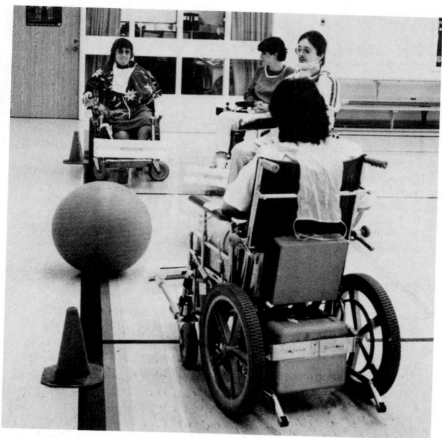

Figure 4 Scoring a goal.

at center court. At no time is any player allowed to use the arms or hands to play the ball. Possession of the ball is awarded to the other team if such an infraction occurs. If the ball is lodged between two opponents so that it is immovable for 3 s, it is considered a dead ball and the play is stopped. The play is resumed with a face-off between the two players. If any player causes the ball to go out-of-bounds, the opposing team is awarded possession at the point where the ball left the playing area. Although incidental contact between wheelchairs is allowed, there is a 2-min penalty given to any player who charges another with his wheelchair, either accidentally or intentionally.

The sport has been most popular in British Columbia, where teams from Vancouver and Victoria have been competing regularly since 1981. Inquiries about the game have been made to the British Columbia group from as far away as Denmark. Inquiries about starting a team in Kitchener, Ontario, have reached Ottawa, as have requests to purchase the bumpers.

Discussion

People who require the use of electric wheelchairs tend to be more restricted in the use of their leisure time. Sedentary activities are generally the norm. For those who were used to more exciting recreational pursuits prior to their injury or those who enjoy more active sports, the options are very limited.

Many people enjoy competition and the feeling that they are part of a team. The camaraderie and social events associated with belonging to a team can also be very satisfying. The sport of motor soccer opens up this vista to persons confined to electric wheelchairs.

The availability of the wheelchair bumper ensures a safer environment for participation. It allows the game to be played faster and more openly without concern for foot safety. This helps keep the action and excitement high.

The potential for development of the sport is there. What is required is the desire and will of the participants to develop that potential.

References

Cowin, L. W., Sibille, J., & O'Riain, M. D. (1984). Motor soccer—The electric connection. *Sports 'N Spokes,* **10**(4), 43-44.

Sibille, J., Layeux, G., & O'Riain, M. D. (1984). Foot shields for wheelchairs. *Archives of Physical Medicine and Rehabilitation,* **65**, 101-102.

Sport for All: Sailing Is Fun

Finn Richard Roeren

Norway, with a population of about 4 million, is a fairly well-organized community in that roughly 80% of the population are members of one or more organizations. Among them, the Norwegian Confederation of Sports with 1.5 million is by far the largest and thus carries much weight in everyday life. The confederation is a nonparty political, independent movement, although to a great extent it is dependent upon economic support from central and local authorities.

The Norwegian Yachting Association is part of this umbrella organization, with 130 yacht clubs and about 35,000 members. Like most national sailing associations, the Norwegian Yachting Association is a member of the important International Yacht Racing Union headquartered in London.

During the period 1960–1970, a new political school of thought emerged in Norway respecting the status of all disabled in the community. In essence, the Confederation of Sports noticed a slowly growing political will to concentrate more upon the individual than upon the handicap. Integration into the local society was a main theme. Adjustments of already existing schools and organizations, such as local sport clubs, suddenly were very much in the picture. Furthermore, the Confederation of Sports studied with great interest the astonishing news coming from the Beitostølen Health Sport Center to the effect that physical activity is good medicine for the disabled to enhance or regain self-confidence.

Based mainly on this background, at its 1976 convention, the confederation proclaimed all sport clubs open to the handicapped so that sport could be for all.

A Practical Course in Sailing for the Handicapped

The following year, 1977, the Bærum Yacht Club outside Oslo decided to do just that. Having no experience in training disabled individuals, the club started a research program that lasted about 3 years. During that time the club was encouraged upon learning that several European countries as well as the United States and Canada had also started to promote sailing for the disabled.

In 1980 the Bærum Yacht Club formed a teaching committee of 11, some of them disabled, with sailing experience. Two 6-week courses in practical training were arranged that year on a trial basis. About 50 individuals aged from 10 to 65 took part. Earmarked for this special purpose, the yacht club bought two ordinary sailboats of Norwegian make, 5.5 m long with a fixed keel and room in the cockpit for one trainer and two to three trainees.

For the very first time, individuals with polio, cerebral palsy, spina bifida, spinal cord paralysis, multiple sclerosis, muscular dystrophy, deafness, and visual handicaps met at an ordinary yacht club. I dare say that all enjoyed it right from the start. Why? Simply because the trainers did not relate to the trainees from a feeling of pity but instead had a deep respect for their courage in learning to sail. Thus they all soon acquired the exciting feeling of being able to conquer the sea together with true friends in the same boat—in a double sense. Right from the outset they emphasized that loss of one faculty just sharpens another. In short, to handle a sailing boat with fixed keel requires 80% sitting still and feeling free while observing and enjoying life. Suddenly, conquering the blue sea seemed within reach of the handicapped.

Only small adjustments had to be made to the sailboats, like special chairs on transverse rails used for trainees with balance problems. Somewhat broader twarts with cushions of foam rubber with closed cells helped wheelchair users with lack of seat musculature to feel comfortable. To aid the blind and poorly sighted, an audio compass of British make was used.

The following year two more boats with fixed keel were bought. In addition, a sailboard course for deaf youngsters was arranged, and it also proved to be a success. This goes to show that nothing is impossible, although such progress takes a bit more time and effort.

Good planning was crucial to the success of these programs. We found that the availability of nearby parking places was essential. Life jackets, of course, were worn when entering the floating stand. Alongside mooring was necessary in most cases, and from time to time a manually driven hydraulic crane was necessary to get a heavy person safely on board.

The basic idea of the sailing course has been to convince people that a handicap of some sort is no barrier to learning to handle a boat alone or with a crew. I am happy to say that we have succeeded so far and look to the future with optimism.

Further Advances in Sailing for the Handicapped

In 1983, the Norwegian Yachting Association formed a committee called Sailing with the Disabled with its primary task to inform and give assistance to yacht clubs and others interested in physical activities among the disabled. To advance new ideas, of course, is always a time-consuming commitment. There are many physical obstacles as well as human feelings to be overcome. However, it has been our experience that there is a sound solution to the most intricate of problems, although it has sometimes been necessary to apply a mixture of optimism, fantasy, and—most of all—tenacity.

On this sound basis, the committee is slowly making progress both in Norway as well as abroad. Last autumn the International Sport Organization for the Disabled (ISOD) approached the Norwegian Yachting Association requesting a full report on its experiences to date. Having perused all pertinent details of this report, it was decided in Geneva that sailing be encouraged as a new summer sport for all disabled. It goes without saying that this decision opens new and exciting aspects in the sport. No doubt this means new life qualities will be brought into the yachting world.

To revert once more to Norway, under the auspices of the yachting association in the summer of 1984 the committee tried out the possibility of engaging amputees on sailboards and tandem sailboards for the blind or poorly sighted. Once more we saw exciting results. On the tandem sailboard, from the aft position the sighted trainer was able to steer and simultaneously to instruct the blind trainee in front. With some training they were both able to navigate the board safely to their own great satisfaction and, of course, much to the surprise of onlookers.

In another development, we have been able to include blind persons in regatta crews. To guide the blind or poorly sighted person in a crew during a regatta on a so-called Olympic course, small watertight radio transmitters with different signals are placed on top of the three buoys to be passed. By listening to the signals picked up by receivers, the blind crewmember gets a good idea of the direction, although the sighted crewmember is mainly responsible for the safe navigation. This is only one of many examples of adaptation possible with the use of modern technology.

To conclude this short review on sailing with the disabled, the underlying idea has been to integrate the handicapped into this sport mainly by using existing groups like local yacht clubs. To form special clubs for disabled yachters we feel is not the right policy. I mention this because in some countries I have noted such a tendency. I hope that future cooperation between the International Yacht Racing Union and the umbrella organization of the four or five international sport organizations for the disabled, The International Co-Ordinating Committee of World Sports Organizations for the Disabled (ICC), will correct this unfortunate tendency.

I have tried to touch upon only the main aspects of our work. Nevertheless, I sincerely hope I have presented a clear picture of where we stand today and that our final aim above all will be full integration. It is my firm belief that international cooperation will lead us all in the right direction.

Navigare necesse est, vivere non est.

Horseback Riding: The Therapeutic Sport

Marcee Rosenzweig

> *I saw a child who couldn't walk*
> *sit on a horse, laugh and talk*
> *then ride it through a field of daisies*
> *and yet he could not walk unaided.*
> *I saw a child, no legs below*
> *sit on a horse, and make it go,*
> *through woods of green*
> *and places he had never been*
> *to sit and stare,*
> *except from a chair.*
> *I saw a child who could only crawl*
> *mount a horse and sit up tall.*
> *Put it through degrees of paces*
> *and laugh at the wonder on our faces.*
> *I saw a child born into strife*
> *take up and hold the reins of life*
> *and that same child, I heard him say*
> *Thank God for showing me the way. . . .*
>
> *John Anthony Davies**

Historic literature dating back to the 17th century relates evidence of horseback riding prescribed as treatment for diseases such as gout and neurological paralysis (Bain, 1965; Baumann, n.d.). However, in 1952 when Liz Hartel won the silver medal in the equestrian events at the Helsinki Olympic Games there was a renewed interest in horseback riding as a sport for the disabled. Hartel was a victim of polio. Both her legs were partially paralyzed, and she could only walk a few steps on crutches. Yet she was able to compete against her able-bodied peers. Those in the audience who were unaware of her disability did not know she was a handicapped individual (Riding for the Disabled Association, 1976).

Having been inspired and encouraged by Hartel's success, a group of pioneers in England began to explore the possibility of horseback riding for all types of handicaps, especially the victims of the polio epidemic. This group eventually evolved into the Riding for the Disabled Association in the United Kingdom.

Simultaneously, horseback riding for the disabled was gaining widespread acceptance throughout Europe. Major centers and facilities were

*From *Reins of Life: Instructional and Informative Manual on Riding for the Disabled* by J. A. Davies, 1967, London: J. A. Allen. Copyright 1967 by John Anthony Davies. Reprinted by permission.

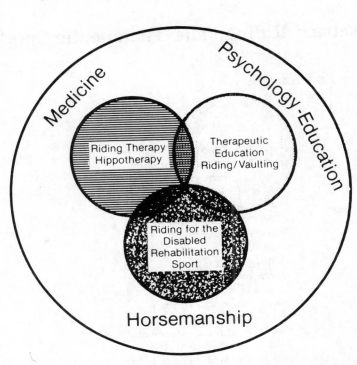

Figure 1   Schematic illustration of the various realms of therapeutic riding. *Note.* From *Therapeutic Riding Medicine Education Sports* (p. 11) by W. Heipertz, C. Heipertz-Hengst, A. Korger, and W. Kuprian, 1977, Stuttgart, Germany: Franckh'sche Verlagshandlung. Copyright 1977. Reprinted by permission.

evolving in Germany and Switzerland. After serious injuries or illnesses, experienced riders summoned up enough courage to resume an old hobby. With the observation that physical impairments showed remarkable recovery, greater interest was taken in the therapeutic value of horseback riding. Centers devoted to rehabilitation through the use of horses began to emerge in Germany in the early 1970s. Today riding instructors and physical therapists employed in these centers must have specialized training and certification. Therapeutic riding has become an accepted form of treatment for orthopedic, neurological, psychiatric, cardiopulmonary, and circulatory disorders (Heipertz, Heipertz-Hengst, Kroger, & Kuprian, 1977).

In the late 1960s facilities for riding for the disabled were established in Canada and the United States. For many years the programs were fashioned after those founded in England. Initially, the emphasis was on teaching functional riding skills, but soon the physical and psychological improvements were recognized as the major benefits.

For example, in Toronto, the Community Association for Riding for the Disabled (CARD) was founded in 1968. The late Dr. Reginald Renault, a doctor of rehabilitation medicine, teamed up with riding instructor Joseph Bauer, a physical therapist, a hemiplegic patient, and a borrowed horse for the purpose of developing a maintenance program following hospital discharge. In the beginning the riding instructor taught functional riding skills with limited therapeutic input. However, as the physical and psychological benefits gained recognition, therapists became an integral part of the teaching team with the assistance of 9 riding instructors, 6 specialized therapists, and 14 well-trained horses. Today CARD provides riding classes for 200 riders from age 2 to 72 years old.

Over the past 5 years therapists with horseback riding knowledge have begun to take an interest in the value of the horse's movement as a therapeutic modality. Study of German organization and methodology has led to the formation of therapeutic riding programs in North America. Professionals from the fields of physical and occupational therapy, special education, speech therapy, psychology, adapted physical education, therapeutic recreation, and gymnastics have all contributed their own expertise and perspective to the growth of riding for the disabled on this continent (Glasow, 1984a).

With an ever increasing knowledge and understanding of the treatment of physical, emotional, and developmental handicaps, there has been a great diversification in the field of riding for the disabled. North American riding programs have utilized the basic schematic divisions that have already been developed in Switzerland and Germany. These terms are represented pictorially in Figure 1 (Heipertz et al., 1977).

Hippotherapy

Hippotherapy literally means "treatment with the help of the horse." It is a therapeutic treatment using the three-dimensional swinging motion of the horse's gait to elicit automatic reactions from the rider. The client sits on a bareback pad using a vaulting surcingle. He or she in no way influences the horse. Hippotherapy must be applied by a therapist with training in the specific techniques that are part of the treatment program. When administered properly it can be used to mobilize the pelvis, lumbar spine, and hip joints, normalize muscle tone, develop equilibrium and righting reactions, and improve head and trunk control. The patient also receives tactile, proprioceptive, and vestibular input from the horse's movement (Glasow, 1984a, 1984b; Heipertz et al., 1977).

The horse is used as a physiotherapeutic treatment modality for patients with central nervous system deficits (e.g., cerebral palsy, multiple sclerosis, head trauma, and stroke) and spinal disorders (e.g., spina bifida, spinal cord injury, and scoliosis).

Riding Therapy

Riding therapy is a type of therapy that uses the horse's movement to achieve specific goals. Unlike hippotherapy, the rider actively performs exercises on the horse's back while responding passively to its gait. The exercises are adapted for the individual's needs. They should be selected, instructed, and supervised by a therapist. The goals of this type of program are muscle stretching, relaxation, and strengthening and improved balance, coordination, and movement patterns. Patients suffering from central nervous system deficits, amputations, spinal disorders, sensorimotor dysfunction, and circulatory diseases benefit from riding therapy (Glasow, 1984a; Heipertz et al., 1977).

Psychologists have been successful in using riding therapy with emotionally disturbed or autistic children, utilizing animal bonding as a basis for treatment (Heipertz et al., 1977).

For riding therapy the rider begins using a bareback pad and vaulting surcingle. Part of the exercise routine may involve vaulting techniques that progress through various developmental sequences. Exercises may also be performed facing backward on the horse. As the rider's ability improves there can be progress to a saddle and perhaps a sports riding program.

Therapeutic Education

Riding/Vaulting

Riding and vaulting for therapeutic education is called *remedial riding*. Not only are functional riding skills taught, but also gymnastic exercises are performed on the horse's back in groups of up to six. Clients with physical, emotional, developmental, and learning disabilities participate in this type of program. In Germany there has been an overwhelming success in reeducating behaviorally disturbed children using remedial vaulting (Heipertz et al., 1977). The objectives of remedial riding are to reduce anxiety levels, develop trust, increase self-esteem, improve concentration, develop the sensorimotor system, learn to adapt to others, and encourage friendships (Glasow, 1984a; Heipertz et al., 1977).

Similar to adapted physical education, riding or vaulting is adapted to the individual needs of each child. Various remedial approaches are used to achieve educational, behavioral, psychological, and physical goals (Glasow, 1984a; Heipertz et al., 1977).

The use of horses in therapeutic treatment and reeducation is unique. Many disabled children and adults suffering from chronic conditions are often "therapy tired." Sometimes they reject conventional physical therapy (Heipertz et al., 1977). However, the horse and the activity of horseback riding are the motivators that can redevelop an interest in regular exercise treatment. Motivation is extremely important in maintaining the cooperation of the patient. If the client is not willing to succeed, there is no treatment that can help.

Another factor remains of prime importance to therapeutic riding. The movement of the horse and its three-dimensional effect on the pelvis cannot be simulated by any other apparatus. This movement moves the rider's pelvic girdle in a fashion similar to normal gait. The motion is both symmetric and rhythmic and can be repeated for a prolonged period of time. In approximately 75% of the clientele seen at CARD there is some form of disability that blocks symmetric, rhythmic input to the pelvis. Without the experience of this quality of movement equilibrium reactions cannot develop (Baumann, 1979).

Recently, a new patient at CARD, whose disability included abnormal tone and weakness on one side of his body, described to his therapist the wonderful sensations he felt experiencing rhythmical movement once again. A young girl suffering from spina bifida was having great difficulty learning to walk. However, after 5 days of horseback riding, the movement of her pelvis and thus her gait improved dramatically. There are many equally exciting stories of the therapeutic progress that can be made through horseback riding.

Rehabilitation Sport

After an extended period of time in a therapeutic riding program many children and adults progress to riding as a sport for the disabled. Often handicapped clients come into the program merely interested in learning functional riding skills. Sometimes they are looking for an activity to help maintain their level of function while coping with a chronic illness.

In a sports riding program the emphasis is on learning and applying functional riding skills with the least amount of adaptation possible (Glasow, 1984a). Stable management and horse care are an integral part of each lesson.

One of the major benefits of weekly horseback riding classes is that handicapped riders are exposed to regular physical exercise. All too often disabled people have spent years confined with little or no physical activity. With the emphasis society places on fitness, participants in riding programs feel better both physically and psychologically.

Other physical improvements have been observed in balance and equilibrium reactions, coordination of upper and lower extremities, relaxation of tight muscles, head and trunk control, and postural tone (Hoskin, Erdman, Bream, & MacAvay, 1974). The position of the pelvis required for a good riding seat is the neutral position of the pelvis required for proper body alignment.

There are many cognitive benefits from sports riding. For dressage, riders must learn shapes and sizes of figures and alphabet letters. They must also develop laterality, directionality, motor planning, and spatial awareness. For jumping or hunting they must develop depth and height perception. Horses often open a new world of reading, writing, and oral dissertation subjects for school-aged children. Learning the parts of the horse and the tack used for riding helps to develop short- and long-term memory.

The psychological benefits of this type of program can be the most important to many disabled riders. First, they are participating in a risk sport.

Psychologists describe a primal need for risk taking. The environment is controlled, yet the risk still exists (Rosenthal, 1975). Next, there is the feeling of self-respect and personal satisfaction from being mounted on a horse. The riders perceive these sensations as they view themselves in the mirrors surrounding the arena. Many disabled riders cannot be distinguished from able-bodied riders. Riding a horse also allows handicapped people to travel in places that are otherwise inaccessible (Heipertz et al., 1977). A young woman who had ridden in CARD's arena all winter came back from her first spring trail ride full of enthusiasm. She was so excited to move among the trees and smell the fresh blooms for the first time in 3 years. Equally important, acquiring a very specialized skill helps to develop self-esteem. The steps to success can be graded small enough to avoid failure. Children who have great difficulty in touching people or objects learn tactonics through stroking horses (Heipertz et al., 1977). Finally, human-animal bonding can take place, allowing clients to interact in a meaningful relationship (Mayberry, 1978).

There are also many social benefits from horseback riding. Interaction with peers is important to promote competitiveness. Interaction with volunteers is important to promote role modeling. It has been found that totally unsociable, emotionally disturbed children will transfer the relationship they develop with the horse to human relationships (Heipertz et al., 1977).

Competition is a major aspect of sports riding (Mayberry, 1978). There are events in dressage, jumping, cross country, and driving. These contests can be on a local, provincial, national, and international level. Riders compete against others with similar abilities. For handicapped individuals who have few other opportunities for competition, their scope of experience and opportunity can be greatly extended. Often they must travel to new and exciting places. Many teenage riders have never been away from their parents. Most important, they must learn to cope with success and defeat.

The importance of stable management and horse care skills cannot be overlooked. Physically, the riders benefit from the activity and exertion required in preparing the horse for riding, putting the horse and all its tack away after riding, and cleaning up the barn at the completion of the lesson. Socially, the riders learn to care for another being and learn to take responsibility for that care. Cognitively, math skills can be improved through lessons based on the concepts of measuring hay and grain for feeding. The skills that can be taught in the barn are as extensive as those that can be taught in the riding arena.

Conclusions

There is therapeutic value in each of the different categories of horseback riding. Recognition of these benefits by the medical profession and the successes experienced by participants have contributed to a general public awareness of these programs. The challenge of the future lies in expanding and developing facilities and training personnel to cope with the demand for horseback riding, the therapeutic sport.

References

Bain, A. (1965). Pony riding for the disabled. *Physical Therapy,* **51**, 263-265.

Baumann, J. U. (1979). Therapeutic exercise on horseback for children with neurogenic disorders of movement. Basel, Switzerland: Neuro-orthopædic Unit.

Glasow, B. (1984a). *Divisions of horseback riding for the disabled: A need for semantics.* New York: Warwick.

Glasow, B. (1984b). *Hippotherapy: The horse as a therapeutic modality.* New York: Warwick.

Heipertz, W., Heipertz-Hengst, C., Kroger, A., & Kuprian, W. (1977). *Therapeutisches Reiten* [Therapeutic riding]. Stuttgart, Germany: Franckh'sche Verlagshandlung.

Hoskin, M., Erdman, W., Bream, J., & MacAvay, C. (1974). Therapeutic horseback riding for the handicapped. *Archives of Physical Medicine and Rehabilitation,* **55**, 473-474.

Mayberry, R. (1978). The mystique of the horse is strong medicine: Riding as therapeutic recreation. *Rehabilitation Literature,* **39**, 192-196.

Riding for the Disabled Association. (1976). *The handbook of the Riding for the Disabled Association.* Kenilworth, Warwickshire: Author.

Rosenthal, S. (1975). Risk exercise and the physically handicapped. *Rehabilitation Literature,* **36**, 144-149.

A Study of Wheelchair Basketball Skills

J. O. C. Vanlerberghe
K. Slock

We are convinced that many excellent tests exist that have been used to measure particular basketball skills; however, they were developed for the able-bodied basketball player. Therefore, we tried to develop basketball tests for wheelchair athletes, adapting test situations from Pauwels (1979) and applying biomechanics in wheelchair basketball described by Vanlerberghe (1964). Brasile (1984) tried to measure basketball skills of wheelchair athletes, but his investigation resulted only in a T-score system for practical use.

We used six tests that measured skills in shooting, dribbling, and passing the ball as set out below.

- Shooting: (a) shot under the basket, rebound—to measure accuracy, and (b) dribbling, shot and rebound—to measure speed and accuracy
- Dribbling: (a) obstacle dribble—to measure dribble ability, and (b) dribble around the wheelchair—to measure ball skills and dribbling skill
- Passing: (a) speed pass—to measure speed of passing the ball, and (b) pass for distance—to measure strength when throwing the ball as far as possible

The principal aim of our tests was to determine the reliability and validity of tests by means of a test-retest system (different trials) in order to focus on each athlete's weaknesses or strengths.

After pretest sessions, we omitted two tests—the pass for accuracy and free throws. In the first test we didn't find any discrepancy between good and bad players, and the results of the second test were not similar at all. Milloen (1977) obtained the same data when testing able-bodied players, and other investigations resulted in a reliability coefficient between .42 and .69.

Procedure

Tests were done between November 1982 and January 1983. Thirty wheelchair basketball players from four different sporting clubs were tested. There were 9 players from one club and 8, 7, and 6 players from the others, respectively. The sample was made up of 12 Class III athletes, 7 Class II athletes, and 11 Class I athletes. In all tests, the athletes were encouraged to score as high as possible.

Description of the Tests

Shot under the basket, rebound (Figure 1).   The subject starts facing the basket from any point in the 5-s area. Any method of shooting is permitted, and the players must get their own rebounds. If they wish to move closer after retrieving a ball, they must do so adhering to the ISMFF dribbling rule. Each player was allowed three trials, and the total number of baskets made within 30 s was counted.

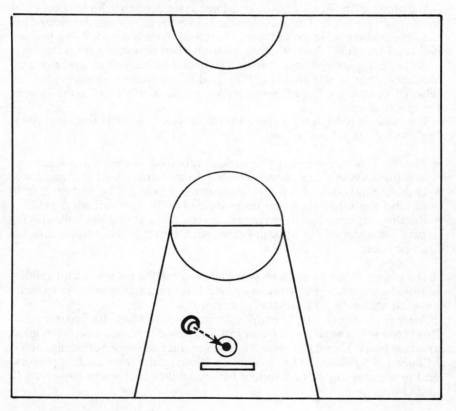

Figure 1 Shot, rebound.

Dribble, shot, and rebound (Figure 2).   The subjects start facing the basket from a point at foul line level and 450 cm from the center of foul line and must adhere to the ISMFF dribble rule and get their own rebounds. Three trials were allowed, and both the time and the number of successful baskets were counted.

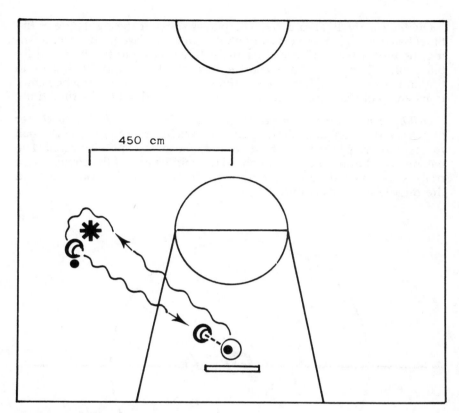

Figure 2 Dribble, shot, and rebound.

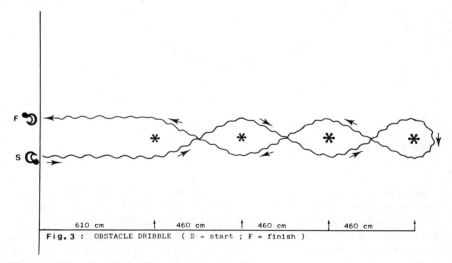

Fig. 3 : OBSTACLE DRIBBLE (S = start ; F = finish)

Figure 3 Obstacle dribble (S = start; F = finish).

Obstacle dribble (Figure 3).   The player starts at the right side of the first obstacle and maneuvers through the course as fast as possible, pushing the wheelchair and dribbling the ball, adhering to the ISMFF dribbling rules. Three trials were allowed by each player, and the time to do the course was noted. But each time the player, ball, or wheelchair touched an obstacle, one additional second was added to the final time.

Dribble around the wheelchair (Figure 4).   The athlete sits in the center of a circle (0 = 200 cm). During 20 s the player tries to dribble the ball from the right side to the left side of the wheelchair and vice versa. The ball must be bounced upon or behind the middle line of the circle. Three trials were allowed, and the number of balls bounced upon or behind the middle line was counted.

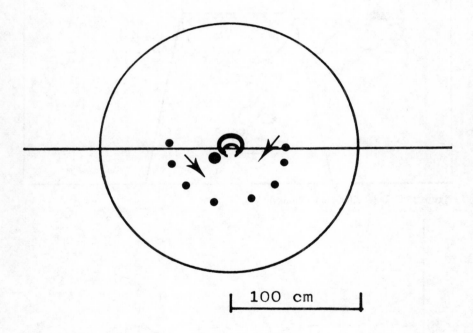

Figure 4 Dribble around the wheelchair.

Speed pass (Figure 5).   The subject places the wheelchair so that the front casters are behind a line that is 200 cm from the wall. The player must pass the ball to the wall and catch it on the rebound in the air as many times as possible within a 15-s time frame. The chest pass is required. Six trials were allowed. Between each trial a 1-min rest period was permitted. One point was scored for each successful completion.

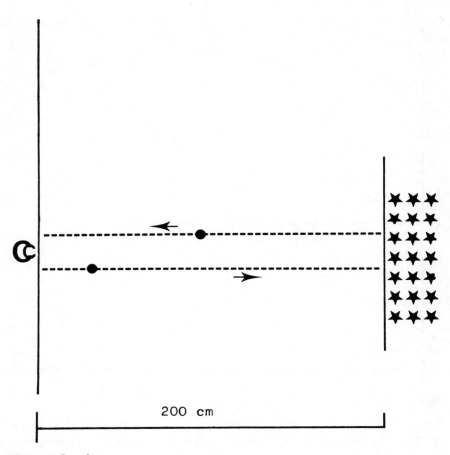

Figure 5 Speed pass.

Pass for distance (Figure 6).   The player places the wheelchair so that the front casters are behind the end line of the field. Using the chest pass, the player tries to pass the ball as far as possible. Six trials were permitted, and each trial was measured and recorded.

Test Administration Hints

1. Directions must be read and a demonstration of the activity must be given to the players as a group prior to their trials.
2. Areas have to be marked off clearly prior to the testing.
3. A whistle to start each trial is necessary.
4. The athlete's score must be counted loud enough so that it can be heard clearly.
5. Subjects have to be alternated to allow for a break between trials.

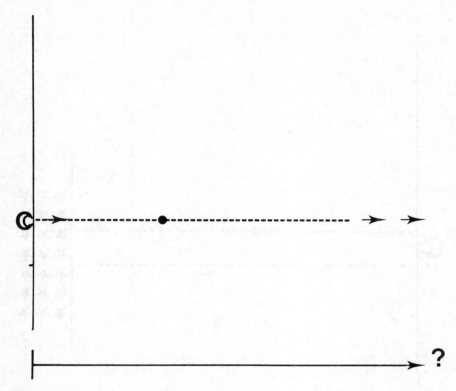

Figure 6   Pass for distance.

6. The following equipment must be available: basketballs, stopwatches, wheelchairs, tape measure, masking tape or chalk, and a layout with dimensions of each test situation.

Procedure of Testing Reliability and Validity of Tests

Reliability

We calculated an intraclass correlation coefficient following a two-way analysis of variance, as shown by Safrit (1973); Safrit, Atwater, Baumgartner, and West (1976); and Guilford and Fruchter (1973). In this way we were able to know three variances (i.e., variance between athletes, variance between trials, and variance of interaction).

F-values make it possible to test hypotheses at the 95% confidence level, H_o: each player has the same average result as against H_1: not all the players have the same results, and H_o: the trials all have the same average test results as against H_1: not all trials have the same average test results.

The intraclass correlation coefficient gives us an idea of the reliability of the tests, if all trials are done on the same day. A reliability coefficient of .70 in the case of sporting skill tests may be considered sufficient (Kühn & Heiny, 1974).

Validity

In order to have a criterion for validity measurements of our testing system, we used Mathews's method (1973). Each coach was asked to give two evaluations about his basketball players. These evaluations helped the authors to evaluate the coaches' knowledge of the athletes with whom they worked.

The first evaluation of basketball skills (dribble, shot, pass) concerned the use of a very well drafted description of all elements in these skills. A 5-point scoring scale was used.

A few weeks later each player in the team was ordered by the coach in a rank order to do the three skills. All values of these evaluations were added, and a new rank order was established.

We calculated the Spearman's rank correlation coefficient to know the association between both evaluation systems. If the judgment of the coach is similar, then there must be a high value of the rank correlation coefficient. Barrow and McGee (1968) used the following limits in determining validity: > .85 = excellent validity; .80 to .84 = very good; .75 to .79 = good; .70 to .74 = acceptable validity; and between .65 to .69 = doubtful validity. We used statistical analysis following Guilford and Fruchter (1973) and Siegel (1956).

Results and Discussion

As there are many different class statuses of athletes, it was of interest to know to what extent the degree of handicap really had an influence on wheelchair basketball. In all tests, Class III athletes had the best results and Class I players, the worst (Table 1). As expected, the variances among players were significant, whereas this was not the case among the different trials. We found the best correlation coefficients in "obstacle dribble," "dribble around the wheelchair," and "pass the ball." However, "speed pass" as well as "pass for distance" were also good (Table 2).

Tests in shooting are not very reliable, especially the "dribble, shot, and rebound" test, because the athlete has to shoot while moving his or her wheelchair. This skill requires very good concentration of the player and needs a continuous adaptation of distance with regard to the basket. This combination of different abilities has an important influence on the result, and we think that the test is too difficult for wheelchair athletes as an evaluation system.

Table 1 Results of Tests for the Total Group (*n* = 30) and Three Classes (Class I, *n* = 11; Class II, *n* = 7; Class III, *n* = 12) of Wheelchair Athletes

Test	Total group			Class III			Class II			Class I		
	Min	Mean	Max	Min	Mean	Max	Min	Mean	Max	Min	Mean	Max
Shot, rebound (no.)	2	6	15	2	7.5	15	3	6	9	2	4.5	8
Dribbling, shot, rebound (s/no.)	37.8 / 1	48.2 / 3.1	62.5 / 5	38.7 / 2	44.0 / 3.3	52.0 / 5	38.9 / 2	47.0 / 3.3	62.5 / 5	43.6 / 1	53.5 / 2.7	62.5 / 5
Obstacle dribble (s)	15.3	21.5	41.0	15.3	18.9	22.4	16.0	19.9	35.1	18.2	25.7	41.0
Dribble around chair (no.)	2	9	13	9	10	13	9	10	13	2	7	9
Speed pass (no.)	10	18.6	25	18	21	25	14	19	23	10	16	20
Pass for distance (cm)	514	960	1,405	620	998	1,405	670	1,019	1,400	514	863	1,129

Note. Min = minimum score; Mean = mean score; Max = maximum score.

Table 2 *F*-values Following a Two-Way Analysis of Variance and Intraclass Correlation Coefficients in Four Sporting Clubs for Six Skills

Tested skill	Club	*F*-values P	T	r_c
Shot, rebound	1	3.35*	1.97	.75
	2	7.21**	0.43	.87
	3	8.50**	2.86	.91
	4	27.74**	7.80*	.97
Dribbling, shot, and rebound	1	72.32**	2.83	.99
		2.31	1.27	.56
	2	91.10**	2.02	.99
		4.94**	1.61	.81
	3	119.78**	0.80	.99
		2.38	1.63	.87
	4	42.11**	4.12*	.97
		2.17	3.04	.57
Obstacle dribble	1	199.68**	1.15	.91
	2	47.13**	2.01	.98
	3	23.94**	1.75	.97
	4	11.05**	0.23	.92
Dribble around wheelchair	1	32.77**	0.15	.97
	2	35.55**	2.70	.98
	3	38.26**	1.20	.98
	4	37.95**	8.17**	.99
Speed pass	1	91.00**	1.84	.99
	2	75.91**	1.87	.99
	3	36.36**	2.23	.97
	4	30.96**	1.62	.97
Pass for distance	1	188.29**	1.28	.99
	2	227.72**	0.78	.99
	3	96.68**	2.56	.99
	4	54.30**	0.89	.98

Note. P = players; T = tests.
*$p < .05$. **$p < .01$.

Table 3 Spearman's Rank Correlation Coefficients Between Both Evaluations of the Coach in Each Sporting Club

Club	Shooting skills	Dribbling skills	Passing skills	Total evaluation
1	.97**	.97**	.97**	.99**
2	.92**	.94**	.95**	.91**
3	.82*	.88*	.88*	.96**
4	.93*	.93*	.10	.80

$*p < .05.$ $**p < .01.$

We note a very strong correlation between the two evaluations of the coaches (Table 3). But an exception must be made in Sporting Club 4 for skills that measure "pass the ball." The coach did not follow any definite policy during the judgment of his basketball players. For that reason we may expect a low validity value, especially for tests that measure passing skills.

Finally, we wanted to know if our tests really measured the premised skills of wheelchair basketball athletes. We may expect that an athlete who obtained very good results in a test situation also would be judged as a very good player by the coach. But even the opposite statement was possible. If that was true, we could conclude, according to Mathews (1973), that the test was valid to measure basketball skills.

So, the coach's knowledge of athletes plays a very important role. In Table 4, we noted high correlation coefficients in Sporting Clubs 1 and 2. We observed lower values in Sporting Club 3 concerning the "shot, rebound" test and the "pass for distance" test. We kept in mind that all players in this club have about the same level of basketball skills. Consequently, the difference in performances resulted in changing places in the rank order, and the correlation coefficient declined.

Conclusions

The results prove that the degree of handicap plays an important part in testing wheelchair athletes for basketball skills. We did the same statistical analysis following the class status and found quite the same trends in variances. Therefore, we recommend not to focus on class status.

We observed a high reliability coefficient between .99 and .75, which allows us to conclude that our tests may be considered as a real evaluation system for wheelchair basketball players, with one exception; "dribble, shot, and rebound" seemed to be a very complex test and, therefore, should be adapted in the future.

Table 4 Spearman's Rank Correlation Coefficients Between Test Results and Each Coach's Evaluation for Six Basketball Skills

Coach's evaluation	Shot, rebound	Dribbling, shot, and rebound	Obstacle dribble	Dribble around wheelchair	Speed pass	Pass for distance
A	.88**-.93**	.66 -.94**	.73*-.91**	.77*-.93*	.41 -.86**	.76*-.82*
B	.65 -.94**	.88**-.99**	.74*-.94**	.78*-.89*	.86*-.99**	.69*-.87**

Note. Ranges represent correlation values for Clubs 1 to 4.
*$p < .05$. **$p < .01$.

The judgment of the coach was reliable and did not have any influence on the correlation coefficients, except in Sporting Club 4, where the rank correlation coefficient between the evaluations was very low. This fact had an influence on validity estimation. Indeed, the tests "speed pass," "pass for distance," and "shot, rebound" did not have high correlation coefficients.

It could be interesting to set up a T-scale to have a usable statistical tool as an indication of the individual skill level (Brasile, 1984). But that was not possible because of the low number of participants. We are convinced that this study can be a contribution to the analysis of skills for wheelchair sports.

References

Barrow, H. M., & McGee, R. (1968). *A practical approach to measurement in physical education*. Philadelphia: Lea & Febiger.

Brasile, F. M. (1984). A wheelchair basketball skill test. *Sports 'n Spokes*, **10**, 36-39.

Guilford, J. P., & Fruchter, B. (1973). *Fundamental statistics in psychology and education*. Tokyo: McGraw-Hill Kogakusha.

Kühn, W., & Heiny, E. (1974). Testbatterie zur Leistungerfassung im Sportspiel Basketball [Test battery for competitive factors in recreational basketball]. *Leistungssport*, **4**, 111-118.

Mathews, D. K. (1973). *Measurement in physical education*. Philadelphia: W. B. Saunders.

Milloen, D. (1977). *Validiteitsstudie van een testbatterij basketbal voor jongens van 12 tot 19 jaar*. Unpublished master's thesis, Leuven University, The Netherlands.

Pauwels, J. M. (Ed.). (1979). *Sportspelen aanleren. Enkele methodologische bijdragen*. Leuven: Acco.

Safrit, M. J. (1973). *Evaluation in physical education*. Englewood Cliffs, NJ: Prentice-Hall.

Safrit, M. J., Atwater, A. E., Baumgartner, T. A., & West, C. (1976). *Reliability theory*. Washington, DC: American Alliance for Health, Physical Education, and Recreation Publications.

Siegel, S. (1956). *Non-parametric statistics for the behavioral sciences*. New York: McGraw-Hill.

Vanlerberghe, J. O. C. (1964). *Sport voor gehandicapten. Poging tot systematisatie van het basketbalonderricht voor paraplegiekers*. Unpublished master's thesis, Leuven University, The Netherlands.

PART VIII

Aging and Physical Activity Concerns of the Elderly

Physiology of Aging
and Adapted Physical Activity

Roy J. Shephard

Physical education as it has developed over the past decade is one of the most demanding of university disciplines. Well-rounded physical educators must be health exemplars, demonstrating a strong personal commitment to the development of fitness and an optimal life-style. At the same time, they must have the interest, the sensitivity, and the empathy to impart these skills to others in either an individual or a group setting. Finally, they must be at the forefront of academic knowledge and research in 10 or more subdisciplines, any one of which would prove a heavy challenge (Shephard, 1983b; Zeigler, 1983).

The demand for broad scholarship is particularly awesome in the emerging specialization of adapted physical education (Crowe, Auxter, & Pyfer, 1981; de Potter, 1981; Eason, Smith, & Caron, 1983; Simri, 1971). Each of the many subdisciplines in which the physical educator has expertise must be reviewed and reevaluated in the context of the pathology, clinical history, medical, and surgical treatment of a myriad of diseases and disorders.

A multidisciplinary approach is particularly essential when considering issues in physical activity and aging (Harris & Frankel, 1977; Shephard, 1978, 1983a; Smith & Serfass, 1981). There is the fascinating question of possible interactions between physical activity and longevity, the seemingly relentless diminution of working capacity with age, and the resultant social isolation and depression, with the associated burden of institutional costs. A deterioration of the special senses, a loss of neurohormonal regulation, impaired immune function, and a poor adaptability to environmental extremes call for specific program adaptations. Often there is a loss of recent memory, and a proportion of patients are affected by Alzheimer's disease or senile dementia. Osteoporosis and a deterioration of balance enhance the risk of fractures. Nutrition is less adequate than in a younger individual, and there may be obesity and maturity-onset diabetes. Cardiovascular disease, including hypertension and strokes, becomes ever more prevalent, lung tissue may be extensively damaged by chronic obstructive lung disease, and malignancies become ever more frequent. Finally, exercise responses are distorted and made more dangerous by a multitude of medications that are prescribed for the elderly. Even a brief survey of these topics (Shephard, 1987) requires a full graduate-level course. This chapter will focus primarily upon implications for the design of physical activity programs.

The Problem of Biological Versus Calendar Age

It is usual to distinguish the "young old," typically aged 65 to 75 years and able to exercise without restriction; the "middle old," typically aged 75 to 85 years, who experience some limitation in their activities; and the "old old," typically over 85 years of age, who require full institutional care (Shephard, 1987). However, there is a tremendous range of calendar ages within each of these functional categories. Physiologists have thus been interested in developing indices of biological age (Comfort, 1969; Heikkinen, 1979). Most functions begin an asymptomatic degeneration around 25 years of age, so that the first phase of unrestricted activity lasts for 50 years or more. The second phase (where activity is somewhat restricted) lasts for 8 to 9 years, whereas the third phase of total dependency lasts for less than 1 year. Numbers are such that by far the largest program demands are from the youngest category. On the other hand, the greatest cost to society arises from people in the second and third categories (Shephard, 1984), and it is in these categories that there is the greatest need for an improvement in the quality of life.

What causes the transition from one age category to another? Sometimes a person develops some obvious pathology—a stroke, a cataract, or senile dementia. In other instances, admission to an institution is for social rather than functional reasons. But often the problem is physiological—the various body systems have deteriorated to the point where the demands of daily living can no longer be met.

Let me illustrate this with respect to maximum oxygen intake. A person becomes fatigued if more than 40% of the maximum oxygen intake is used over an 8-hr day (Shephard, 1977). By the age of 65 years, the average 40% loadings correspond to energy expenditures of 16 and 11 kJ/min for men and women, respectively. In many 65-year-old people, oxygen transport is already so limited that the activities of daily living are becoming fatiguing. The rate of functional loss accelerates as a person moves beyond 65 years. The effort tolerance drops below 8 kJ/min somewhere between 75 and 85 years, and independent living is no longer possible.

A similar difficulty develops in other body systems. The maximum isometric force of the arm muscles is no longer adequate to lift the loads encountered around the house, the quadriceps becomes too weak to lift the body mass from a chair or toilet seat, and the loss of flexibility prevents performance of key tasks such as climbing into or out of a bath.

The Problem of Atrophy Versus Inherent Aging

Are the effects of age upon performance the result of an inherent, genetically determined deterioration of cell function, or can they be averted through a vigorous program of adapted physical education? This question is difficult to answer because activity habits and age are closely intertwined. However, most studies suggest that exercise does not change the inherent slope of the aging curve (Shephard, 1987). On the other hand, the training response, a functional gain of some 20%, has tremendous practical significance for a frail and sedentary older person. It can be equivalent to 20 years of rejuvenation—a benefit that could be matched by no other treatment or life-style change.

The Problems of Clinical and Subclinical Disease

A large number of chronic diseases become more prevalent as the population ages. Brown and Shephard (1967) found that 29 of 62 older females had some form of chronic disease; in 17 of the 29, the disorder affected the cardiorespiratory system, with a 10 to 14% loss of maximum oxygen intake. Likewise, the Canada Fitness Survey (1983) screened out 55% of volunteers over 65 years of age, although interestingly only 19% considered themselves as unfit to take the test. The type of exercise that can be prescribed for any given elderly group is influenced markedly by the extent to which such subjects have been excluded from the sample.

Many old people are also affected by subclinical pathological changes. Montoye (1975) found that by the age of 65 years, 30% of the population of Tecumseh had abnormal exercise electrocardiograms (ECG). This raises the intriguing possibility that much of the deterioration in myocardial function that has been attributed to age is really due to the steady progression of subclinical disease (Weisfeldt, Gerstenblith, & Lakatta, 1985). However, if the heart continues to function normally, why do even healthy volunteers show a steady, age-related decline of oxygen transport? Possibly the performance of the healthy elderly person is limited by respiratory symtoms rather than by a ceiling of cardiac function; nevertheless, the usual reasons for halting exercise (muscle weakness, deteriorating coordination, and impending loss of consciousness) remain suggestive of an inadequate cardiac output.

Implications for Program Design

Safety

The cardiac risk of all-out competition probably increases with aging, but the real problem with most older patients is excessive caution rather than overexertion. Vuori, Suürnakki, and Suürnakki (1982) concluded that the chances of provoking a cardiac incident were relatively much greater in a middle-aged person than in someone who was older.

"Abnormal" electrocardiograms can be very alarming to a cardiologist who is accustomed to examining younger patients. However, given the high incidence of false-positive tracings and the strong likelihood that moderate, progressive activity will improve the quality of an older person's life, ECG appearances are not usually a valid reason to restrict the activity of a senior citizen (Shephard, 1983a). At most, moderation of exercise should be advised as symptoms or signs of cardiac decompensation are appearing.

Leg, ankle, and back injuries remain too frequent in the elderly exerciser. As in other areas of life, moderation is the rule. Fast walking should replace jogging, since the impact stress on the knees and spine is then only about a third as high. Hard surfaces should be avoided, and the volume of training should leave the subject only pleasantly tired the next day (Shephard, 1977, 1983a). Specific movements to avoid remain controversial. Violent efforts and sudden twisting seem undesirable, whereas straight leg lifts, traditional knee bends, and hyperextension of the back have all been criticized (MacCallum, 1980). Nevertheless, the activities performed should take the major joints of the body through their full range of motion on a regular basis.

Limitations of vision and balance, with an increased liability to postural hypotension, are strong theoretical arguments against pursuits where there is a danger of collision, falling, or drowning. However, in practice the risks are quite low. At the Baycrest Centre in Toronto 14,000 people per year exercise in a pool heated to 32 °C, but there has not yet been an episode of postural hypotension (Greife & Kremer, personal communication, 1985).

The fun of team sports can be extended to elderly players, given age-specific leagues and simple modifications of the rules. The main difficulty with such activities is that the pace of exercise may then be determined by the opponents, and it is here that skillful officiating becomes important (Shephard, 1983a).

Extremes of heat and cold are less well tolerated by an old person (Shephard, 1987). Cardiac deaths are increased under hot and humid conditions, whereas cold and dry air may provoke both bronchospasm and angina; the dangers of frostbite and hypothermia also increase with age (Shephard, 1987).

Practical Programming

The general principles of training for a young old person are much as at an earlier age (Shephard, 1983a), although obesity, musculo-skeletal weakness, and a poor heat tolerance may restrict the daily volume of training. Fortunately, there is a slow but steady response to a high-frequency, low-intensity program (Badenhop, Cleary, Schoal, Fox, & Bartels, 1983; Sidney & Shephard, 1978). In a totally sedentary 70-year-old, benefit can be obtained from any increase of activity—for example, gentle walking, possibly split into two or three 10-min sessions per day. Recreational swimming, folk dancing, lawn bowling, and (for the disabled) even chair exercises can contribute to aerobic conditioning. As age increases, the prescription must be progressively adapted. At 65 years, 80% of the population can move without difficulty, but by the age of 80 years a high proportion of patients have mental or cardiac problems (Heikkinen & Kahty, 1977). Recommendations that are made must take account of biological age, social situation, and any specific medical limitations.

The aerobic component of the prescription must be progressive, advancement of the intensity and duration being gauged from the individual's reactions to a given dose of exercise. A good warm-up is needed to minimize musculoskeletal injuries and cardiac arrhythmias. Exercises to strengthen wasted muscles and increase bone mineral should also be a significant part of the prescription. An extended warm-down is also needed because of poor venous tone and a tendency to postural hypotension after exercise. An appropriate prescription does not overtire the patient. If there is excessive pain or stiffness, microtraumata are developing, and activity must be moderated until the condition improves. Note that the healing process becomes progressively slower in older individuals.

Isometric exercise is a controversial issue in the elderly. It has been argued it will cause a dangerous rise of blood pressure (Lind & McNicol, 1967). However, contractions of less than 10-s duration have little effect upon blood pressure yet seem sufficient to stimulate muscle hypertrophy (Hettinger, 1961). Isometric activity can thus be a useful supplement to aerobic conditioning. Gentle stretching exercises are also needed to develop flexibility at the major joints.

Adaptations to Specific Pathologies

Specific medical abnormalities call for a more cautious approach to exercise (Shephard, 1987). Nevertheless, increased physical activity can be helpful in conditions such as angina, hypertension, intermittent claudication, and chronic obstructive lung disease (Shephard, 1978).

A careful history of medication is needed. Sometimes (as in an insulin-dependent diabetic), the exercise prescription may modify the demand for medication. The widely used beta-blocking agents may also cause local muscle fatigue and invalidate the normal heart rate–based exercise prescription.

Motivation

Participants need continual encouragement to persist with their prescription. The exercise that is recommended must be perceived as safe, convenient, and appropriate for the individual's age. The class leader must have a real empathy for both the needs and the potential of an older person. Classes that are grouped by biological age boost both real and perceived safety, simultaneously overcoming some of the self-consciousness that is a barrier to renewed activity.

Some people are seeking social interchange and fun, so this should be an integral part of the program. However, the prime rewards are an upgrading of health and fitness. At first it is easy to demonstrate an improvement of scores on simple tests of fitness. However, the rate of progress diminishes as the standard for a fit person is approached. At this stage, attention can be drawn to items that are still improving (for instance, the distance walked without fatigue), and scores can be presented as the maintenance of a 10- or even a 20-year advantage of biological age (Shephard, 1983a).

Medical Supervision

The risk of a cardiac emergency in any given hour of physical activity is very low, even in the elderly (Shephard, 1981), whereas the cost of medical supervision of geriatric exercise classes is prohibitive (Shephard, 1984). The role of the physician should thus be restricted to development of exercise guidelines, encouragement of exercise during office visits, and identification of specific subgroups where exercise is contraindicated or requires special supervision.

Treatment of any cardiac emergencies that may arise is best assured by educating the general public in techniques of cardiac resuscitation. Older individuals should be encouraged to exercise in pairs, and the possibility of a cardiac incident should be discussed quite openly. Beyond the age of perhaps 80 years, patients should have the right to indicate that they do not wish to be resuscitated if an emergency occurs (Gordon & Hurowitz, 1984).

Conclusion

Available evidence does not suggest that an exercise prescription will extend the average life span. However, a more appropriate measure of outcome is the quality-adjusted life span, and in such terms we are well justified in commending physical activity to the elderly.

Adapted programs of physical activity for the elderly must be adjusted not for calendar age but for biological age and health status. Regular exercise cannot retard the fundamental processes of aging, but it can offer the equivalent of 10 to 20 years of rejuvenation, countering a deterioration in cardiovascular and muscular function and enhancing the quality of life. Adaptations of programming must be made for specific pathologies, but immediate medical supervision of all elderly patients is both costly and unnecessary. The key to an appropriate prescription is an amount of exercise that the older person enjoys, that induces only pleasant tiredness, but yet initiates a progressive improvement of physical condition.

Acknowledgment

Studies in aging at the University of Toronto, Faculty of Medicine have been supported by a University of Toronto research development grant.

References

Badenhop, D. T., Cleary, P. A., Schoal, S. F., Fox, E. L., & Bartels, R. L. (1983). In *Medicine and Science in Sports and Exercise*, **15**, 496-502.

Brown, J. R., & Shephard, R. J. (1967). Some measurements of fitness in older female employees of a Toronto department store. *Canadian Medical Association Journal*, **97**, 1208-1213.

Canada Fitness Survey. (1983). *Fitness and lifestyle in Canada*. Ottawa: Fitness and Amateur Sport.

Comfort, A. (1969). Test-battery to measure aging rate in man. *Lancet, 2*, 411-414.

Crowe, W. C., Auxter, D., & Pyfer, J. (1981). *Principles and methods of adapted physical education and recreation* (4th ed.). St. Louis: C. V. Mosby.

de Potter, J.-C. (1981). *Activités physiques adaptées* [Adapted physical activities]. Bruxelles: Editions de l'Université de Bruxelles.

Eason, R. L., Smith, T. L., & Caron, F. (1983). *Adapted physical activity: From theory to application*. Champaign, IL: Human Kinetics.

Gordon, M., & Hurowitz, E. (1984). Cardiopulmonary resuscitation of the elderly. *Journal of the American Geriatric Society, 32*, 930-934.

Harris, R. J., & Frankel, L. J. (Eds.). (1977). *Guide to fitness after fifty*. New York: Plenum Press.

Heikkinen, E. (1979). Normal aging: Definition, problems and relation to physical activity. In H. Orimo, K. Shimada, M. Iriki, & D. Maeda (Eds.), *Recent advances in gerontology* (pp. 501-503). Amsterdam: Excerpta Medica.

Heikkinen, E., & Kahty, B. (1977). Gerontological aspects of physical activity—Motivation of older people in physical training. In R. Harris & L. J. Frankel (Eds.), *Guide to fitness after fifty* (pp. 191-205). New York: Plenum.

Hettinger, T. (1961). *Physiology of strength*. Springfield, IL: C. C. Thomas.

Lind, A. R., & McNicol, G. W. (1967). Muscular factors which determine the cardiovascular responses to sustained and rhythmic exercise. *Canadian Medical Association Journal, 96*, 706-712.

MacCallum, M. (1980). Practical programmes for older persons. In R. C. Goode & D. J. Payne (Eds.), *The coming of age of aging* (pp. 83-111). Toronto: Ontario Heart Foundation.

Montoye, H. J. (1975). *Physical activity and health: An epidemiologic study of an entire community*. Englewood Cliffs, NJ: Prentice-Hall.

Shephard, R. J. (1977). *Endurance fitness* (2nd ed.). Toronto: University of Toronto Press.

Shephard, R. J. (1981). *Ischaemic heart disease and exercise*. London: Croom Helm.

Shephard, R. J. (1983a). Management of exercise in the elderly. *Canadian Journal of Applied Sports Sciences, 9*, 109-121.

Shephard, R. J. (1983b). Professional and scholarly dimensions of physical education: A reaction. *Canadian Association for Health, Physical Education and Recreation Journal, 50*(2), 20.

Shephard, R. J. (1984). *Fiscal implications of a fit Canada: Guidelines for social planning and research*. Ottawa: Fitness and Amateur Sport.

Shephard, R. J. (1987). *Physical activity and aging* (2nd ed.). London: Croom Helm.

Sidney, K. H., & Shephard, R. J. (1978). Frequency and intensity of exercise for elderly subjects. *Medicine and Science in Sports*, **10**, 125-131.

Simri, U. (1971). *Sport as a means of rehabilitation*. Natanya, Israel: Wingate Institute.

Smith, E. L., & Serfass, R. C. (1981). *Exercise and aging: The scientific basis*. Hillside, NJ: Enslow Publishing.

Vuori, I., Suürnakki, L., & Suürnakki, T. (1982). Risk of sudden cardiovascular death (SCVD) in exercise. *Medicine and Science in Sports and Exercise*, **14**, 114-115.

Weisfeldt, M. L., Gerstenblith, G., & Lakatta, E. G. (1985). Alterations in circulatory function. In R. Andres, E. L. Bierman, & W. R. Hazzard (Eds.), *Principles of geriatric medicine* (pp. 248-279). New York: McGraw-Hill.

Zeigler, E. (1983). A proposal for the reunification of our professional and scholarly dimensions. *Canadian Association for Health, Physical Education and Recreation Journal*, **50**(2), 17-19.

Psychosocial Factors Influencing Intentions to Exercise in a Group of Individuals Ranging From 45 to 74 Years of Age

Gaston Godin
Roy J. Shephard

Older people are increasingly reluctant to exercise (Canada Fitness Survey, 1982). In order to reverse this undesirable trend, it is necessary to identify both the variables influencing behavior and the rules linking these variables in a causal sequence leading to behavior (Godin & Shephard, 1983).

One comprehensive schema, developed to explain social behavior at the level of individual decision making, is Fishbein's model (Fishbein & Ajzen, 1975) (Figure 1). According to this model, the proximate determinants of the intent to adopt a given behavior are the individual's personal attitude toward performing the behavior in question and the influence of the social environment upon this behavior. A person does not adopt a given pattern of behavior because he or she has specific personality traits, has been educated in a particular fashion, or has a given cultural background. Instead, the act is carried out because the individual believes that its performance will lead to more "beneficial" than "harmful" consequences or because of a perception that "significant others" think he or she should adopt that behavior. External variables influence behavior only by

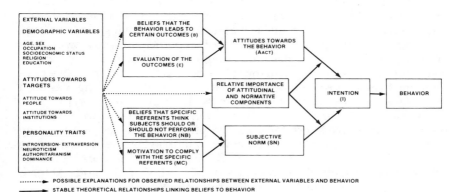

Figure 1   Schematic representation of Fishbein's model (from Ajzen & Fishbein, 1980).

influencing those attitudinal and normative considerations that are the ultimate determinants of behavior. The model is predicated on the assumption that most human behavior of interest to social specialists is to some degree under volitional control and hence is determined by behavioral intent.

Fishbein's model seems quite robust when describing health-related behaviors, including exercise (Godin, Cox, & Shephard, 1983; Godin, Valois, Shephard, & Desharnais, in press; Riddle, 1980). The prime objectives of the present study were to understand and predict intentions to participate in active sports or vigorous physical activities among a sample of older individuals and to see whether older and younger individuals differ in their belief structures.

Methods

Subjects

A total of 90 subjects were randomly selected from a group of 2,500 University of Toronto current and retired employees who had returned a brief questionnaire about exercise preferences. The sample was stratified by sex and age (45 to 54 years, 55 to 64 years, and 65 to 74 years).

Questionnaire

Fishbein model variables were developed as suggested by Ajzen and Fishbein (1980). The intentional (I) component was measured on a likely-unlikely 7-point scale by answering the question "I intend to participate in active sports or vigorous physical activities long enough to get sweaty at least twice a week, in my leisure time in the future." The attitude-toward-the-act (Aact) component was assessed by summing scores from 7-point semantic differential scales. Behavioral beliefs ("b") and the corresponding evaluations of their consequences ("e") were each measured using fourteen 7-point scales. Individual "b" scores were multiplied by the corresponding "e" values, and the product was summed (Σ b • e). The subjective norm (SN) variable was measured by having subjects agree or disagree with the proposition "I think that participating in active sports or vigorous physical activities long enough to get sweaty at least twice a week during my leisure time in the future is something that people whose opinions I value most believe I should do." A similar wording was used to assess each of five normative beliefs (NB). Motivation to comply (MC) was evaluated by agreement with questions of the type "I would like to participate in active sports or vigorous physical activities the way (my physician) thinks I should." Each NB was multiplied by the corresponding MC and the products were summed Σ NB • MC). Two-week test-retest reliability coefficients showed values of .73, .81, .71, .85, and .70 for I, Aact, SN, Σ b • e, and Σ NB • BC, respectively.

The immediate past exercise behavior of subjects was measured by having them answer the 6-choice question "How often did you participate

Table 1 Activity Habits of Men and Women

Leisure time exercise	44–54 years		55–64 years		65 years +	
	Men (*n* = 15)	Women (*n* = 15)	Men (*n* = 10)	Women (*n* = 15)	Men (*n* = 15)	Women (*n* = 15)
Strenuous[a] (time/week)	0.5	0.4	1.2	0.1	1.2	0.6
Moderate[b] (time/week)	3.0	3.4	2.1	2.9	3.6	1.8
Light[c] (time/week)	4.2	2.8	3.0	4.1	3.1	4.2
Total[d]	31.8	28.4	30.3	27.7	38.2	27.0

Note. Subjects were given examples of activities in each category. However, the MET estimates were formulated for younger individuals, and it is conceivable that older subjects performed the specified activity at a lower energy cost.
[a]Average 9 METs for a minimum of 20 min.
[b]Average 5 METs for a minimum of 20 min.
[c]Average 3 METs for a minimum of 20 min.
[d]Total = (Strenuous × 9) + (Moderate × 5) + (Light × 3).

in active sports or vigorous physical activities long enough to get sweaty, during your leisure time within the *past four months?*"

Prior experience of sport and physical activity was measured by having subjects answer the 6-choice question "How often have you participated in active sports or vigorous activities long enough to get sweaty, during your leisure time since you became an adult?"

Subjects were finally asked to indicate years of schooling and diploma obtained.

Results

The average age of the subjects was 60.2. Intention to exercise scores were 1.66, 1.64, and 0.87, respectively, in the three age categories. The mean intention was stronger for men (1.61) than for women (1.14), although this was not significant. Men were also more active than women (Table 1). Older males reported a higher level of physical activity than the two younger male groups, and for women levels of physical activity were relatively stable across age (Table 1). This may reflect a volunteer bias, or older people may have perceived a given level of activity as more strenuous when it demanded a larger fraction of their aerobic power.

A multiple regression analysis of intentions to exercise versus Fishbein's model components (Aact and SN), immediate past exercise behavior, prior experience of sport and physical activity, educational levels, and

Table 2 Average Exercise Belief Scores

Beliefs about exercise	Intention to Exercise	
	Low (n = 16)	High (n = 70)
Look younger	0.06	1.29**
Fill recreation time	-0.25	0.99**
Control body weight	0.06	1.29**
Be healthy	1.94	2.50*
Live longer	1.25	1.10
Relieve tension	1.63	1.66
Be tiring	1.69	0.90
Be more energetic	1.38	2.07*
Improve physical appearance	0.63	1.56*
Feel good	1.81	2.14
Meet people	0.44	0.91
Time-consuming	1.25	1.17
Improve thinking ability	0.69	1.11
Be physically fit	1.44	1.90

Note. All scales range from +3 to -3. Hotelling test ($F = 3.24$, 14 and 69 df, $p < .01$).
*$p < .05$. **$p < .01$.

two-way and three-way interactions yielded a cumulative R^2 of 0.364. Attitude and the two-way interactions of SN with education, past behavior, and sex carried significant beta weights (.389, .207, .141, and .136, respectively); SN had more influence upon intentions to exercise in less educated subjects.

In accordance with Fishbein's theory, the zero-order correlation between Aact and Σ b • e was .522 ($p < .001$), whereas a value of .350 ($p < .001$) linked SN with Σ NB • MC. A multivariate analysis of variance (MANOVA) showed that high and low intenders differed significantly with respect to exercise beliefs ("b") ($F = 3.24$, 14 and 69 df, $p < .01$) and (less significantly) in normative beliefs ("NB") ($F = 2.01$, 5 and 78 df, $p < .08$). High intenders (Table 2) were more certain that carrying out vigorous physical activities a few times a week during their leisure time would help them to "look younger" ($p < .01$), "fill their recreation time" ($p < .01$), "control their body weight" ($p < .01$), "be healthy" ($p < .05$), "be more energetic" ($p < .05$), and "improve their physical appearance" ($p < .05$). High intenders also believed more strongly that "close friends" ($p < .05$) and

Table 3 Average Normative Belief Scores

	Intention to Exercise	
Normative beliefs	Low (n = 14)	High (n = 70)
Physician	0.43	1.21
Close friends	0.07	1.10*
Most members of the family	0.36	1.37*
Society	1.14	1.00
Physical educators	1.21	1.90

Note. All scales range from +3 to −3. Hotelling test (F = 2.01, 5 and 78 df, p < .08).
*p < .05.

"most members of the family" (p < .05) thought that they should exercise regularly (Table 3). Verification of the cognitive structure in "b," "e," "NB," and "MC" showed no significant differences among age groups, sexes, or levels of education.

Discussion

In our volunteer sample, intention to exercise was independent of age over the range 45 to 74 years. Four terms influenced intention to exercise: attitude and the two-way interactions of subjective norm with education, past behavior, and sex. Less educated subjects were influenced by societal norms, but more educated people tended to exercise independently of external influences.

The absence of an age influence in either overall behavioral intentions or its cognitive components is in agreement with the Canada Fitness Survey (1982), which documented similar reasons for being physically active in people from 10 to 69 years of age. However, Sidney, Niinimaa, and Shephard (1983) noted that certain attitudes toward physical activity as measured by Kenyon's inventory varied with age. Specifically, the elderly placed more value on the "aesthetic experience" and "health and fitness" and less value on the "pursuit of vertigo" than did high school students.

This information could be reconciled with the present report in several ways. First, the difference in mean age was much larger in the study of Sidney et al. (1983). Second, the theories of attitude used were not the same; Kenyon's inventory assumes that physical activity is a socio-psychological phenomenon and assesses its perceived instrumental value. It provides a traditional measure of general attitudes toward objects rather than a personalized format of attitude toward a given behavior, an approach that is relatively unsuccessful in predicting specific behaviors such as participation in vigorous physical activity (Godin & Shephard, 1986). In contrast, we found that attitude toward the act (Aact) was significantly correlated with the immediate past exercise behavior (past 4 months, $r = .36$, $p < .001$). A further consideration is that Sidney et al. (1983) made multiple comparisons of group means and differences in subdomains in univariate fashion, where in the present study belief structure was investigated only if a significant MANOVA was demonstrated for differences considered jointly.

The ability of past behavior to influence behavior is widely acknowledged in learning theory (Triandis, 1977). In the realm of physical activity, Godin et al. (1985, in press) found that prior experience helped to explain variability in exercise intentions and behavior.

The contribution of sex to exercise intention supports the view that more variability is explained for the male. This finding is congruent with our previous observations on younger men and women (Godin & Shephard, 1985), suggesting that the cognitive structure underlying intention differs between sexes.

The difference of attitudinal and normative beliefs between high and low intenders has particular importance. Those promoting physical activity for this age group should lay particular stress on building beliefs that vigorous physical activity will help participants "look younger," "fill recreation time," and "control body weight." Attention should also be focused upon "close friends" and "members of the family," because they not only help to convince at least the less educated and older low intenders that they should exercise regularly but also play an important role in sustaining exercise compliance (Heinzelman, 1973; Oldridge, 1982). The limited influence of the physician with respect to this important aspect of life-style is a matter of concern. The Canada Fitness Survey (1982) also stressed the negative role of the health professional, noting that many older people who considered themselves capable of exercise were denied permission to undertake a simple submaximal step test.

Finally, it should be stressed that only 36% of the variance in intentions was explained by our behavioral model. While this is moderately satisfactory in the context of social psychology, much of intention remains unexplained, and care should be shown in generalizing findings from a selected group of volunteers to a more representative sample of the elderly. Further research is needed to understand why some older citizens exercise regularly whereas others remain sedentary.

Acknowledgments

This work was supported by a research development grant from the University of Toronto; principal investigators were R. Beamish, M.E. Berridge, J.V. Daniels, J.F. Flowers, G. Godin, R.C. Goode, P. Klavora, M.R.

Pierrynoski, M.J. Plyley, E. Thompson, P. Tiidus, K.A. Wipper, and R.J. Shephard.

References

Ajzen, I., & Fishbein, M. (1980). *Understanding attitudes and predicting social behavior*. Englewood Cliffs, NJ: Prentice-Hall.

Canada Fitness Survey. (1982). *Fitness and aging*. Ottawa: Fitness and Amateur Sport.

Fishbein, M., & Ajzen, I. (1975). *Belief, attitude, intention and behavior: An introduction to theory and research*. Don Mills, Ontario: Addison-Wesley.

Godin, G., Cox, M., & Shephard, R. J. (1983). The impact of physical fitness evaluation on behavioural intentions toward regular exercise. *Canadian Journal of Applied Sport Science*, **8**, 240-245.

Godin, G., & Shephard, R. J. (1983). Physical fitness promotion programmes: Effectiveness in modifying exercise behaviour. *Canadian Journal of Applied Sport Science*, **8**, 104-113.

Godin, G., & Shephard, R. J. (1985). Psycho-social predictors of exercise intentions among spouses. *Canadian Journal of Applied Sport Science*, **10**, 36-43.

Godin, G., & Shephard, R. J. (1986). The importance of type of attitude to the study of exercise behavior. *Psychological Reports*, **58**, 991-1000.

Godin, G., Valois, P., Shephard, R. J., & Desharnais, R. (in press). Prediction of leisure time exercise behavior: A path analysis (LISREL V) model. *Journal of Behavioral Medicine*.

Heinzelman, F. (1973). Social and psychosocial factors that influence the effectiveness of exercise programs. In J. P. Naughton & H. K. Hellerstein (Eds.), *Exercises testing in coronary heart disease* (pp. 275-287). New York: Academic Press.

Oldridge, N. B. (1982). Compliance and exercise in primary and secondary prevention of coronary heart disease: A review. *Preventive Medicine*, **11**, 56-70.

Riddle, P. K. (1980). Attitudes, beliefs, behavioral intentions and behaviors of women and men toward regular jogging. *Research Quarterly for Exercise and Sport*, **51**, 663-674.

Sidney, K. H., Niinimaa, V., & Shephard, R. J. (1983). Attitudes towards exercise and sports: Sex and age differences, and changes with endurance training. *Journal of Sports and Science*, **1**, 195-210.

Triandis, H. C. (1977). *Interpersonal behavior*. Monterey: Brooks/Cole.

Adapted Physical Education, Aging, and the Postindustrial Society

Roy J. Shephard

It is now widely held that automation is removing the need for physical work in industry. In the present chapter, I examine this hypothesis, considering whether technological advances have changed the need for adapted programs designed to restore the physical condition of the older worker. Specific questions to be addressed include:

1. Does a decline of physical working capacity currently limit the performance of a 65-year-old worker?
2. What tests can be used to measure the condition of the individual?
3. How valuable are adapted programs of physical activity?
4. Is modern technology modifying working capacity or health?
5. How large a working capacity will be needed by future generations of older workers?

Current Working Capacity of the Elderly

An acceptable 8-hr work load varies with the quality of the industrial environment and details of the task to be accomplished. But observations on voluntary pacing (Hughes & Goldman, 1970) suggest that a reasonable ceiling is an expenditure of 40% of the maximum oxygen intake ($\dot{V}O_2$max) over a working day. What limit does this set to the performance of work?

By the age of 65 years, the maximum oxygen intake has dropped to about 24 ml/kg • min in a woman and 27 ml/kg • min in a man. Assuming respective body masses of 55 kg and 70 kg, the absolute aerobic power amounts to 1.32 l/min in a woman and 1.89 l/min in a man; 40% of this figure is 0.52 l/min and 0.76 l/min. We know that an oxygen consumption of 1 l/min is equivalent to an energy expenditure of about 21 kJ/min (Shephard, 1982), so that the average work ceiling is 11 kJ/min in a woman and 16 kJ/min in a man. The coefficient of variation of maximum oxygen intake is about 20%, so that even lower ceilings of 6.6 kJ/min for a woman and 9.6 kJ/min for a man will be encountered 1 time in 40. Relating such figures to the generally accepted energy costs of light and moderate work, we might conclude that most physical tasks are too hard for an older employee.

A second type of limitation is imposed by declining muscular strength. Celentano and Nottrodt (1984) concluded that the majority of heavy tasks encountered in the Canadian Armed Forces involved lifting and carrying. In 70% of occupational categories, there was an occasional need to lift 36 kg to 183 cm and a regular need to lift 18 kg. Although this demand fell within the capacity of most young male recruits, it would become excessive if soldiers were allowed to continue active duty to the age of 65 years. Moreover, female recruits, although able to satisfy the aerobic requirements of jogging and running around a parade ground, were quite unable to lift the required loads. Nevertheless, it is interesting that some men with apparently inadequate strength and some women had been accepted for employment in many of the trades that were analyzed.

The exercise physiologist thus faces a paradox. Neither aerobic power nor muscular strength seems adequate for heavy work, yet complaints of industrial fatigue are relatively rare among older workers. There are several possible explanations:

1. Symptoms may be suppressed through fear of dismissal. This is increasingly likely as automation boosts the reserves of unemployed young adults.
2. The pace of work may have been exaggerated when energy costs were originally measured. Physiologists have usually used the Kofranyi-Michaelis respirometer to evaluate industrial tasks. Oxygen consumption is then measured over a period of 5 to 10 min (Durnin & Passmore, 1967). However, in a normal working day the specified tasks are usually interspersed with periods of much lighter work. Moreover, the published energy costs have been determined on volunteers, and such individuals may have demonstrated a need of peer approval by working faster than normal while measurements were being made.
3. The nature of the work has changed since the original measurements were made in the early 1930s. Modern equipment may cause people to work faster (Edholm, 1970), but in general it has also reduced energy costs (Shephard, 1985).
4. The aging worker may avoid an excessive rate of working. A task may be undertaken more slowly or, if it is machine paced, longer rest pauses may be taken. Years of experience may also have increased mechanical efficiency, while seniority may allow the assignment of the heaviest tasks to younger workers.
5. It can be argued that heavy work has helped to maintain personal fitness. However, in practice those employed in heavy work do not have a larger maximum oxygen intake than those engaged in light activities (Allen, 1966). Presumably, the typical heart rate reached at an acceptable industrial ceiling (40% of aerobic power) is insufficient to have any training effect (Shephard, 1977).

Assessing Working Capacity

Objective indices of physical working capacity used in legal battles over mandatory retirement, employment of women, and the like are generally based upon task-specific measures of performance. Let us suppose that we wish to decide whether a paunchy aging police constable should be allowed to remain on active service. A battery of occupationally appropriate tests is set, and the policeman is required to complete all of them. For example, he might be asked to clear a 2-m wall, to drag a simulated casualty 30 m across a highway, and to handcuff a mannequin stuffed with resisting springs, completing all of these tasks within a specified time (Wilmore & Davis, 1979). Likewise, a soldier might be asked to lift a series of 36-kg ammunition boxes onto a flatbed truck within a specified time (Nottrodt & Celentano, 1984).

Such tests have an inherent construct validity—that is, they appear to measure an attribute that is of potential value to the employer. But, unfortunately, the scores suffer from a limited reliability. Results improve with practice and depend greatly upon the immediate environmental conditions. A further problem arises from biological variation—a given individual's working capacity is by no means constant from day to day; in any given test, performance may be depressed by intercurrent infection, by recent fatiguing activities in work or leisure, and by circadian and circaseptan rhythms (Strydom, 1978; Yamaji, Sakamoto, Nakaguchi, Kitamura, & Shephard, 1981).

Surprisingly, laboratory tests are often no more satisfactory than the field tests of performance. Submaximum predictions of aerobic power, for example, may show a coefficient of variation of 20 to 25%, far too large to say whether an individual worker is in good or in poor physical condition (Shephard, 1987). Direct measurements of maximum oxygen intake, with a test-retest variation of about 4%, are a little more precise, but they would be costly to carry out on every worker who disputed his or her retirement date. Moreover, whether direct or indirect measurements of maximum oxygen intake are used, day-to-day fluctuations of up to 0.5 l/min arise from factors such as intercurrent disease (Wright, Sidney, & Shephard, 1978). Thus, if one proposes to introduce $\dot{V}O_2$max data into legal testimony, it is wise to show that the employee was well rested and in good general health at the time of testing.

Laboratory lifting tests seem particularly susceptible to the learning of technique. Nottrodt and Celentano (1984) concluded that data obtained from an incremental lifting task accounted for only about a half of the variance in work performance; their scores on the lifting frame proved no more useful information than merely weighing the subject. Half of the variation in lifting remained unexplained, and this component of the total variation was large relative to the 20% difference of performance between a satisfactory and an unsatisfactory recruit.

Value of Adapted Conditioning Programs

Given that aerobic power and strength both seem inadequate at the end of a normal working career, how far can the situation be improved by a suitably adapted program of physical conditioning? Much depends on the extent to which work itself has conserved function. Most jobs do little to conserve fitness. Progressive training can then boost both aerobic power and muscular strength by at least 20% (Wright, Sidney, & Shephard, 1978); indeed, we have seen occasional postcoronary patients who have increased their oxygen transport by more than 100% over 3 to 4 years of progressive endurance training. Moreover, even a 20% gain of working capacity can make a tremendous contribution to a reduction of fatigue. Both maximum oxygen intake and muscular strength decline by about 10% per decade, so that the end result of such training is equivalent to at least a 20-year rejuvenation of the worker.

Influence of Modern Technology on Health

Occupational studies suggest that the ever-declining energy demands of industrial work may have contributed to our 20th-century epidemic of ischaemic heart disease (Paffenbarger, 1977). If we plot the general course of the cardiac epidemic, it now seems to be waning, at least in North America. It is thus unlikely that further automation will add directly to the burden of cardiovascular disease in our society. However, it may do so less directly, by alienating the population, creating a feeling of anomie or lack of meaning, and encouraging acceptance of an adverse life-style. One expression of this trend is the recent shift of ischaemic heart disease from the white-collar sector to blue-collar employees.

The impact of modern technology upon health can be seen particularly dramatically in Canada's northland; there, some populations have moved from the life of neolithic nomads to a 20th-century postindustrial society over the space of 10 or 15 years. Cross-sectional and longitudinal studies of the community of Igloolik (69° 40'N) have shown that this process of ac-culturation is associated with a substantial reduction of aerobic power and muscular strength and the accumulation of subcutaneous fat; in future, the aging Inuit, like white people, will need to maintain their physical condition by deliberate programs of active leisure.

A further hazard arising from a weakened physical condition is an in-creased risk of injury. Back problems are a major source of disability in Western society, and there is some evidence that the incidence of such problems is increased by the introduction of machines that normally lift and carry heavy loads. The worker who sustains injury is usually a person for whom lifting is an infrequent task (Guthrie, 1963).

A final health concern is worker satisfaction. Much ill-health reflects not organic disease but rather a dissatisfaction with the conditions of life in an impersonal and automated society. While new equipment can sometimes add interest and extend the range of a worker's skills, often the physical and mental demands of automated operations are so low that the work becomes intensely boring. An older person may also face problems of the opposite sort because new machinery is not understood, the pace of opera-tion is too fast, or the required level of responsibility exceeds the indi-vidual's competence (Coburn, 1981). Suitably adapted programs of leisure activity can counter some of these problems (Shephard, 1983c). Arousal is restored if the employee is bored, a means of detente is provided if the work load is excessive, and overall life satisfaction is increased.

Physical Demands of a Postindustrial Society

Substantial changes of technology are rapidly infiltrating even traditional heavy occupations. Can we thus assume that in our postindustrial society the declining physical capacity of the older worker is no longer an obstacle to continued employment (Livingston & Robinson, 1984; Robinson, Livingston, & Birren, 1985)? There seems little question that the energy costs of traditional heavy work have dropped dramatically in recent years. On the other hand, a compressed working week, "moonlighting," and strenuous "do-it-yourself" projects have maintained or even increased the weekly energy expenditures of some elderly persons.

Many of the tasks that are still heavy work involve walking, lifting, carrying, and the climbing of stairs (for example, mail carrying, Shephard, 1983a; and marine surveying, Shephard, 1983b). The walking speed of a mail carrier can slow as one gets older, although a standard speed is frequently discussed in contract negotiations. Marine surveyors are often former sea captains. They make a late start in their second career, and their age of retirement is thus extensively debated. In theory, the pace of inspection of a ship could be varied with the person's age. However, the idle capital represented by a modern container vessel at anchor is such that in practice there is strong pressure to complete a marine survey at high speed. Notice that the occupation of mail carrier is currently threatened by the introduction of electronic mail systems. Marine surveying would be more difficult to automate, although a power-operated viewing platform could conceivably help the inspection of large cargo holds.

Robots are rapidly displacing human operators on many production lines. This may have important implications for the physical demands placed upon future generations of older workers. However, the current generation remains in traditional, nonautomated crafts (Sachuk, 1971), and persons with outdated skills have been relegated to relatively arduous "odd jobs" around a factory. As new machinery is introduced, it is generally the youngest employees who learn how to operate it. The traditional skills of the older worker have ever less relevance, and the only options become retirement or acceptance of unskilled and unsatisfying manual work (Shephard, 1987).

What contribution can adapted physical education make to this situation? The elderly person is undoubtedly at a serious disadvantage in the shrinking postindustrial job market. There is thus a need for socialization into leisure. Recreational pursuits will need to be accepted not as a weekend luxury or even an interjob episode but rather as a permanent way of life. Unfortunately, many older people have difficulty in making this adjustment. The Protestant work ethic is strongly entrenched. There are learned expectations of a long working week and little play. Much re-education will be necessary. The leisure allowed by our postindustrial society must become a means of self-fulfillment rather than a source of disgrace (Shephard, 1985).

Finally, let us note that the sport and recreation initiatives needed by the unemployed older person are labor intensive. They can offer employment opportunities to a substantial number of those who have been displaced from traditional work by the process of automation (Shephard, 1984).

References

Allen, J. G. (1966). Aerobic capacity and physiological fitness of Australian men. *Ergonomics*, **9**, 485-494.

Celentano, E., & Nottrodt, J. (1984). Analyzing physically demanding jobs: The Canadian Forces Approach. In D. A. Attwood & C. McCann (Eds.), *Proceedings of International Conference on Occupational Ergonomics* (pp. 421-424). Toronto: Human Factors Association of Canada.

Coburn, D. (1981). Work alienation and well-being. In D. Coburn, C. D'Arcy, P. New, & G. Torrance (Eds.), *Health and Canadian Society* (pp. 420-437). Toronto: Fitzhenry and Whiteside.

Durnin, J. V. G. A., & Passmore, R. (Eds.). (1967). *Energy, work and leisure*. London: Heinemann.

Edholm, O. G. (1970). The changing pattern of human activitiy. *Ergonomics*, **13**, 625-643.

Guthrie, D. I. (1963). A new approach to handling in industry. A rational approach to the prevention of low back pain. *South African Medical Journal*, **37**, 651-656.

Hughes, A. L., & Goldman, R. F. (1970). Energy cost of hard work. *Journal of Applied Physiology*, **29**, 570-572.

Livingston, J., & Robinson, P. K. (1984, March). Age, health, and productivity. In *Report of a seminar sponsored by the National Policy Center on Employment and Retirement*. Los Angeles: Andrus Gerontology Center.

Nottrodt, J. W., & Celentano, R. J. (1984). Use of validity measures in the selection of physical screening tests. In D. A. Attwood & C. McCann (Eds.), *Proceedings of International Conference on Occupational Ergonomics* (pp. 433-435). Toronto: Human Factors Association of Canada.

Paffenbarger, R. (1977). Physical activity and fatal heart attack: Protection or selection? In E. A. Amsterdam, J. H. Wilmore, & A. N. deMaria (Eds.), *Exercise in cardiovascular health and disease* (pp. 35-49). New York: Yorke Books.

Robinson, P., Livingston, J., & Birren, J. E. (Eds.). (1985). *Aging and technological advances*. New York: Plenum Press.

Sachuk, N. N. (1971). The aging worker's abilities and disabilities in relation to industrial production. In J. Huet (Ed.), *Work and aging* (pp. 147-162). Paris: International Centre of Social Gerontology.

Shephard, R. J. (1974). *Men at work: Applications of ergonomics to performance and design.* Springfield, IL: C.C. Thomas.

Shephard, R. J. (1977). *Endurance fitness* (2nd ed.). Toronto: University of Toronto Press.

Shephard, R. J. (1982). *Physiology and biochemistry of exercise.* New York: Praeger.

Shephard, R. J. (1983a). The daily work-load of the postal carrier. *Journal of Human Ergology, 11,* 157-164.

Shephard, R. J. (1983b). Equal opportunity for a geriatric labor force. Some observations on marine surveying. *Journal of Occupational Medicine, 25*(3), 211-214.

Shephard, R. J. (1983c). Physical activity and the healthy mind. *Canadian Medical Association Journal, 128*(5), 525-530.

Shephard, R. J. (1984). *Fiscal implications for fit Canada: Guidelines for social planning and research.* Ottawa: Fitness and Amateur Sport.

Shephard, R. J. (1985). Technological change and the aging of working capacity. In J. Birren, P. Robinson, & J. Livingston (Eds.), *Aging and technological advances.* New York: Plenum Press.

Shephard, R. J. (1986). *Health and fitness in industry.* Basel: Karger.

Shephard, R. J. (1987). *Physical activity and aging* (2nd ed.). London: Croom Helm.

Strydom, N. B. (1978). Environmental variable affecting fitness testing. In R. J. Shephard & H. Lavallee (Eds.), *Physical fitness assessment: Principles, practice and applications* (pp. 94-101). Springfield, IL: C. C. Thomas.

Wilmore, J. H., & Davis, J. A. (1979). Validation of a physical abilities field test for the selection of State Traffic Officers. *Journal of Occupational Medicine, 21,* 33-40.

Wright, G. R., Sidney, K. H., & Shephard, R. J. (1978). Variance of direct and indirect measurements of aerobic power. *Journal of Sports Medicine and Physical Fitness, 18,* 33-42.

Yamaji, K., Sakamoto, H., Nakaguchi, M., Kitamura, K., & Shephard, R. J. (1981). Biological rhythms of PWC_{170} and maximum oxygen intake. *Journal of Human Ergology, 10,* 213-219.

Obstacles to Participation in Physical Activities of the Canadian Elderly Population

Jean Claude Pageot

My purpose in this study is to identify the main parties involved in the field of fitness in the elderly and the role these parties play in the Canadian delivery system. In addition, I attempt to list the various obstacles preventing the expansion of fitness programs as well as methods that have been suggested by respondents to eliminate these obstacles.

Method

Sample

The sample comes from national, provincial, regional, and local organizations concerned with the elderly population. However, only those organizations offering direct services to the aged in the areas of programming, leadership, consultation, evaluation, and documentation were selected for the purpose of the sample. It also included educational and health-oriented organizations as well as various levels of government.

Questionnaires were mailed to a total of 3,023 organizations. Some 22.9% of these organizations responded. As the number of respondents reflects quite faithfully the distribution of the Canadian elderly population, the results can be considered as representative of the Canadian scene.

Questionnaire

The questionnaire was mainly composed of closed questions. However, after each series of questions, space was provided to allow the respondent to make additional comments or to elaborate on a particular response.

The section on obstacles to participation asked the opinion of the elderly and of the representatives of the organizations.

Results

Profile of Respondents

The respondents were classified into 15 categories corresponding to structures that are generally accepted in Canadian society. The categories were then subdivided into four sections (abbreviations in parentheses are those used in figures):

1.0 Public Sector

    1.1 Provincial and federal governments and their agencies (Prov. + fed.)

    1.2 Municipal recreation departments (Mun.)

    1.3 Educational institutions (Ed. inst.)

    1.4 Hospitals (Hosp.)

2.0 Associations

    2.1 Regional, provincial, and national senior citizens' associations (SC assoc.)

    2.2 Professional associations composed of people who work with the elderly (Prof. assoc.)

    2.3 Community associations directly involved with the well-being of the aged (Comm. assoc.)

    2.4 Associations specializing in physical activities and physical fitness (Phys. assoc.)

3.0 Local seniors' organizations

    3.1 Senior citizens' clubs (SC clubs)

    3.2 Centers for the elderly (Cent. eld.)

    3.3 Homes for the aged (Homes)

4.0 Other organizations

    4.1 Recreation centers (Rec. cent.)

    4.2 Community centers (Comm. cent.)

    4.3 Private clubs (Priv. clubs)

    4.4 Other organizations (Other)

Senior citizens' clubs and municipal recreation departments constitute the largest proportion of respondents. They represent 34% and 28% of

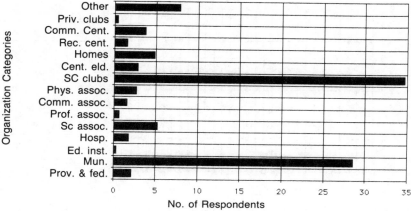

Figure 1 Distribution of sample.

the sample, respectively. Senior citizens' associations, homes for the aged, community centers, and centers for the elderly together account for the next largest proportion of respondents. The smallest number of respondents comes from the educational sector, private clubs, and professional and community associations (see Figure 1).

The geographic distribution of the respondents parallels closely that of the elderly Canadian population. Saskatchewan, however, is an exception; the percentage of respondents of this province is much larger. Saskatchewan ranks sixth in terms of percentage of population aged 65 or over but is second with 20.2% in terms of respondent organizations (Stone & Fletcher, 1981, p. 41).

Nearly half the respondents live in a center with a population less than 15,000, while 21% live in a city of more than 100,000. The remaining percentage is equally distributed between these two extremes. This shows that the sample is equally representative of both rural and urban areas.

Over half of the organizations serve less than 100 people, whereas another 25% serve 250 people or less. This indicates that the majority of organizations operate on a small scale.

Roles of Organizations

Very few large organizations indicated that creating physical activity programs was their main role. This responsibility seems to lie in the hands of local organizations for the elderly, such as clubs and centers (see Figure 2).

On the other hand, it is interesting to note that the majority of respondents feel that their principal role is to provide leadership and stimulus for the elderly or for senior citizens' organizations. Second in importance is providing literature to the elderly and related organizations.

Many respondents indicated that one of their top priorities was to evaluate physical activities and physical fitness programs. This function often

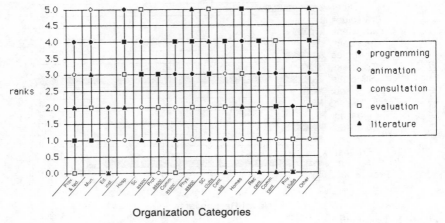

Figure 2   Ranking of role priorities.

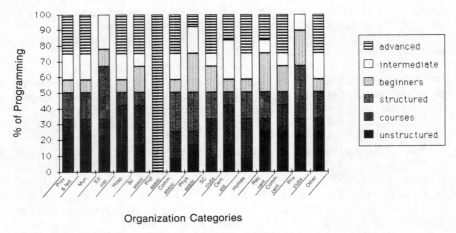

Organization Categories

Figure 3   Percentage of programming devoted to various types of activities.

takes priority over developing and running their own programs. Generally speaking, there is a tendency to let the elderly take charge of their own activities and to help them in this regard only if the need exists and if they request assistance.

Among the organizations that do offer programs, physical activity courses tend to be favored. Structured and supervised activities are the second choice, whereas unstructured activities that generally reflect a certain life-style are not very popular except among local senior citizens' organizations (see Figure 3).

The majority of organizations focus their attention on beginners. The elderly at the intermediate and advanced levels receive little attention. This attitude indicates once again that either the development of an active

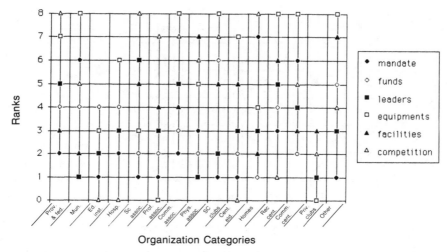

Figure 4   Ranking of obstacles by organizations.

life-style is still not a priority with these organizations or that organizations are not yet able to meet such needs.

Obstacles Faced by the Organizations

Generally speaking, the major obstacle preventing the elderly from becoming or remaining physically active seems to be the lack of qualified personnel. Organizations that have direct contact with the elderly, such as recreation departments and senior citizens' clubs, face this obstacle most often. The problem is also shared by the educational sector and organizations specializing in physical fitness. The lack of personnel is a less serious problem, however, for organizations operating at higher levels, such as governments and regional and provincial associations for the elderly (see Figure 4).

The lack of funds seems to be a problem common to almost all organizations and is related to another obstacle, the lack of equipment. Residences for the elderly suffer the most from this problem, followed by senior citizens' clubs.

It is interesting to note that the majority of respondent organizations state that physical fitness for the elderly does not constitute part of their mandate. However, recreation departments, community centers, and homes for the aged do acknowledge that they have a role to play in this area. This is troubling because it once again brings to light the problem of responsibility. Who should take the lead in this area, and who should be the privileged parties who follow in their footsteps? Senior citizens' clubs and educational institutions do not see themselves in either of these roles.

There is a connection between the fact that the majority of respondents do not feel that physical fitness for the elderly is their mandate and another

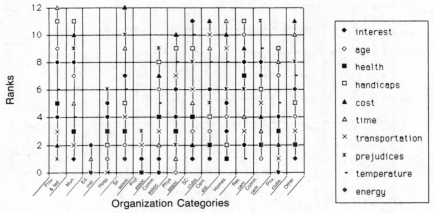

Figure 5   Ranking of obstacles by elderly clients of organizations.

barrier, the lack of support. Organizations emphasize the fact that they receive little recognition for their efforts and little help when they require it. They feel that they have been left to their own resources but, at the same time, are being judged and evaluated. This causes enormous pressure among these organizations. Facilities do not seem to be a problem. A number of respondents, such as recreation departments, residences for the elderly, and various centers, did, however, indicate that they would like to have more facilities.

If recreation centers and private clubs are disregarded, it would not appear that the market is saturated, because competition among organizations is considered almost nonexistent. This perhaps also illustrates that the demand is still not very great and that everyone is hoping that someone else will take action first, as discussed above.

Obstacles Faced by the Elderly

The reason most frequently given to organizations by the elderly for not participating in physical fitness activities is a lack of interest. A few exceptions were found in community centers, specialized associations, and hospitals. In the last two cases, those who avail themselves of the services offered are either already motivated to do so or require physical activity to speed their recovery (see Figure 5).

Health problems are the second most common reason given by the elderly for not participating in fitness programs offered by organizations. However, the exception is the recreation centers, which the elderly population frequents specifically to be active and entertained. It is impossible to determine here whether nonparticipation is due to genuine health problems or whether it is only that some of the elderly perceive their health as an obstacle.

The third obstacle is transportation to and from the place where activities are held. If institutions that house the elderly are excluded from data, then

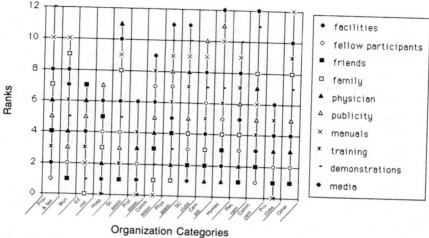

Figure 6   Ranking of solutions to obstacles by organizations.

transportation becomes the second largest obstacle, after lack of interest.

Several other reasons for nonparticipation were also given, but they affect more specifically one or several types of organizations. Clients often tell community centers, hospitals, and senior citizens' associations that they feel they are too old to participate in such activities. Recreation centers and departments have noted that participation fluctuates according to the temperature outside.

The cost of participating in activities does not seem to be an obstacle to participation. Only activities offered by government bodies, senior citizens' clubs, and private clubs may be prohibitively expensive. Moreover, elderly participants are for the large part satisfied with services rendered; the exception is with those rendered by specialized organizations.

Discussion

It does not appear that it will be easy to find solutions for improving physical activities programs and eliminating the major obstacles because no real concensus has emerged from the responses received.

It seems that the best way of ensuring the success of a program is to ensure that the group includes motivated coparticipants so that everyone helps and motivates one another. However, neither the community and specialized associations nor the educational sector really believes that this is the best solution. They lean more toward the influence family members can have on the participant (see Figure 6). Except for the educational setting, the support of friends would appear to be another element of the solution. On the whole, if these solutions were implemented, they could serve to improve the social environment of elderly persons, which might help create a favorable climate for participation in physical activity.

By advising the patient to do more exercise, the physician could contribute to improving the social climate. Senior citizens' associations and clubs, however, question this solution.

Over half of the respondent organizations suggested that by improving their facilities, by making them more suitable and pleasant, they could in turn improve the environment in which activities are held.

The production of audiovisual materials and an instruction manual on physical fitness do not seem to be considered terribly worthwhile; in terms of effectiveness, they are ranked 11th and 10th, respectively. Only the educational sector believes strongly in the manual, and only professional associations think highly of audiovisual materials.

While the lack of leaders has been identified as a major obstacle in developing programs, the training of leaders is ranked only eighth in terms of importance in this regard. Regional and provincial senior citizens' associations, followed by government bodies and the educational sector, are the strongest supporters of leader training.

Conclusion

Although there is a consensus to identify the lack of qualified personnel as the major problem to develop physical fitness programs, there is no solution suggested by respondents to overcome this obstacle. In the near future, more studies should be implemented in this area, especially in using the elderly themselves as leaders.

Because some organizations, such as municipal recreation departments and residences for elderly, already accept an active role in the provision of physical activities for the elderly population, different levels of government should entrust this task to them and give them the necessary support.

Studies should be conducted to determine the best means of integrating physical activities into the life-style of the elderly population. This integration will allow them to better adjust to their new situation upon retirement and transfer their values to something else, as demonstrated by Coutier, Camus, and Sarkar (1977), Gibbs (1982), and Weiner (1982).

It is also necessary to determine why so few elderly individuals adopt the role of leader in the programs in which they participate. The type of training they need to be more efficient, on the other hand, has been studied by Boyd (1982).

Finally, results suggest that physical activities and physical fitness programs should have a social and recreational aspect so that participants feel more like active members of society. Soucy and Gagne (1978) have shown that the best way to include a new activity in one's life-style is by making it fun and pleasurable. Being active and having fun improve self-image (Beck, 1982; Gissal, Ray, & Smith, 1980; Hogan, 1982; Wright, 1977).

References

Beck, L. L. (1982). Recreation and the elderly. *Momentum*, 7(2), 9-19.

Boyd, C. A. (1982). Health, physical education and recreation and the aging process. *Florida Journal of Health, Physical Education, Recreation and Dance,* **20**(2), 10-21.

Coutier, D., Camus, Y., & Sarkar, A. (1977). *3ème age: Mouvement et animation physique* [The third age: Movement and physical animation]. Paris: Institut National du Sport et de l'Education Physique.

Gibbs, R. (1982). Living longer and growing younger. Exercise prescription for the elderly. *Australian Family Physician,* **11**(10), 775-781.

Gissal, M. L., Ray, R. O., & Smith, P. L. (1980). Fitness trail: A healthful activity for older adults. *Therapeutic Recreation Journal,* **14**(2), 43-48.

Hogan, P. I. (1982). Leisure satisfaction, physical activity and older adults. *Leisure Information Newsletter,* **9**(2), 9-11.

Soucy, M., & Gagne, D. (1978). *Participation des Quebecois aux activités de loisirs* [Quebec participation in leisure activities]. Quebec: Haut Commissariat à la Jeunesse, aux Loissirs et aux Sports.

Stone, L. O., & Fletcher, S. (1981). *Aspects of population aging in Canada.* Ottawa: National Advisory Council on Aging.

Weiner, A. (1982). Leisure education for retirement. *Life Long Learning: The Adult Years,* **6**(2), 14-23.

Wright, A. (1977). *Assessment of the effects of a developmental motor activity programme on the self-image of aged females.* Ottawa: D. H. W.

PART IX

Programs for Seniors

Dance-Movement Therapy With the Elderly at Baycrest Centre for Geriatric Care

Pamela Weingarden-Albert

Dance-movement therapy provides a new and innovative approach to improving the functioning level of the individual, both within the institutional setting and within the mainstream of the community. Dance-movement therapy addresses the psychotherapeutic use of movement to facilitate the physical and emotional growth of the individual. This approach is based on the integration of body and mind, in which movement becomes the main therapeutic tool for change. This is based on the principle that one's thoughts and feelings are exhibited in physical movement. In other words, one's emotions are manifested in the body.

Dance-movement therapy views the relationship between body and mind as a system. When there is a disruption in the unity of flow, psychological or physical conflict sets in. The movement patterns that one develops are unique to each individual and become a representation of one's personality, serving as an expression of one's internal representations. Often, one's range of movement may be inadequate or unproductive.

Quite often verbal communication is not possible, be it too threatening or due to a medical cause. Increasing or changing one's use of movement can improve one's ability to recognize and express thoughts and feelings. Quite often emotions remain repressed at an unconscious level; movement can serve as a means of transcending repressed affect to a conscious level.

Since emotional states are in fact exhibited on a body level, the attainment of self-awareness on a movement level can result in personal awareness and growth. This is achieved through redefining body boundaries, integration of upper and lower body, recognition of body parts, self-acceptance, and through the release of bodily tensions.

Dance-movement therapy is a process that helps one achieve changes on a body level, resulting in physical and emotional growth. It helps unlock stored emotions by exploring and expanding one's range of movement, releasing tension, and providing creative channels for the expression of thoughts, memories, feelings, and conflicts. It can enhance one's ability to move authentically, facilitating the emergence of self and impulses. While working with a group or individual the dance-movement therapist serves as a facilitator of themes and emotional content that evolve from members themselves. Thus dance-movement therapy serves as an effective means of facilitating personal discovery and growth.

Setting

The setting for this discussion is Baycrest Centre for Geriatric Care. Baycrest consists of a hospital, the Jewish Home for the Aged (JHA), the Terrace (a residential complex), the Wagman Centre (a community center), and a day treatment program. Instead of a purely medical approach, Baycrest addresses the medical, social, and community needs of the elderly, providing a continuum of care (Jesion, 1984).

More and more individuals are living to an age where they need quality care within the community. Baycrest is able to provide the necessary support systems for the elderly. Previously, the emphasis was on the medical treatment. At this time, there is a growing realization of the need for providing an active, enriching life for the elderly.

The focus of Baycrest is not on therapy but on socialization and community involvement. Although there are a vast number of activities, interest groups, and adjunctive therapies, there are still some individuals whose needs aren't being served. Dance-movement therapy can provide an alternate means of fulfilling and enriching the lives of residents. Even in rehabilitation, there are often emotional needs that are left unmet. The following section will discuss how dance-movement therapy has been effectively incorporated into Baycrest's programs and concept of care.

Dance-Movement Therapy Goals

The purpose of this section is to outline the goals that dance-movement therapy addresses while working with the elderly. One common problem is that of loss, either the loss of a spouse or loved one or physical loss. It is important to find an outlet for expressing the loss as well as a means of filling that void.

Emotional states that accompany loss are denial (e.g., if a limb is amputated), anger, and frustration. Feelings of depression, guilt, and helplessness may also result from loss. If people are depressed, they may lose their will to live or fail to take care of themselves and carry on with daily activities. Through the use of specific movements, one is able to discover a nonverbal means of expressing feelings around loss. Imagery is used quite often, such as pushing a hand to the center of the circle to symbolically push away troublesome thoughts and feelings. It is not uncommon to see a wheelchair-confined old person thrashing out at others physically or verbally. An example of an appropriate method of channeling this type of behavior is squeezing a nurf ball in the hands or clenching and pulling a sheet of material.

The nurf ball activity relates to another goal—reality orientation. Confusion or disorganization can be present as a result of physical or emotional deterioration in the elderly. Direct movements, such as squeezing a ball with two hands simultaneously or tapping of arms and legs, can provide a means of cognitive reorganization in confused patients through sensory stimulation. Studies have shown (Tinnins, 1981) that continuously lying in a bed or sitting in a wheelchair can result in a lack of reality orientation or even in a form of psychosis. For example, after a certain amount of time the patient can begin to feel as if the bed or chair is an extension of the self. In a group situation, direct movements such as reaching an arm straight out in front and looking at the person across the circle provide an effective method for regaining reality orientation.

Socialization is usually an important goal. Quite often referrals are made because the elderly either feel alienated or alienate themselves from others. If verbal communication has become too threatening or is no longer possible due to a medical cause (e.g., loss of sight or hearing), movement can provide an alternative means of relating to others.

Depending on one's origin, verbal communication may be impossible due to a language barrier. For example, one woman I worked with spoke only Russian. I met with her daughter so that her daughter could translate for us as well as learn another way of being with her mother. I asked her daughter to tell her that I wished we could speak the same language. Her mother responded by saying, "It doesn't matter, we can talk all we want like this," as she proceeded to show her daughter the ritualistic ways we developed of swinging our arms together.

This example also brings up the importance of physical touch and closeness. It is usually unacceptable to hug acquaintances. Everyone needs some expression of physical and sexual warmth and love. Because we are working on a movement level, it becomes acceptable to hold each others' hands or tap elbows, providing the physical warmth and comfort that every individual requires. A common exercise is to give oneself a hug. The purpose of this is to teach the group members that they can take care of themselves or provide themselves with comfort and love. Thus dance-movement therapy achieves this by providing a supportive caring environment.

Often it is difficult for the elderly to accept their physical and emotional limitations. This can result in a defeatist attitude, focusing only on loss of functioning. Allowing the group members to take a leadership role in the group can enable them to focus on what they can do. Thus a negative outlook is switched to a positive self-image. This new ability to accept oneself may enable the person to feel more relaxed and happier about the present. It is strongly believed that attitudes and will to live are directly related to the ability to maintain or improve one's level of functioning.

An important part of the aging process is reminiscence. Reminiscing provides a way of overviewing one's life. It is often those past memories that enable someone to smile or breathe free of tension. Images often accompany movement, such as rowing a boat or pulling the cord of a bell. Introducing images also elicits the sharing of fond memories.

Common symptoms of depression are a lack of motivation and isolating behavior. On a body level, the person may seem stuck or immobile. The use of movement can result in activating and motivating a person enough to carry on with daily life. An example of the type of movement is a general body warm-up for the purpose of improving circulation, stimulating the body and using breathing and getting the body working as a unit.

An example is stretching one's arms high up in the air and then low to the ground. Another example is opening and closing fingers and toes or rolling wrists and ankles. The key often lies in the group unity that develops as the group members work as a unit.

Another goal that is quite common in rehabilitation, as with the stroke recovery group at Baycrest, is to redefine or strengthen body boundaries. An example is the denial of the loss of a limb. The use of movement can provide a way of accepting new body boundaries and of feeling good about one's existing capabilities. Often with stroke patients, there is a loss of awareness of one side of the body. By using both sides of the body simultaneously (e.g., grasping two hands together) or using the forgotten side of the body to move, the patient is able to redefine body image.

Another goal in rehabilitation is improving gross and fine motor control movements, such as tapping both hands simultaneously or tapping hands and feet simultaneously, which can facilitate the development of skills. Tapping each finger and thumb is an example of improving fine motor control. Moving one arm stretched sideways at horizontal position toward the center of the body is an example of improving eye-to-hand coordination.

The last goal to be discussed is often overlooked, and it is one of the most important goals of dance-movement therapy—that is, to have fun; to provide the elderly with a nonthreatening environment where they can laugh, share, and experience the quality of life; to provide a place where learning and socialization can be accompanied by fun.

Description of Dance-Movement Therapy Groups

This section will briefly outline five dance-movement therapy groups held at Baycrest, which are as follows: (a) special needs, (b) two music and movement groups in the JHA, (c) a Terrace residents' group, and (d) a hospital group.

Special needs. This group, open to Wagman Centre members, meets once a week for 50 min. The group began as a place for people recovering from stroke and other medical conditions to meet and share their problems, experiences, and goals. The group meeting is followed by a therapeutic swim program. The purpose of the group has not changed, but movement is now used as the main therapeutic tool to achieve many of the goals outlined in the previous section. The goal grows closer as the members are able to share feelings about their situations. Verbal sharing usually follows the movement expression. It is nice to see the group members helping each other as they work together to improve their skills.

Music and movement. There are two groups to be discussed from the JHA: an off-the-floor group and an on-the-floor group.

The off-the-floor group is held in the arts and crafts room. Residents from different floors join to achieve individual and group goals. General goals are to improve socialization, to activate and motivate residents, to achieve a better sense of well-being, to provide an appropriate outlet for expressing emotions, and to reminisce about their past.

The on-the-floor group consists of four women who have a limited range of movement and are very frail and weak. Movement is achieved on a more individualized level. The JHA is realizing a growth in the need for more on-the-floor programs. There seem to be more and more residents who are no longer able to leave the floors due to a deterioration in functioning level. It has been found that most group situations are not appropriate for reaching these people.

Dance-movement therapy provides the alternative for communicating with many of these residents because movement can happen on such a subtle level. Their smiles that greet me when I arrive and their relaxed bodies when the group finishes exemplify the satisfaction they attain from these programs.

Movement to music. Many of the residents who attend the Terrace group talk about needing an outlet for reducing stress. This is described in the form of headaches or tense, stiff bodies. Another common problem is an inability to sleep at night. Because we all have individual movement patterns that work as coping mechanisms, they are able to discover these in the group and use their specific movement activity or exercise to help them relax in their apartments. Other common goals are activating and motivating, alleviating depression, and improving their ability to think and focus in the here and now.

Chronic and long-term care. Initially there were six patients in the chronic and long-term care group, but as more patients began to pull their wheelchairs down to the room, we opened the sessions to all interested patients on the floor. Like the stroke recovery group, much of our time is geared toward physical rehabilitation, whereas the JHA groups focus more on maintaining a preventative intervention.

Quite often chronic care patients tend to lose any hope of getting better. Through the movement intervention, they are often able to work on improving their capability and are left with a positive attitude about their daily lives. The group also provides them with a warm, caring environment and provides them with an outlet for expressing the sudden changes in their lives.

Conclusion

In summary, dance-movement therapy provides an effective means of serving the physical and emotional needs of the elderly, both within the institution and in community settings.

The purpose of Baycrest Centre as a whole is to address medical, psychiatric, and social problems of the elderly. Dance-movement therapy with the elderly include the following goals:

- Dealing with the issue of loss and mourning
- Providing a structured and appropriate outlet for expressing anger, frustration, and tolerance
- Facilitating cognitive reorganization in confused patients through sensory stimulation
- Improving socialization skills and peer interaction
- Providing a supportive, caring environment
- Increasing self-awareness of existing capabilities
- Improving self-esteem
- Providing a place to reminisce
- Alleviating depression
- Redefining and strengthening body image
- Improving gross and fine motor coordination
- Improving hand-to-eye coordination
- Providing a place to relax and enjoy

The groups to whom these goals were applied in this discussion include a special needs group, an on-the-floor and off-the-floor group in the JHA, a hospital group, and a group for Terrace residents.

In all these areas, dance-movement therapy has provided an alternative means of improving the physical and emotional functioning level of the elderly. It offers innovative and exciting solutions to the provision of high quality services for the elderly in the future, both within the community and in an institutional setting.

References

Jesion, M. L. (1984, Autumn). The geriatric hospital: A new concept in care for the elderly. *Health Management Forum*, pp. 37-46.

Tinnins, L. W. (1981). *Developmental overview of psychiatric disorders.*

Relaxation-Concentration Training for Older Adults

Tadeusz Pasek
Juri V. Daniel

Degenerative changes due to aging manifest themselves in increased impairment of seeing, hearing, touching, moving, concentrating, reasoning, and other functions essential to a healthy and enjoyable life-style. Psychosocial stressors such as loneliness, helplessness, depression, anxiety, deprivation, and changing self-perception are often additional sources of distress and ill health. The aging process may be viewed as consisting of primary or chronological aging, which is largely genetically determined, and secondary aging, which is speeded up by emotional tension, physical trauma, disease, and other insults to the body. Selye (1974) called secondary aging a result of all the stresses to which the body had been exposed to during a lifetime; in a sense, an accelerated version of primary or "normal" aging. Some of the above-mentioned changes, particularly those of secondary aging, can be slowed by stress management techniques and life-style changes. Increased attention has been given to techniques that (a) minimize the frequency of the stress response, such as social engineering, personality engineering, and cognitive reappraisal; (b) minimize the intensity of the stress response and reduce emotional reactivity, such as the various meditational forms, biofeedback, neuromuscular relaxation, and autogenic relaxation; and (c) utilize stress and promote body consciousness, such as body awareness activities and exercise, preferably ego-void exercise. Certain stress management techniques overlap categories and relaxation-concentration training based on yoga has this potential to be an effective technique in reducing the frequency of the stress response, reducing its intensity, and utilizing stress as well as promoting body consciousness.

The beneficial physiological effects of yoga have been well documented by Funderburk (1979). Other investigators have also shown that relaxation-concentration training based on yoga can improve both the intellectual and physical performance of older adults by improving not only selected physiological factors but also psychological factors such as mood, depression, and anxiety (Dolezalova, 1978; Pasek, Nowakowska, Fellmann, Hauser, & Sluzewska, 1981; Vahia et al., 1973).

Relaxation-Concentration Training

Relaxation-concentration training consists of a series of specific static postures; slow, controlled breathing; and some meditation to divert attention from external stimuli. These postures are light isometric exercises, suitably modified for different groups, performed in a state of concentration on certain parts of the body. Contrary to other forms of physical education, these exercises consist of repeating a relatively simple set of postures with the same physical load. Most of these postures (*asanas* in yoga) are known in calisthenics or gymnastics; however, the technique for performing them is different. Attention is focused on integrating relaxation into the exercises while performing postures for several or a dozen seconds, gradually increasing to several minutes. A feeling of "melting away" while concentrating should be the aim. These exercises are above all mental, and, according to Romanowski et al. (1969), remaining in a constant posture for a certain definite time under recommended conditions "produces a hyperaemia of the relevant organs and an enhanced interoceptive impulsation from these regions. This, with regular and appropriately dosed training, produced a specific interoceptive autonomic stereotype." This autonomic stereotype is in the opposite direction to the andrenogenic type of the chronically distressed. According to Pasek and Romanowski (1972), only through appropriate procedures in relaxation-concentration postures and breathing exercises can what they call "guided" biological rhythmicity, as a factor of beneficially stabilizing the nervous system, be produced.

Furthermore, the accompanying slow, controlled relaxation-concentration breathing is believed to have an energizing role, that is, a role of assimilating energy more efficiently from the external environment. These breathing exercises and the concentration involved manifest themselves in changes of spontaneous electrical activity of the brain (Funderburk, 1979). Investigations in biophysics and theoretical biology are furthering the understanding of the interrelationship between environmental electromagnetic forces and physiological processes of the human organism (Inyushin, 1969; Sedlak, 1972). In building the theory in this interrelationship, Sedlak (1972) refers to the concept of bioplasma in this way:

> The plasma in a living organism would be a system of delocalized particles which have a special spatial organization; it would constitute the substrate of life dynamics and the foundation of its energetics. It may be that only in conditions of integrity of an organism is its bioplasma maximally stable. A disturbance of this state would bring about instability of the biological plasma. This plasma is exposed to the action of various electromagnetic forms of energy and here a certain similarity with prana [cosmic energy according to yoga] may be observed. It seems possible that the bioplasma processes may be controlled with the consciousness. (p. 45)

Investigations by physical educators in Poland (Pasek, 1973; Pasek et al., 1981; Pasek, Romanowski, Eberhardt, & Jasser, 1971; Romanowski et al., 1969) have shown that the equilibrium of the sympathetic nervous system of relaxation-concentration trainees displays tendencies toward the parasympathetic dominance and toward a more effective metabolic balance. Concomitant psychological investigations suggest that these exercises improve mood, reduce anxiety, and reintegrate the psychological dimensions of a practitioner. These physiological and psychological "effects" presumably reduce the intensity and frequency of the stress response.

Stress arousal is a psychophysiological response to psychosocial and environmental stressors. Each stressor produces an immediate stress response but may also leave a residual in the body. Response to subsequent stressors is then augmented by the residual left from previous responses having a cumulative effect. Over time, response overactivity may result from the inability to dissipate residual stress. The relaxation-concentration training sessions, although relatively short-term phenomena in themselves, tend to have a carry-over influence beyond the training sessions. Thus in addition to temporarily reducing physical arousal the training brings about a more chronic parasympathetic dominance.

Relaxation-concentration training was developed by Romanowski and Pasek from yoga to facilitate acceptance in a Western culture. It was developed from yoga exercises (Aundh, 1956; Kuvalayananda & Vinekar, 1963; Sivananda, 1958a, 1958b) with differentiated simplifications for different groups, including older adults.

From a general physiological viewpoint, relaxation-concentration training aims to (a) increase movement of intervertebral joints, improving circulation in the vertebral column; (b) improve circulation to the brain; (c) massage inner organs by means of pressure; (d) affect various glands and organs by means of pressure; (e) affect various glands and nerve plexuses, particularly the visceral plexux; and (f) produce a hypometabolic homeostatic state of calm and relaxation.

The effectiveness of the method depends on regular practice and the competence, interest, and personality of the instructor to arouse and maintain motivation yet have a calming influence. Surroundings that maximally enhance concentration have been found to be helpful, and special music can further the creation of a suitable atmosphere.

Relaxation-Concentration Training for Older Adults

Within the system of relaxation-concentration training, Romanowski and Pasek have introduced a set of simplified exercises suitable for older adults of varying physical fitness and with varying personal or medical restrictions.

This simplified set of exercises consists of the following elements: (a) introductory relaxation-meditation in a kneeling position, (b) rhythmic-concentrating exercises according to Suryanamaskar (yoga movement exercise), (c) fundamental yoga relaxation in lying position (Yoganidra), (d) simple and easy energizing and integrating postures, (e) ending relaxation in lying position (Yoganidra) and consolidation of the effects of the

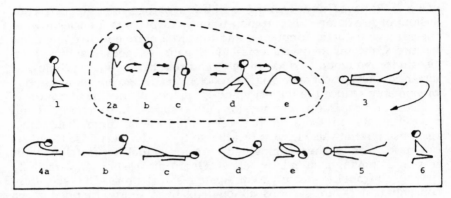

Figure 1   Relaxation-concentration training set for older adults.*

set, and (f) pleasant "awakening" to normal activity through breathing-meditating in a kneeling-sitting position.

More specifically, the regeneration-rehabilitation unit lasting 40 min consists of the following (consult Figure 1):

1. Respiratory meditating exercise in a kneeling-sitting position, with cushions reducing joint discomfort if necessary (4 min, Figure 1:1)
2. Simplified rhythmic-concentrating exercises—Suryanamaskar (4 cycles, approximately 8 min, Figure 1:2a, 2b, 2c, 2d, 2e)
3. Relaxation—Yoganidra, stressing the feeling of "melting away" into the surroundings and absorption of energy, with calm and harmony emanating from it (10 min, Figure 1:3)
4. Yoga postures—Pascimatana (Figure 1:4a), Bhujangasana (Figure 1:4b), Sasankasana (Figure 1:4c), each three times (8 min)
5. Relaxation as in Item 3 but gradual "bringing back" with suitable music (6 min, Figure 1:5)
6. Breathing-meditating in kneeling-sitting position ending the set (4 min, Figure 1:6)

Depending on the fatigue of participants, exercises in prone position can be altered with several or a dozen seconds of relaxation in the prone position called Makarasana in yoga.

It should be noted that in this modification of the system for older adults, the precision of postures is not as important as performing them in as comfortable and as relaxed a manner as possible. The body will yield and adapt slowly and pleasantly. The sensation the participant should feel is some pleasant strain.

Although long-term effects can only be achieved after some time, the response of participants to the training should be carefully and consistently monitored. In general, the exercises should stimulate and regenerate

*1, 6—breathing and meditating postures; 2a-e—rhythmic-concentrating gymnastics (Suryanamaskar); 3, 5—relaxing postures (Yoganidra); 4a-c—energizing and integrating postures.

the body yet have a calming effect. There should be no fatigue, sweating, or sign of distress, and the main warning signs are disturbances in breathing, circulation, and the nervous system (e.g., shortness of breath, light-headedness, anxiety).

Summary

Benefits of relaxation-concentration training in health promotion and stress management have been demonstrated convincingly in Poland by the originators of this technique. It is a useful method for the general population, including older adults, and has also been used successfully in the rehabilitation of mental patients in Poland showing improvements in neurosis, situational reactions, and personality disturbances (Pasek, 1981; Pasek et al., 1981).

The development of relaxation-concentration training and the observed benefits from consistent participation in this system point to its potential as a stress management technique on a broader scale than presently practiced. It is also a very suitable life-style modifier and stress reducer for older adults, with relatively high cost effectiveness.

References

Aundh, R. (1956). *The ten-point way to health*. Bombay: Taraporevala.

Dolezalova, V. (1978). *Experience with the application of yoga in the rehabilitation of psychiatric patients*. Paper presented at the 1st Conference on the Application of Yoga in Rehabilitation Therapy, Kosice-Saca, Czechoslovakia, 1978. (Published in *Slovenska Lekarska Spolecnost v Bratislava*, pp. 71-74)

Funderburk, J. (1979). *Science studies yoga: A review of physiological data*. Honesdale, PA: The Himalayan International Institute of Yoga Science and Philosophy.

Inyushin, V. M. (1969). *Sastav biologiczeskoj plazmy i niekotoryje vaprosy fotobioenergietyki* [Concept of biological plasma and some problems of photobioenergetics]. Alma-Ata, USSR: Kazachskij Gosudarstviennyj Universitet, Biologiczeskij Fakultiet.

Kuvalayananda, S., & Vinekar, S. L. (1963). *Yogic therapy*. New Delhi: Ministry of Health, Government of India.

Pasek, T. (1973). System cwiczen relaksowo-koncentrujacych wzorowany na systemach wschodnich na podstawie doswiadczen wlasnych [System of relaxation-concentration exercises according to Eastern systems, developed on the basis of the author's experiences]. *Wychowanie Fizyczne i Sport*, **2**, 132-136.

Pasek, T. (1981, September). *Relaxation-concentration training as a form of rehabilitation of psychiatric patients*. Paper presented at the 6th World Congress of the International College of Psychosomatic Medicine, Montreal.

(Published in Abstract 425, 107, *Psychiatria Polska*, 1982, **16**, 371-375, in Polish)

Pasek, T., Nowakowska, C., Fellman, B., Hauser, J., & Sluzewska, A. (1981, September). *The evaluation of the yoga-type relaxation-concentration training on patients with psychogenic mental disturbances.* Paper presented at the 6th World Congress of the International College of Psychosomatic Medicine, Montreal. (Printed in Abstract 514, 129, *Psychiatria Polska*, 1982, **16**, 365-370, in Polish)

Pasek, T., & Romanowski, W. (1972). Rola sterowanych rytmow w przeciwdzialaniu i zwalczaniu stanow rozkojarzen psychonerwowych [Role of steered rhythms in the prevention of psychoneurological disturbances]. *Medycyna Lotnicza*, **39**, 133-135.

Pasek, T., Romanowski, W., Everhardt, A., & Jasser, S. (1971). Problematyka wplywu cwiczen relaksowo-koncentrujacych wzorowanych na jodze na odpornosc [Problems of the influence of relaxation-concentration exercises based on yoga on resistivity]. *Wychowanie Fizyczne i Sport*, **4**, 141-146.

Romanowski, W., Pasek, T., Szwarc, H., Gradowska, T., Turos, B., Sikora, J., Ronikier, A., Kocjasz, J., Eberhardt, A., & Jasser, S. (1969). Proba fizjologicznej i psychologicznej oceny wplywu na organizm cwiczen wedlug systemu jogi [Studies on physiological and psychological evaluation of the yoga system exercises]. *Wychowanie Fizyczne i Sport*, **3**, 139-170.

Sedlak, W. (1972). Joga w swietle wspolczesnej biofizyki [Yoga in the light of biophysics]. *Zeszyty Naukowe KUL*, **2**, 43-48.

Selye, H. (1974). *Stress without distress.* New York: The New American Library.

Sivananda, S. (1958a). *Science of pranayama.* Rishikesh: Yoga Vedanta Academy.

Sivananda, S. (1958b). *Yoga asanas.* Rishikesh: Yoga Vedanta Academy.

Vahia, N. S., Doongaji, D. R., Jeste, D. V., Kapoor, S. N., Ardhapurkar, I., & Nath, S. R. (1973). Further experience and the therapy based upon concepts of patanjali in the treatment of psychiatric disorders. *Indian Journal of Psychiatry*, **15**, 32-37.

Encouraging Interaction Between Long-Term Care Patients and Community Children

Louise M. Toffoli McLaughlin

The most prevalent stereotyped characteristic of long-term care patients is that of helplessness. These patients are perceived as incapable of active participation; thus they are encouraged to sit back and let others care for them. Many view these patients as a burden on society, not as a valuable resource.

These opinions must be clearly acknowledged as fallacious, after which more meaningful programs for long-term care patients can be implemented. Programming must give direction and a sense of purpose to these patients. Recreation therapy should be a leader among disciplines in innovative programming. What better way to challenge patients and bring meaning back into their lives than by encouraging interaction between themselves and children as a form of recreation therapy?

Recreation therapy is defined as a process that focuses on the healthy aspects of a patient and that modifies leisure activities, when necessary, to assist patients in meeting their leisure needs. This chapter will focus on those needs that can best be met through interaction with children, needs such as sense of purpose and achievement, sharing emotional satisfaction, permission to assume responsibility, the opportunity to assist others, and sense of self-worth and love.

Children can be the spark that ignites new life for these patients. Long-term care patients have knowledge to share and their contributions to the growth and development of children can be of great value. Intergenerational programming should be a priority if the patients as well as community children indicate an interest. Prior to beginning such a program one must take steps to ensure its success by setting guidelines, listing priorities, identifying goals, and recognizing benefits to participants.

Selection of Participants

Clear guidelines for selection of the patients and children must be established if maximum therapeutic value is to be achieved. Not all patients and children will be appropriate as participants (Dunkle & Mikelthun, 1982). A recreation therapist should consider the following criteria for patients selection prior to including them in an intergenerational program:

- An interest in children and willingness to spend time relating to them and communicating with them
- Agreement to participate actively—they aren't selected to be entertained
- Freedom from active illness—medical approval from the attending physician is essential
- Alertness and awareness of their involvement—confused patients will not gain therapeutic value from the experience, and their confusion may frighten and upset the children.
- Sufficient social and physical skills to permit actual active participation in activities
- Interest in experiencing new challenges
- Ability to be appropriately dressed—they should not be allowed to wear hospital gowns

Some characteristics of the children that should be considered are as follows:

- No fear of old age or disabilities
- Ability to encourage interaction with patients
- Emotional security
- Ability to sit quietly for table games and small group activities (Excessively active children may disrupt the group activities, upset the patients, and make interaction between participants more difficult.)
- Enjoyment of new experiences
- Supportive and consenting parents who recognize the potential benefits to participants

Program Goals

Once the population has been identified and the leisure needs of the participants understood, the programs can be formulated. The goals and objectives for each therapy program must be clear if the programs are to be successful. The following goals may be considered when implementing intergenerational programs:

- Including long-term care patients and community children in a mutually beneficial program
- Providing an environment where participants learn from one another
- Providing innovative and meaningful intergenerational programs and encouraging broader application of them in other areas of activity
- Providing consistency in attendance and participation whenever possible to ensure that patients' and children's communication is heightened and that they gain maximum therapeutic value from the program
- Stimulating patients while simultaneously acquainting children with the special needs of the elderly and disabled
- Providing small group settings in order to decrease apprehension of participants

- Allowing patients opportunities to correct children's misconceptions of elderly and disabled persons' capabilities
- Increasing and practicing the leisure skills of participants

Intergenerational programming, if carefully planned, can provide meaningful experiences for patients and children (Dunkle & Mikelthun, 1982; Greenblatt, 1982; Rath & Trocchia, 1981). Rath and Trocchia (1981) also believe, as do I, that participants should aid in the planning process. Durst (1983) commented, "Participant involvement in the planning process is essential as it is a greater commitment and enjoyment for all concerned" (p. 21). Both the patients and children gain from meaningful interaction with one another. Tice (1981) stated, "The interaction provides a two-way street benefiting all who participate" (p. 21).

Benefits to Participants

First, let us consider some of the benefits for children by exposure to and interaction with long-term care patients. Rath and Trocchia (1981) indicated one of the benefits to children as follows: "The opportunity to interact on an ongoing basis with a loving older person may dispel fears and stereotyped notions of the aged now and later in their lives" (p. 59). Tice (1981) stated, "The presence of older people and their unique attributes exert an influence on the child's self-concept and feelings of self-worth, ability to think creatively and independently, academic skills, historical and cultural perspectives, attitudes toward work and leisure and understanding of aging" (p. 22).

Patients can assist in making children feel happier, feel more secure, enrich their learning experiences, and feel more comfortable near elderly and disabled individuals. The Baum, Newman, and Shore (1982) study indicated that children often have misconceived notions of the elderly, and intergenerational programming can change this.

Many children seldom see elderly relatives such as grandparents due to family units being separated by greater distances now than in the past (Baum et al., 1982). An intergenerational program can provide children with the elderly companionship that may be missing. Long-term care patients have the time to talk, listen, and give that special hug to children. Children do not always want advice, just an interested listener. Seniors are most often nonthreatening and openly forgiving. The caring and love that elderly so generously give is graciously received by children. What better way to benefit both populations?

Long-term care patients contribute to children's learning experiences, growth, and development, but patients too are the recipients of numerous benefits. Intergenerational programming allows them opportunities for meaningful relationships with children, many of whom become adopted grandchildren (Vujovich, 1984; Yuknavage, 1981). Patients know that children tend to accept them for themselves, and this increases patients' self-concept and positive state of mind. If others feel good about us, we feel good about ourselves.

Patients need to make contributions to their community and feel that they still have a lot to offer that is worthwhile. This must not be an exercise in tokenism. How better than to aid the community by teaching and working with the children? Rath and Trocchia (1981) offered children opportunities to be exposed to and to be familiar with the elderly. In describing some of the outcomes of their work they reported the following observations: "Each of the surrogate grandmothers is now part of a meaningful and gratifying personal relationship with a child. They feel proud to be contributing individuals who can reach out and do for others and they are no longer isolated in the final stages of their lives" (p. 59). Feelings of isolation and loneliness can be overcome through carefully planned and monitored intergenerational programming (Vujovich, 1984; Wallach, Kelley, & Abrahams, 1979). Rath and Trocchia (1981) observed that "many older people felt that their lives had become useful and of value again" (p. 22). Patients' lives gain a new found purpose and direction. Long-term care patients greatly need opportunities to socialize with others, and unfortunately this does not occur enough in institutions. Children's innocent openness permits the elderly to socialize in a nonthreatening environment. It is readily apparent that this greatly enhances communication skills. Patients respond to children's spontaneity.

Both children and patients mutually benefit from the time they spend together. Often lasting relationships and a strong bonding occur. Programs clearly illustrate that unique qualities exist in relationships between such patients and children (Greenblatt, 1982; Yuknavage, 1981).

Procedure

Patient-child oriented programs must be imaginative and stimulating to maintain the interest and enthusiasm of participants. The recreation therapist must be prepared to offer challenging therapeutic experiences that will enhance the growth and development of each child as well as assist patients in achieving their highest level of healthy functioning.

The programs should occur once or twice per week at the same time and location to allow for consistency. There should be a minimum of one staff member for each group of five or six children as well as one recreation therapist for each group of six or seven patients. The participants should commit to regular attendance to ensure that all participants become comfortable and familiar with one another. The possibilities for programs are endless if the recreation therapist focuses on the wide scope of leisure activities.

All program suggestions should be carefully considered prior to acceptance. The following program ideas may not always be appropriate for all long-term care patients. Think carefully about your population's needs and skills prior to implementing any of the following suggestions. Discuss programs with your patients and determine those of greatest potential interest.

- Encourage Boy Scout and Girl Guide groups to visit patients to work together on requirements for specific badges. The Riverdale Hospital, Toronto, invited 20 Brownies to work on their "friend of a disabled" badge. Patients were informed of the badge requirements, ages of the children, and other information prior to the visit. The encounter was meaningful to all concerned. One can schedule regular group meetings at an institution so that patients can regularly work with the Scout and Guide groups.
- A weekly or biweekly program organized by patients to allow local mothers and their preschoolers the opportunity to have an afternoon out. Mothers would enjoy conversation with other mothers and patients, infants would have the companionship of their peers as well as the exposure to seniors, and patients would participate in planning and implementing play activities for the children. Thus one can effectively address the devastating isolation of old age.
- A patient group and day-care children could arrange to meet regularly. The two groups would share in the planning of activities as well as being active participants in the chosen activities. Small groups are preferable. Large groups inhibit interaction due to the number of participants. Small groups encourage intimacy but prevent dependence of a patient on a child or vice versa that may occur in one-on-one sessions. If a patient dies or is discharged, the child may have trouble dealing with the trauma. With respect to the elderly, they may feel a void once the child leaves day care. This experience of loss is not negative, as it is an unavoidable fact of life. With an intimate group there are always familiar faces to look to for support.
- Long-term care patients could be a great asset to the education system if asked to visit schools, participate in lectures to teens and university students, volunteer their services as teacher aides, and assist in educating community children on the needs of institutionalized individuals. Tice (1981) commented, "Working side by side in the classroom, old and young serve as natural teachers to one another" (p. 21).
- We have big brother and big sister groups. Why not supportive grandparent groups for underprivileged children?
- School groups, summer camp groups, local youth clubs, to mention a few, are child-centered groups that often plan community projects. Why not have long-term care patients share their skills and expertise in working on these projects with children? Volunteers are always needed.
- An exciting Santa's Workshop at The Riverdale Hospital, Toronto, was developed to provide a meaningful and rewarding experience for patients while meeting basic needs of community children. Patients repaired donated used toys and clothing and gave them to needy children. Patients often need the assistance of an extra pair of hands or clearer eyesight, so why not have fortunate children assist them on such a worthy project?

- Patients could regularly volunteer their services as guides for groups of children touring patient institutions. The children could learn first-hand what institutional life is all about as well as becoming acquainted with elderly and disabled people. The patients' role as a guide would be extremely challenging and rewarding if the visits by children were carefully planned. Also, the patients would have to have the support of well-trained recreation therapists to assist with the planning.

The above mentioned programs are only a few of many innovative possibilities that can be planned for long-term care patients and community children. We do both groups an injustice when we bring them together to merely entertain one another. Patients and children gain a feeling of self-worth when able to interact with one another as well as help each other. Active involvement is essential. Durst (1983) reported on the importance of participant involvement: "The successful intergenerational programmes are those which respect the needs and wishes of all, and those which allow for participation on a variety of levels" (p. 21).

Discussion

There is a definite therapeutic value of bringing long-term care patients and community children together in meaningful intergenerational programming. It is unfair to dismiss or diminish the knowledge and experiences that patients can bring to children merely because these individuals are patients and live in long-term care institutions. Programs must be developed and implemented in an attempt to end the isolation of old age while bringing valuable learning experiences to children. Recreation therapy can and must provide these programs. Durst (1983) wrote, "The wealth of knowledge and expertise contained in the older population is often an untapped resource in the community" (p. 20). The recreation therapist is in a position to be the catalyst for interactions that will enhance the lives of long-term care patients and community children.

References

Baum, M., Newman, S., & Shore, B. (1982, Summer). Learning about aging through intergenerational experiences. *Gerontology and Geriatrics Education, 2*(4), 313-316.

Dunkle, R., & Mikelthun, B. (1982, Winter). Intergenerational programming: An Adopt-a-Grandparent Program in a retirement community. *Activities, Adaptation and Aging, 3*(2), 93-105.

Durst, K. (1983, February). Inter-generational programming and the older adult. *Recreation Canada, 41*(1), 20-21.

Greenblatt, F. (1982, Fall). Adopt-a-Grandchild Program: Improving attitudes of adolescents toward the aged. *Activities, Adaptation and Aging, 3*(1), 21-25.

Rath, S., & Trocchia, J. (1981, Summer). Nursing home residents as surrogate grandparents for preschool children. *Activities, Adaptation and Aging,* **1**(4), 55-59.

Tice, C. (1981, May-June). Creating caring communities: Linking the generations. *Aging,* pp. 20-23.

Vujovich, J. (1984, January-February). Child day care livens a nursing home. *Geriatric Nursing,* pp. 31-33.

Wallach, H., Kelley, F., & Abrahams, J. (1979). Psychosocial rehabilitation for chronic geriatric patients: An intergenerational approach. *The Gerontologist,* **19**(5), 464-470.

Yuknavage, P. (1981, May-June). Intergenerational issues. *Aging,* pp. 15-19.

Aquatic Exercise Program for the Aged in Nursing Homes

Dean R. Gorman
Barry S. Brown
Michael Daniel
Charles Daniel

It seems well established that proper exercise is good for people, no matter their age. A senior citizen has much to gain from starting an exercise program and more to gain from continuing that program through the lifespan. Research continues to substantiate that contention, as do the testimonials of participants with a perceived increase in quality of living. The real key, though, is in the proper exercise. The principles of duration, intensity, frequency, overload, and progression apply to all exercise and will not be repeated in this section. Our purpose here is to examine a specific mode of exercise—exercise in the water.

Water exercise offers advantages that may make it the exercise of choice for a great number of people. The body is lifted to some extent by the water, thereby decreasing the amount of stress on the weight-bearing joints. The extent of lift, or buoyancy, is dependent on the percentage of body fat, body size, and proportion of the body in the water versus out of the water. Many people are not able to walk, jog, or participate in other forms of exercise because of deteriorated or weak ankles, knees, hips, and back, but many of these people can exercise in the water. Those suffering from arthritis may be able to rejuvenate damaged joints while improving cardiovascular, respiratory, and muscular fitness. Non–weight-bearing joints (wrists, shoulders, neck) can be moved against the resistance of the water without the added strain of supporting the total weight of the body part. Water therapy has long been a part of rehabilitation programs, but it is only recently that we have begun to capitalize on these features of water exercise and place it in an exercise program. The decreased stress on the skeletal structure, along with the resultant decreased incidence of injury, will lead to even greater use of water exercise, especially with an aging population.

In the past many people felt that water exercise could only attract a limited population because of the necessity of swimming ability. However, swimming ability is not a prerequisite for entrance into a water exercise program. (Please note that the term *water exercise* is used in this section rather than the term *swimming*.) The benefits of exercise can be obtained in the water without swimming at all. No swimming skills are required to start a water exercise program. Certainly this is an environment in which certain safety measures must be taken, and we would not advocate placing undue danger on anyone. Lifeguards with training in handling emergency situations should be present at all times, and the pool setting should be controlled so that there is a sense of calm and control around participants who have doubts about their swimming ability. But a great beauty of water exercise is the ability to meet the standards of beneficial exercise while keeping the feet on the bottom in relatively shallow water or with the hand firmly in contact with the side of the pool. Many successful water exercise workouts have been accomplished with the hair dry and intact and makeup still on.

Also, with the emphasis on water exercise rather than on swimming, more people can use a facility at the same time, and more socializing can be done because the head is out of the water and one is not practicing the lonely art of swimming laps. In fact, water workouts are now being choreographed to music and may soon sweep the country the way dance and exercise to music have done recently.

Water exercise is not without its disadvantages. This form of exercise has its problems as well. Let's first look at the obvious: A swimming facility is needed. Water exercise is not as convenient as walking or jogging, where very little is needed in the way of a facility, nor is it as cheap to purchase the necessary equipment as stationary cycling. But pool availability is not as big a problem as it once was. Many care facilities for the elderly now build pools into their complexes. Many YMCAs, YWCAs, Boys' or Girls' Clubs, universities, and community centers have pools and are willing to make arrangements for exercise sessions; and there may be access to private facilities such as health clubs. The initial capital outlay for this exercise facility is larger than one would encounter in other forms of exercise, but it is not one that is usually made by an individual. So this is only a different kind of obstacle and certainly not one that is insurmountable. The facilities are there, and in most cases the costs are not forbidding.

One factor that is often overlooked or ignored in other forms of exercise must be accounted for in water exercise: support and safety personnel. Lifeguards are a necessity for water exercise. A person engaging in other forms of exercise may be considered to have assumed the risk for accident or emergency. In a swimming pool, that risk is assumed by the pool management. Consequently, lifeguards and supervisory personnel must generally be accepted as another factor to consider in establishing a water exercise program.

Many people enter into exercise programs with fat and weight loss as one, if not the primary, motivation. A caloric imbalance caused by any type of exercise will help in a fat/weight reduction program. But one thing must be understood—swimming does not promote the same degree of fat and weight loss as do some other forms of exercise. Water exercise will help in a weight reduction program, but it may not result in the losses that the same amount of, say, walking or jogging will cause. The reasons for this are not fully understood. Certainly it is due in part to the fact that water exercise is a non-weight-bearing (or at least reduced weight-bearing) exercise. That is, the body weight is not the resistance that must be moved in exercising, so less actual work is done in movement and less calories are burned per unit of time. Also, the body seems to have a mechanism for retaining some fat as insulation against the cooler environment in the water. It is debatable whether or not that fat is a necessity, but genetically it appears that we fall back on prehistoric protective devices in this case. Nevertheless, the increased caloric expenditure caused by water exercise, combined with prudent dietary measures, will aid a person in a fat and weight loss program.

Before Getting in the Water

A number of safety precautions should be covered prior to beginning an exercise program. The first concern is that participants not unknowingly place themselves in a dangerous situation. The more that is known about a participant, the more individualized the exercise can be, and, therefore, greater benefit is realized. But another concern that cannot be minimized is the legal liability of the instructor and sponsoring organization. No precaution can legally overcome negligence. But obtaining participant information and professional opinions of health status and fully informing participants will go far to establish that a program has taken prudent safety measures.

First, any participant over the age of 35 should have a medical examination by a physician. If that person has had an exam within the previous year, it still may not be adequate if the examining physician did not know that the patient would be undertaking exercise. The physician should be given a notice that states the exact nature of the exercise program, so that the degree of stress the patient will face is known.

The physician can then decide the extent of examination called for at that time. Each physician has a preferred base of medical history and areas of examination. The form, which should be kept on file, should provide indications that the physician found nothing to indicate that the patient should not participate in the program. (Many physicians are not willing to state that a person should participate, only that no reason was found that they should not. The wording might affect insurance reimbursement for the exercise program. Local attitudes and policies will dictate the exact wording on the form.)

Second, the instructor and other program personnel need information about the participant. A medical history questionnaire should be passed out, one similar to that found in *YMCArdiac Therapy* (Fry & Berra, 1981).[1] A form of this type might be used in conjunction with the medical exam. In any case, information on family history, medications, past exercise habits, injuries, infirmities, and primary risk factors should be known by program management.

Third, the participant should know exactly what will be expected in the program. Any informed consent form[2] should include not only a description of activities but also the risks and benefits that might result from participation. It should be clearly understood by instructor and participant alike that intensity, duration, and even continuation of exercise is purely voluntary. This presents a challenge for the instructor; there is a fine line between motivating participants and removing the voluntary nature of the exercise.

The Exercise Program

This type of exercise program should adhere to all the principles of exercise prescription and exercise leadership previously discussed. We will now look at some of the water exercises you can use; they should be used in the correct way, as dictated by those principles of exercise. This will be only a sampling of some of the exercises you might use. There are other sources,[3] but your imagination may be your most prolific source. If an exercise fits within the framework of the exercise principles, use it.

Warm-Up Exercises

The warm-up exercises can also be used as cool-down exercises. For many people in poor physical condition, the warm-up exercises may also serve as cardiovascular exercises. Whatever the case, the instructor and the participant must work together to stay within the guidelines for exercise. All the exercises are designed to be performed in water that is waist to chest deep.

Morning stretch. Stand comfortably in waist-deep water, feet shoulder-width apart. Reach high above the head and stand on the toes and stretch as much as is comfortable. Drop down into a relaxed crouched position and shake; relax.

Leg loosener. Stand on the left leg and lift the right knee, letting the bottom part of the leg hang loosely. Make circles with the bottom part of the leg for 10 s and reverse direction for 10 s; then change legs and repeat.

Calf stretcher. Stand facing a side wall and lean forward, placing hands on the wall. Keeping the heels in contact with the bottom of the pool and the knees, hips, and back straight, walk away from the wall until you feel a stretching in the calf. Stop and hold for 10 to 15 s; relax and repeat.

Side stretcher. Stand with left side toward the wall and left arm bracing against the wall. With right arm extended over the head and body aligned in proper posture, lean to the left slowly, stretching the right side. Stretch to the point of discomfort and hold for 10 s; relax and repeat. Do the same for the right side.

Front thigh stretcher.   Stand with left side to the wall, bracing yourself with your left hand. Grasp the right ankle with the right hand, just below the buttock. Pull and lift the leg to the rear until the point of discomfort, holding for 10 s; relax and repeat. Do for both sides.

Hamstring stretcher.   Stand facing the side wall. Place the left foot as high on the wall as possible. Bending at the hips, lean forward as far as possible, keeping the legs straight and holding for 10 s; relax and repeat. Repeat twice for right leg. (Caution: This exercise might be dangerous in subjects with low back pain or spinal fusions.)

Hamstring and lower back stretch.   Hang onto the wall with the feet on the wall, about hip height. Lower the left leg toward the bottom of the pool, against the wall, and press back with the right leg, rounding the back and stretching the right hamstring, holding for 10 s; relax and repeat. Do twice for each leg.

Toe touch.   Standing on left leg, lift the right leg straight in front of you and touch as near the toes as possible with the left hand. Alternate legs (can be done standing still).

Tummy tuck.   Hang onto the wall with your back to the wall. Draw your knees up toward the chest while flattening the lower back against the wall, holding for 3 to 5 s; relax and repeat.

Tummy twister.   Hang onto the side of the pool with back to the wall. Let the legs float up in front of the body until laid out on top of the water. Twist over to the left hip and then twist back to the right hip; repeat.

Leg press.   Facing the wall, hold onto the wall and float away. Keeping the legs straight and the back straight on top of the water, press the legs down to a standing position; float back and repeat.

Push aways.   Lean forward and place your hands on the wall, keeping the knees, hips, and back straight. Lower the chest to the wall and push away; repeat as in push-ups (the greater the forward lean, the harder the push away).

Arm pulls.   Stand with knees bent so the water is almost shoulder depth. Placing one arm straight out in front and the other straight out behind, pull/push against the water and alternate positions; repeat.

Kickboard press.   Place the hands flat on top of a kickboard directly in front of the body. Maintaining proper posture, press the kickboard underwater until the arms are extended, then let it rise back to the top slowly; repeat.

Kickboard swings.   Stand with the feet spread comfortably, establishing a good base. With a kickboard to the left of the body, place the left hand at the bottom of the board and the right hand at the top. Pulling with the right arm, pushing with the left arm, and twisting with the body, swing the kickboard around to the right side; turn it upside down so the right hand is on the bottom, left hand on the top, and repeat back to the left; repeat.

Cardiovascular Conditioners

Split jumps. From a standing position, jump slightly and spread the legs (right leg in front, left leg in back). Immediately jump and return to the starting position, then jump and split with right leg in back and left leg in front, then back to starting position. Continue (legs may also split to the side; exercise may be done by alternating the two different movements).

Flutter kicks. Hold onto the side of the pool and brace with one arm. Begin kicking with the legs, swinging them wide apart, and alternating (may be done on front or back).

Ski slalom. Keeping the feet together, jump up and bounce the feet to the right side. Immediately bounce back up and bounce the feet across to the left side. Imagine that you are jumping over a bench; the higher the bench, the greater the work.

Walk/March/Jog. Move through the water at whatever pace suits you.

Charleston kick. Stand with feet shoulder-width apart, arms by the sides. Bounce slightly and kick the left heel up to the left hand. Go back to the starting position, bounce slightly, and kick the right heel to the right hand. Continue to alternate.

Cool-Down Exercises

Wedding march. Walk slowly. As the trail leg passes, pause. As you step forward the next trail leg pauses, then steps forward.

Wiggle through. Bend the knees so that the shoulders are underwater, then begin wiggling the shoulders and the upper body, and move across the pool.

Easy kicks. Lean back against the wall and let the body float up. Begin doing an easy frog-kicking motion, moving slowly and not pressing the water.

Summary

The principles of water exercise for the aged retain the same safeguards and progressions as in any age group. Innovative exercise routines are continuously being developed and can be used successfully as long as they adhere to scientifically validated guidelines. Even jogging in the deep end of pools has become possible and desirable with the advent of the

"Wet Vest,"[4] a newly developed water jacket that allows cardiovascular conditioning without pressure exerted on the knees, ankles, and hip. The gains to be realized through water exercise will allow the elderly to live young as late in life as possible.

Notes

1. A medical history questionnaire also may be obtained from the authors upon request at the following address: Dean R. Gorman, Adapted Physical Education, HPER 308N, University of Arkansas, Fayetteville, AR 72701.

2. An informed consent form may be obtained from the authors upon request at the address given in Note 1.

3. A list of sources may be obtained from the authors upon request at the address given in Note 1.

4. Information on the "Wet Vest" can be obtained from the authors upon request at the address given in Note 1.

Reference

Fry, G., & Berra, K. (1981). *YMCArdiac Therapy*. Chicago: National Council of the YMCA of the U.S.A.